D1534695

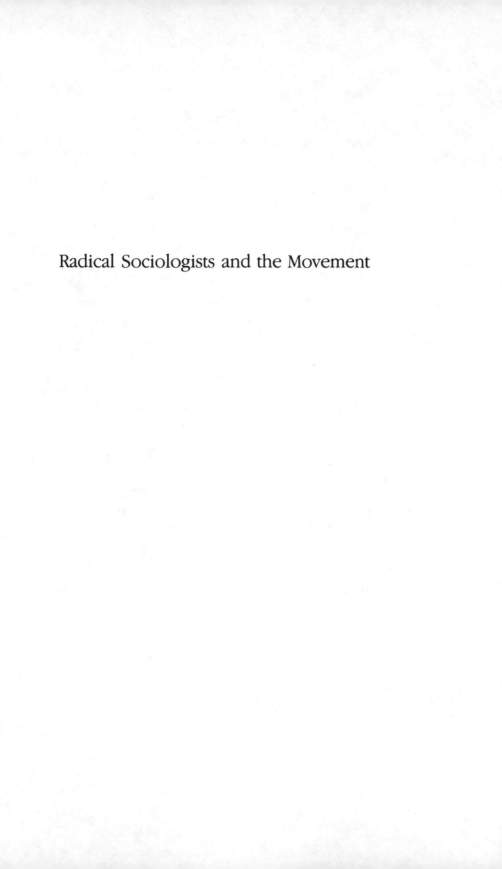

Radical Sociologists and the Movement

Radical Sociologists
and the Movement

Experiences, Lessons, and Legacies

Edited by
Martin Oppenheimer,
Martin J. Murray, and
Rhonda F. Levine

 Temple University Press • PHILADELPHIA

$ 7.50

Temple University Press, Philadelphia 19122
Copyright © 1991 by Temple University, except Chap. 14, which is © Howard J. Erhlich
All rights reserved
Published 1991
Printed in the United States of America

The paper used in this publication meets the minimum requirements of American National Standard for Information Sciences—Permanence of Paper for Printed Library Materials, ANSI Z39.48-1984 ♾

Library of Congress Cataloging-in-Publication Data

Radical sociologists and the movement : experiences, lessons, and
  legacies / edited by Martin Oppenheimer, Martin J. Murray, and
  Rhonda F. Levine.
      p.   cm.
    Includes bibliographical references.
    ISBN 0-87722-745-4 (alk. paper)
      1. Sociology—United States. 2. Radicalism—United States.
  I. Oppenheimer, Martin. II. Murray, Martin J. III. Levine, Rhonda F.
  HM22.U5R33   1991
  301'.0973—dc20   90-32841
                                                              CIP

Contents

PART III   *Sociology in Action*

PART IV   *Documents*

Acknowledgments

THE EDITORS would like to acknowledge the cooperation of the Eugene Collective of the journal *Critical Sociology* (the former *Insurgent Sociologist*) in the production of this book, which is based in part on volume 15, number 2 (Summer 1988) of *Critical Sociology*, and of the authors in that issue who willingly revised and expanded their essays for this book. The inspiration for that thematic issue came originally from a conversation with Evan Stark. Special thanks to the American Sociological Association for permission to reprint Martin Nicolaus's "Fat-Cat Sociology," previously published in *The American Sociologist*. Comments by William G. Domhoff and other reviewers were very helpful in giving final shape to this book. We would also like to thank Sally McCarthy for secretarial assistance and Liza Murphy for research assistance. Almost needless to say, we are grateful to the "new" authors for their contributions as well. This effort will earn no one great glory within the sociological establishment; it is truly a labor of love and comradeship for all the participants, and that is reward enough.

Radical Sociologists and the Movement

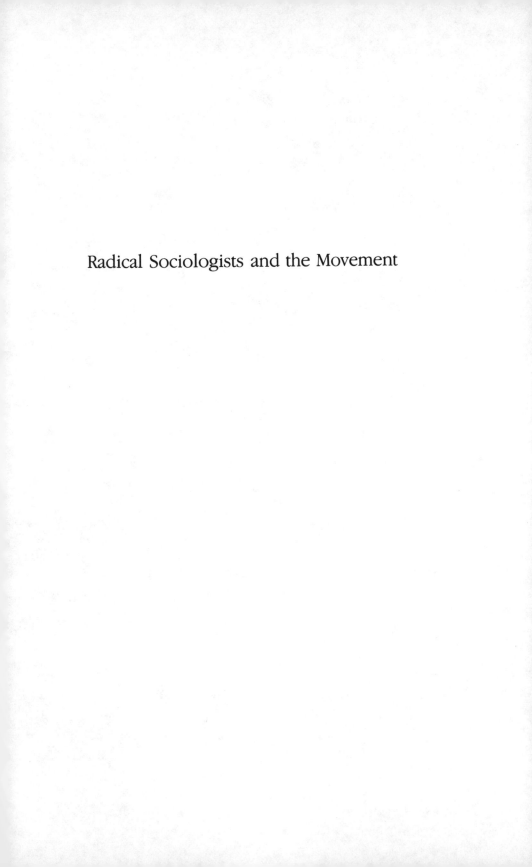

Introduction

The Movement and the Academy

Martin Oppenheimer, Martin J. Murray,
and Rhonda F. Levine

> We must reveal by our work the meaning of structural trends and historic
> decisions; . . . we must reveal the ways in which personal troubles are
> connected with public issues. . . .
>   The first job of the intellectuals today is to be consistently and alto-
> gether unconstructive. For to be constructive within the going scheme of
> affairs is to consent to the continuation of precisely what we ought to be
> against. (Mills 1958, 153, 157–58)

AS MUCH AS any other statement, these two quotations, four and a half
pages apart, from a small book by C. Wright Mills, *The Causes of World
War III*, constituted the battle cry of radical sociology in the United
States. The interrelationship of the social and the individual—social psychology in its true sense—that is implied in Mills's words (and in much
of his work) also constituted the trademark of much of the New Left.
Mills's call to make the connection between the personal and the political
(transmuted into the New Left slogan that the personal *is* the political)
resonated within left sociology far more profoundly than did the broad
historical sweep of Marxist theory, at least until around 1970.

C. Wright Mills was an intellectual outcast. Unlike the overwhelming
majority of his contemporaries, he did not welcome the celebrated coming of the "end of ideology," the dominant idea that class conflict and the
struggle for socialism were no longer necessary in the advanced capitalist
world. He did not worship at the altar of conformity and normative consensus. Mills popularized the term "power elite" to describe the enormous growth of corporate, governmental, and military power in the
United States. For him, gigantic multinational corporations were not
"soulful," as some of his contemporaries suggested. The huge military
establishment was not a necessary deterrent against the Soviet threat, nor
was big government a benefactor distributing goods and services in accordance with the common good. Mills went against the prevailing intel-

3

lectual grain by rejecting the scientific ideal of "value-free" sociology. His insistence that personal troubles (from the general malaise of alienation to specific problems like divorce, suicide, alcoholism, drug addiction) were intimately intertwined with public issues (unemployment rates, the quality of social life, and education, not to mention war) put him at odds with the intellectual establishment of the 1950s.

It should not be surprising that the young intellectuals of the early New Left turned to mavericks like Mills for ideas missing in the bland formulas of the reigning paradigm. He inspired a generation of young scholars who came of intellectual age during the 1960s to ask unpopular questions, to challenge dominant world views, and to invent new approaches. Radical sociology owes its intellectual debt to scholars such as Mills, Herbert Marcuse, and Norman O. Brown, all of whom were shunned by the academic establishment. Mills exemplified populist, radical thought. His work had a significant impact on the growth of 1960s New Left thinking and strongly influenced the development of radical sociology. Marxist theory developed later, blending with earlier populist strains.

Alternative Visions

This book is organized as a set of autobiographical essays written by people whose radicalism developed in and around the academic discipline of sociology. These essays epitomize what Mills called the "sociological imagination"—that is, the intimate connection between history and biography. These two interrelated themes permeate these essays: the historical focus—how critical, radical, Marxist, and humanist sociology developed and matured in the political and social milieus of the 1960s; and the biographical focus—how the socioeconomic and political conditions of the era acted as an intellectual incubator, serving to radicalize a significant number of sociologists who, in turn, contributed to shaping a countervailing intellectual tradition in the field of sociology, a tradition that departed significantly from the conventional wisdom of the structural functionalists of the 1950s and early 1960s. Individuals develop radical consciousness for a variety of reasons that are rooted in the dialectic between biography (the idiosyncratic) and history (the broad environment). We hope with this book to further our understanding of how that process works.

How "typical" of radical sociology are the people represented here? Although they represent a range of experiences typical of the era, they do not constitute a "sample" in the sense that term is understood within sociology. We have tried to enroll a cross section of our colleagues. Clearly this particular cross section significantly overlaps with the professional network to which the editors belong. However, although any number of other writers could have been included, there are really no competing or even alternative networks within radical sociology today.

Broadly defined, radical sociology encompasses a variety of intellectual developments that are now permanent fixtures within the discipline of sociology. These perspectives were nurtured in the enormous outpouring of creative and original thinking that characterized the academic environment of the 1960s. Radical sociology forms only a single dimension of a considerably broader and wider historical process of reevaluation that engulfed all academic fields during the 1960s.

One underlying aim of this collection is to investigate how a vibrant intellectual countertradition emerged within mainstream sociology. This countertradition is not by any means homogeneous. It encompasses a range of theoretical frameworks that have been influenced (but not defined) by Marxism, a plethora of subject areas, and a mixture of methodological and epistemological assumptions. The contributors are active sociologists who participated in various ways during the 1960s and afterward in the formation of an intellectual political culture. Russell Jacoby in his provocative and stimulating work *The Last Intellectuals* (1987) perhaps overstates the degree to which those who participated in the formation of this intellectual political culture have failed to become "public intellectuals" because they are safely ensconced within the narrow confines of the university. Jacoby has overlooked how college professors, including sociologists, continue to speak out on both local and global issues and have continued to participate in community struggles, yet perhaps not in the visible, vocal ways that would attract huge media attention.

The reasons why individuals develop a politically radical consciousness have continued to haunt the academic establishment. The contributors to this volume express, in the form of reflective biographical essays, why and how they turned to radical interpretations of world events—the persistence of racial and gender inequality, power relations, the permanence of privilege and poverty, the causes and consequences of war, and so forth. Equally important, they describe how their intellectual views were shaped by the political culture of "the movement" of the 1960s, and they explain why they maintain their radical perspective today. For every handful of celebrated academics who have expressed second thoughts by renouncing their 1960s radicalism, there are hundreds of active intellectuals who have stayed the course. They have grappled with their 1960s beliefs, refining and modifying their approaches to pressing political and social issues of the present day but not abandoning *tout court* the creative impulses that inspired them in the first place.

Although individual theorists like Paul Sweezy, Paul Baran, Herbert Marcuse, C. Wright Mills, and the like made significant contributions to radical thought, critical-thinking sociologists did not treat these figures as above reproach but instead made use of their work as a starting point for analysis, not the end point of truth. Armchair critics like Edward Shils (1988, 17–18) suggest otherwise, arguing that these early contributors were in reality perpetuating a "vulgar" Marxist-Leninist-Stalinist totalitarian outlook under the guise of "emancipationist wrinkles." He warns us against these wolves in sheep's clothing. This indictment is patently untrue. Moreover, what Shils and others like him overlook is that as long as the powerful and privileged refuse to take seriously all oppression, real as well as perceived, then the ideas that they espouse will be called into question.

It may be useful at this point to hint at some common threads that seem to be woven into many of these autobiographies. In terms of politics, there is the thread of antiauthoritarianism. Contrary to some popular myths about the New Left, our particular group seems deeply committed to democratic values and participative strategies, and hostile to "vanguardist," elite structures. In terms of social psychology, these essays in sum seem to support the theory that "strain" or contradiction between a society's expressed ideals and its reality leads to questioning and ultimately to radical critique. Rather than dramatic conversion, many of the authors seem to have become radicals as the culmination of a slow process of exposure to real-life conditions (in several cases in the Third World) that exposed the myths on which they had been raised. The contradictions of race and gender in the United States have been of particular significance in this regard.

FROM SOCIOLOGY LIBERATION MOVEMENT TO THE LIBERATION OF SOCIOLOGY

The Eastern Sociological Society held its 1968 annual meeting in Boston. The assassination of Martin Luther King, Jr., the day before the meeting began, had triggered fears of another long hot summer. Standing in front of the convention hotel, we could hear the fire sirens from the direction of the black neighborhoods. A sense of desperation filled the air. The movements to end the two major crises of the day—the war in Vietnam and lingering racial discrimination and oppression at home—seemed to reach an impasse that spring and summer. Robert Kennedy's assassination and the police riot at the Democratic national convention in Chicago were still to come.

By 1968, if not before, many intellectuals and established academics had reached the conclusion that the established social science disciplines not only were failing to address the pressing political and social issues of the day but, worse, were contributing to the status quo by avoiding controversial subjects. In a more sinister vein, numerous academics, universities, and private think tanks actually participated in the war machine abroad and the containment of the aspirations of the oppressed at home by selling their knowledge, expertise, and advice to various governmental agencies. A typical example was the Michigan State University Group (MSUG) project, designed to train Ngo Dinh Diem's police force in South Vietnam, build the civil administration, and permanently entrench the U.S. military in this "bastion of anti-Communism." Radical intellectuals sought to expose the complicity of these individuals and institutions in carrying out the dirty work of the vast "counterinsurgency" effort.

In July 1968, a small group of graduate students (mainly enrolled at Columbia University) formed the Sociology Liberation Movement (SLM). One of its principal tasks was to turn the spotlight on professional sociologists who were assisting the war effort in Indochina and thwarting popular movements at home. The SLM first appeared publicly at the annual convention of the American Sociological Association (ASA) in Boston a month later. Sociologists who were actively participating in the antiwar, student, black liberation, and various other political movements of the late 1960s focused their attention on the SLM. It quickly emerged as an organizational vehicle through which one could question the relevance of sociology as it was practiced at the time and could explore ways of addressing the concerns of "real" people. The SLM sought to develop an alternative vision of sociology, one that avoided the "trivial and obscure undertakings upon which professional sociology was built," as *The Insurgent Sociologist* editorialized (1977).

The SLM soon faded into obscurity, yet it left a vibrant legacy that continues to this day. From the late 1960s through the early 1970s, radical sociologists conducted countermeetings that ran parallel to the official ASA format. The journal *The Insurgent Sociologist* originated in this intellectual environment as an alternative outlet for the kind of critical scholarship that was ignored within the professional establishment. Regional caucuses, such as the Eastern Union of Radical Sociologists (later reorganized as the East Coast Conference of Socialist Sociologists), the Western Union of Radical Sociologists, the Union of Radical American Social

Scientists (URASS), and others were organized as alternatives to regional professional sociologists' associations. From 1969 to 1972, the SLM acted as an umbrella coordinating caucus within the ASA. Its successor, the Radical Caucus, still operates at ASA annual meetings.

The development of a distinctly radical perspective in the field of sociology was not an isolated phenomenon. Similar caucuses developed in literally dozens of regional and national professional associations. This "long march" through practically every academic field of scholarly inquiry was sufficiently widespread that it merited the attention of the Carnegie Commission on Higher Education (Bloland and Bloland 1974). One report presented to the Carnegie Commission correctly pointed out that these hastily formed caucuses were by no means all defined by radical politics. Many were initiated to voice the growing concern of their members about the Vietnam War and to transform the rhetoric about "social responsibility" into reality. A significant number of these caucuses later turned toward a more radical interpretation of their particular academic disciplines. Radical groupings within the Modern Language Association, the American Philosophical Association, the American Political Science Association, and the American Economic Association were perhaps the best-known examples of this tendency. In addition, the Radical Historian Caucus, formed within the American Historical Association, eventually transformed itself into the Middle Atlantic Radical Historians' Organization, which continues to publish the journal *Radical History Review*.

Just as significantly, a number of caucuses emerged with the expressed purpose of representing the special concerns of women, minorities, and other underrepresented or disadvantaged constituencies. This development occurred within academic sociology as well. Black and women's caucuses (today formally institutionalized within the ASA) sprang up around the same time as the SLM. In some academic fields, caucuses (along with their official journals and other publications) were formed around pedagogy as such, a reflection of the interest of the New Left in democratizing and revamping the educational process itself (Norton and Ollman, 1978). The journal *Radical Teacher*, which is still in existence, emerged out of this effort. Perrucci (1973) identified eighteen radical professional organizations in the early 1970s, ranging in size from the huge Medical Committee for Human Rights (with an estimated fifteen thousand members) to the SLM. Bloland and Bloland (1974) provide data on the formation of three large radical caucuses in their respective academic professions: the Caucus for a New Political Science within the American Political Science Association; the radical caucus that formed in the Modern Language Association; and Scientists and Engineers for Social and Political Action, which developed within the American Physical Society.

Equally important, a number of radical organizations originated outside the confines of particular academic associations: the National Social Welfare Workers Movement, Science for the People (publisher of a magazine by the same name), the Committee for Social Responsibility in Engineering, Concerned Asian Scholars, Computer Professionals for Peace, and others. In addition, a variety of independent research collectives and groups developed, including the North American Congress on Latin America, the Africa Research Group, the Pacific Studies Center, the Indochina Resource Center, and the Health Policy Advisory Center. Numerous legal resource centers, some of them loosely connected through the National Lawyers Guild, flourished during the late 1960s and 1970s.

So we see that the radical impulses that emerged within academic sociology were not unique. Still, the movement that developed within the profession did exhibit peculiar features that distinguished it from similar efforts in other fields. The inaugural issue of *The Insurgent Sociologist*, published as a preconvention clarion call just before the 1969 annual ASA meetings, loudly proclaimed that the aim of the SLM was "to destroy the power structure of the profession, eliminate the power elite that controls the profession through its undemocratic structure, and redefine sociology to correspond to social reality" (1977, 2). In retrospect, this bold proclamation was unrealistic and far-fetched. Yet it did reflect the widespread sentiment that the ASA was out of touch with a growing number of critical, radical, humanist, and Marxist sociologists. In time, the ASA altered its structure to accommodate some of those who pressured the organization from below.

THE POLITICAL AGENDA OF RADICAL SOCIOLOGY

Early issues of *The Insurgent Sociologist* (published in newsletter format) proclaimed that it functioned as "the newsletter of the Union of Radical Sociologists and the Sociology Liberation Movement." The fourth issue, published in April 1971, contained, among other items, Carol Andreas's and Henry Etzkowitz's responses to Reinhard Bendix's 1970 ASA presidential address. The ASA had refused to publish these replies in any of its officially sponsored journals. *The Insurgent Sociologist* published a continuing barrage of articles exposing "counterinsurgency scholars" and, of course, provided coverage of the politically motivated firings of radical scholars, including David Colfax and Marlene Dixon. In November 1971,

The Insurgent Sociologist began publishing as a regular journal, head-quartered at the University of Oregon, and in 1987 changed its name to *Critical Sociology.*

Almost from their inception, radical caucuses in all academic disciplines were confronted with two internal issues that ripped apart the initial illusion of unity and solidarity. Despite the proclaimed goals of equality and justice, practically every radical caucus was characterized by a virtual absence of African-American and other racial-minority members. Equally important, despite significant participation of women in the work of radical sociology, a radical "old boys' network" maintained positions of power and authority. In 1969, the annual New University Conference meeting was almost completely preoccupied with issues raised by the Women's Caucus. In 1975, the *Invisible Socialist University Newsletter* (published by the East Coast Conference of Socialist Sociologists) admitted that "a number of feminist socialists . . . are no longer part of our scene." Feminists tended to shy away from the radical caucuses, arguing that male chauvinism remained deeply entrenched despite the radical rhetoric. Many radical women felt more comfortable with the more mainstream Sociologists for Women in Society.

The period between 1972 and 1976 witnessed a growth of radical sociology that increasingly developed a theoretical identity with Marxism, including variants of neo-Marxist theorizing that originated primarily within the European New Left. *The Insurgent Sociologist* mirrored these developments by publishing Marxist scholarly work in a variety of substantive areas. In its early stages, very few sociology graduate programs in the United States offered substantive areas of inquiry oriented to, or by, radical sociology. In time, however, Marxist approaches to various intellectual problem areas gained considerable legitimacy, because of both a high quality of scholarship and the perceived relevance for the problems of the real world. By the late 1970s, a significant number of sociology departments employed Marxist and radical faculty, despite the fact that many of these appointments were merely token efforts to assuage curious students.

In 1976, the Marxist Sociology Section was officially inaugurated as one of about twenty subgroupings within the ASA. This section has maintained a stable membership of more than four hundred for over a decade, symbolizing the legitimation of Marxist and radical perspectives within the mainstream of the sociology profession. Flacks's 1982 verdict thus appears to be accurate: "It is clear that Marx has been restored to sociology in a way that would have been very surprising a decade ago. We find the radical sociologist in the 1970s not devoting his or her time to documenting a critical view of society but instead trying, as Marx did, to comprehend the contradictions in society that create the basis for effective strategies of social transformation" (45). Flacks implies here a less active and more contemplative role for contemporary Marxists within the academy. This is not an unmixed blessing, as he points out: "The very acceptance of Marxism . . . creates a fundamental dilemma for radicals in sociology. The more they are engaged in fruitful work within the academy, the more . . . likely it is that the connection between neo-Marxism and political practice will become problematic" (46). In short, perhaps part of the price for survival within the academic establishment for radical sociologists has been the withdrawal from political practice.

Many have refused to pay this price, continuing in their efforts to link their sociological understanding to social action both within and outside the university. Yet many radical sociologists who behaved as "good professionals" were fired for political reasons anyway. By the mid-1970s, despite the seemingly "academic" quality of their work, numerous Marxists, feminists, and radical sociologists came face to face with university and departmental administrations that deployed every means at their disposal to fire them.

The future of radical sociology as a vibrant and exciting intellectual option is inextricably linked to the growth of political and social movements in the United States. In the absence of social and political movements, radical sociology cannot hope to occupy more than an exotic niche within the profession.

REINVENTING THE 1960s: A GROWTH INDUSTRY

In contemporary popular culture, "the sixties" has become a fluid historical period defined less as a distinctive time span than as a set of symbols, values, and attitudes. A host of recent films, television programs, and books have chronicled the origins and development of the civil rights movement, the student movement, the anti–Vietnam War movement, the feminist movement, and the growth of the "counterculture." These efforts to analyze, interpret, and explain the sixties have produced mixed results. All too often, they have been mildly distorted—or worse. In some instances, the sixties are treated simplistically as a time of unrestrained license that eroded the traditional values of American life and undermined the educational system (Bloom 1987).

There are exceptions. In his refreshing glimpse at the period, Todd Gitlin (1987) creatively blends personal narrative with historical analysis. Because he treats the decline of the movement as synonymous with the collapse of Students for a Democratic Society in 1969, Gitlin fails to understand how the movement managed to outlast his own personal retreat from full-scale political participation. Yet the problems with Gitlin's interpretation of the 1960s era pale in comparison with the distortions of the period found elsewhere.

John Bunzel's edited volume entitled *Political Passages* (1988) and Peter Collier and David Horowitz's *Destructive Generation* (1989) exemplify this trend toward reinventing the political character of the 1960s movements through the distorting lens of late 1980s neoliberalism and conservatism.

Yet these two books have more directed aims. At one fundamental level they represent impassioned defenses of American capitalism and the American middle-of-the-road political institutions. By systematically criticizing all efforts to change it, the contributors to these volumes defend the *status quo*. Many of these first-person essays recounting political journeys away from the political left and toward the center and right masquerade as thoughtful and reasoned appreciations of the liberal democratic vision of the "open society." This defense of "good" liberalism against "bad" radicalism obscures real understanding of how capitalism works on a world scale.

Both Edward Shils and Jeffrey Herf (who currently teaches in the Strategy Department at the Naval War College in Newport, Rhode Island) vilify the radicalism of the 1960s as the childish play of idealistic and foolhardy youth. Herf (1988) recants his former radical beliefs, dismissing them as the flotsam and jetsam of youthful folly and misadventure. He proclaims that he was somehow hoodwinked by the spirit and tenor of those turbulent times. While announcing his allegiance to traditional liberal values, he manages to defend the corrupt and inept Saigon regime (because of its alliance with the United States). Shils's contribution is equally macabre. For him, the 1960s era was "a damaging decade" in which a whole intellectual generation was lured by the "temptations of spurious ideals" (1988, 1). "I myself thought," Shils informs us, "that [U.S. engagement in military activities in Southeast Asia was] justified, and I still regret that it had to be halted without success" (19). For Shils, the preservation of the governmental, academic, familial, military, and economic institutions of the U.S. justified the military destruction of Indochina. And he does not restrict his attacks to "youthful demonstrators." "Administrators were culpable by their cowardice; teachers were culpable for their instigation and encouragement of the troublemakers" (21). In the end, Shils offers nothing more than a tired rehash of Cold War anti-Communism blended with a 1980s defense of the need for authority. Above all, he proclaims the need to safeguard the values of tradition, nationhood, normalcy, and civility (31). We shall see how hollow these preachments about civility turn out to be.

In *Destructive Generation: Second Thoughts About the Sixties* (1989), Peter Collier and David Horowitz engage in a vitriolic orgy of self-criticism mixed with dire warnings. "The clock is running out on democracy and freedom," they shout. These born-again conservatives have come full circle, condemning all shades of contemporary liberalism as mere window dressing for the Communist Menace lurking in the background.

In contrast to all these neoconservative revisionist histories, the contributions to this volume form part of a more sympathetic rediscovery and reappraisal of the 1960s. Our essays seek to shed light on one particular segment of "the movement"—the development of radical sociology. Others have dealt with radicalism in some of the disciplines, including sociology, focusing primarily on theoretical issues in each field (see for example Flacks 1982). But the history of what really happened, at least as it is remembered by the participants, has not been systematically explored. Equally important to sociologists is the traditional issue of how and why some of us became movement participants. What remains unexplored is how those individuals who were involved in building the political movement in the 1960s also participated in forming a radical critique of the prevailing ideas that defined the academic disciplines.

ORGANIZATION OF THIS BOOK

Radical Sociologists and the Movement is divided into four parts. The first focuses on the history of radical sociology and the broader movement of which it was a significant part. The second concentrates on the issues of "political socialization," or how particular individuals came to develop a radical political consciousness. The third investigates what it is that radical sociologists actually do in their sociological practice, both within and outside the academy. The final part presents two documents that symbolize and express key moments within the development of radical perspectives in sociology. Each of these parts is preceded by a short introduction that locates the individual essays within their particular historical contexts.

REFERENCES

Bloland, Harland, and Sue M. Bloland. 1974. *American Learned Societies in Transition: A Report Prepared for the Carnegie Commission on Higher Education.* New York: McGraw-Hill.

Bloom, Allan. 1987. *The Closing of the American Mind.* New York: Simon and Schuster.

Bunzel, John, ed. 1988. *Political Passages: Journeys of Change Through Two Decades, 1968–1988*. New York: Free Press.

Collier, Peter, and David Horowitz. 1989. *Destructive Generation: Second Thoughts About the Sixties*. New York: Summit Books.

Flacks, Richard. 1982. "Marxism and Sociology." In *The Left Academy*, ed. Bertell Ollman and Edward Vernoff. New York: McGraw-Hill.

Gitlin, Todd. 1987. *The Sixties: Years of Hope, Days of Rage*. New York: Bantam Books.

Herf, Jeffrey. 1988. "The New Left: Reflections and Reconsiderations." In *Political Passages: Journeys of Change Through Two Decades, 1968–1988*, ed. John Bunzel. New York: Free Press.

Insurgent Sociologist. 1977. Vol. 1, nos. 1–4 (Winter).

Jacoby, Russell. 1987. *The Last Intellectuals*. New York: Basic Books.

Mills, C. Wright. 1958. *The Causes of World War III*. New York: Ballantine Books.

Norton, Theodore Mills, and Bertell Ollman, eds. 1978. *Studies in Socialist Pedagogy*. New York: Monthly Review Press.

Perrucci, Robert. 1973. "In the Service of Man: Radical Movements in the Professions." In *Professionalisation and Social Change: Sociological Review Monograph No. 20*, ed. Paul Halmos. Keele, U.K.: University of Keele.

Shils, Edward. 1988. "Totalitarians and Antinomians." In *Political Passages: Journeys of Change Through Two Decades, 1968–1988*, ed. John Bunzel. New York: Free Press.

PART I

The History of Radical Sociology

The essays in this part comprise personal recollections of radical sociology and the sixties movements of which it was a part. Dick Flacks reflects on the formation of the Sociology Liberation Movement and the establishment sociology it sought to challenge. He makes it quite plain that the university and established sociology departments were by no means immune from the logics of imperialism, militarism, and capitalism. Flacks concludes that participants in the movements of the 1960s helped to redefine the intellectual terrain of sociology and reshape the role and relationships that characterize the university. Yet these achievements were accompanied with certain losses. As radical sociology became part of established sociology, a sense of community among radical intellectuals was lost.

Alfred McClung Lee reminds us that the radical roots of sociology can be traced back to the 1870s. His particular involvement in radical sociology helps illuminate crucial developments in the profession, such as the Society for the Study of Social Problems, the Sociology Liberation Movement, radical caucuses within the American Sociological Association, regional radical caucuses, and the Association for Humanist Sociology. Lee's position as active participant and former office holder in the American Sociological Association, the Society for the Study of Social Problems, and the Association for Humanist Sociology, gives him an unusual vantage point for recalling turning points in both the profession and the discipline.

Like Flacks, Carol A. Brown recollects the early years of the Sociology Liberation Movement but with a slightly different focus. She also notes the formation of the black, gay, women's, and Chicano caucuses. Brown reflects on sexism within radical sociology, a problem that persists today. She argues that the legitimacy of radicals within the profession began with the formation of the Marxist Section of the American Sociological Association.

15

Evan Stark provides a firsthand look at establishment sociology with particular reference to the University of Wisconsin at Madison. He celebrates the "collective imagination" of those who participated in the 1960s movements and presents the social reality of the conditions that radicals were fighting against. Sociology was a far different field two decades ago.

The first attempt to build a radical sociology department at a major university occurred at Washington University (St. Louis) in the late 1960s. By 1972 all the radical faculty had either been fired or left on their own accord. Henry Etzkowitz discusses the fate of this short-lived experiment and ponders the lack of unity among radicals as a major factor in its demise. He bemoans the fact that with the incorporation of radical perspectives within mainstream sociology, a self-conscious radical sociology no longer exists.

The development of a radical sociology was part of the broader movements of the 1960s. Martin J. Murray provides a window into radical activity around the University of Texas. He reflects on the relationship between the university and the community in terms of political activity and questions the enduring legacy of radical politics in Austin.

Chapter 1

The Sociology Liberation Movement: Some Legacies and Lessons

Dick Flacks

TWENTY YEARS AGO, in August 1968, some of us came together to form what we called the Sociology Liberation Movement. What follow are some recollections and reflections about that time, and an effort to point a few lessons.

The idea for the Sociology Liberation Movement began to germinate at least a year earlier. In 1967, some of us at the San Francisco meetings of the American Sociological Association (ASA) got together to push a resolution opposing U.S. involvement in Vietnam. The result was a rather stormy business meeting. The very idea that a "scientific" organization would take a stand on a public issue was considered anathema. I think the outcome of that event was that the question was sent to a mail ballot of the ASA voting membership, and the resolution thus failed. But the debate opened a political cleavage in the organization, revealing what appeared to be a deep ideological and, to a great extent, generational polarization. That cleavage traveled a fault line that dated back at least to the 1930s, when Robert S. Lynd asked his sociological colleagues, "Knowledge for what?" It traveled through the postwar period when the "scientific" model of the discipline was consolidated, and sociology began to be dominated by the hope that it would flourish as a state-sponsored profession—a view challenged by a marginalized few whose hero, of course, was C. Wright Mills.

By the early 1960s, at least a few of us then in graduate school were inspired by Mills's *The Sociological Imagination* and by two anthologies, *The New Sociology* and *Sociology on Trial*, and to question the prevailing paradigms and practices of the field.[1] At the same time, the unfolding events of the 1960s seemed to provide daily evidence that the vaunted "science" of sociology was quite unable to grasp what was actually happening in society.

The ASA debate on the Vietnam issue revealed that the "scientific" model was not only intellectually dubious but morally compromising; the

17

alleged need for scientific neutrality made it illegitimate for the professional association to take a collective stand. The debate created the impression that the dissident wing of the discipline was up against a monolithic "establishment" unified by commitment to a shared paradigm and by a willingness to cultivate their roles as servants of power.

Such perceptions of the state of sociology were of course profoundly reinforced by the deepening polarization of academia and of society as a whole in the months that followed. More and more, those who identified with the black struggle and with the student movement felt compelled to take sides in what seemed increasingly to approach a revolutionary situation. Even if one did not take literally the image of revolutionary apocalypse, those who identified with the New Left found it hard to escape the sense that a massive turning was necessary—and possible.

In early spring of 1968, I helped organize an event at the University of Chicago called the New University Conference (NUC). It brought together a large number of radical faculty and graduate students, for the purpose of providing support to an increasingly embattled student movement and formulating some strategic directions for challenging the established structures of the disciplines and the prevailing practices of academic life. NUC established itself as an ongoing organization; one of its strategies would be the formation of what were called radical caucuses in the disciplines.

Shortly after this conference, the Columbia revolt began—and out of that came a group of sociology graduate students eager to carry forward the challenge to academia. Somehow NUC sociologists and Columbia graduate students linked together to organize what we called the Sociology Liberation Movement. The idea was to find ways to shake up the discipline and challenge its establishment, starting with the annual ASA meeting in Boston, where we planned to develop a series of workshop discussions on the theme "Knowledge for Whom?"

The ASA president that year was Philip Hauser, who had recently chaired the department at the University of Chicago, where I was one of the few untenured members. When I arrived in Boston I found a message summoning me and other SLM organizers to a meeting with Hauser and other ASA officials the next morning in the penthouse suite of the convention hotel. I do not remember whether we had asked for such a meeting; in any event, it had certainly been sparked by our announced intention to challenge Hauser's choice for keynote speaker: Wilbur Cohen, Secretary of Health, Education, and Welfare. We found the choice ironic; Hauser, who represented an ASA leadership that had denounced the effort to pass an antiwar resolution, was now inviting a top member of the war administration to be an honored guest of the ASA. The participants in a discussion panel to follow Cohen's talk had already been announced; we knew it was unlikely that administration policy would receive any significant criticism from them.

Hauser began by announcing that if we planned to disrupt the convention we would be arrested. I was stunned by his ferocious threat. We had not planned any disruption; we had only asked that one of our group be on the discussion panel following Cohen's address, and we had asked people to wear black armbands to the keynote speech. Hauser seemed furious that we would in any way mar his presidential moment. In the end, however, calmer ASA heads prevailed and we were given the right to name a member of the panel.

We chose Martin Nicolaus, who had recently written a brilliant piece on Marx's *Grundrisse*, and who was remarkably and fearlessly eloquent in person. When his time came, Nicolaus presented a dramatic, slashing attack on what he called "fat-cat sociology" (see Chapter 15). It had to be one of the more electrifying moments in the history of the ASA, and it did quite a bit to establish the reality of our position. In retrospect, it provided an opening for "radical sociology."

These events in Boston coincided with the Democratic convention in Chicago, television images of which flickered continuously throughout the days at ASA. People watched in frustrated impotence as police beat demonstrators in Grant Park and in front of the Chicago Hilton. At the business meeting, a motion was put forward to withdraw ASA conventions from Chicago for the next decade (three were scheduled during that period). This time, moral outrage prevailed over "professional" neutrality, and the motion was adopted. And it was not an empty symbolic gesture. In the days that followed, many other organizations followed ASA's lead in cancelling conventions in Mayor Daley's city—much to the chagrin of the Chicago press.

Scenes from the Revolution at the University of Chicago

In 1968, we assumed the worst: Society was bound to get more repressive; what happened that summer on the streets of Chicago was just a foretaste of things to come. The black rebellion would become more militant, more explicitly revolutionary, more threatening; the war in Vietnam signified a spreading Third World revolutionary uprising; more and more American young people would refuse to be used as cannon fodder in putting down domestic rebellion and global revolution.

We imagined that sociology as discipline and profession was useful to the emerging apparatus of repression, and that sociologists would al- low—and even welcome—their mobilization to such use. There was evi- dence of this. For example, there was Project Camelot, a large-scale De- fense Department effort to use social science techniques to analyze Latin American revolutionary movements. Less blatantly, there was the annual national student survey launched by Alexander Astin, under the auspices of the National Council in Education. He explained that the survey could be used to develop profiles of protest-prone students to aid colleges' admissions screening. Since I had done empirical research on the social backgrounds of student activists, this sort of claim made me painfully aware that, whatever the researcher's original intentions, one's work could readily be used to increase the sophistication of agencies of social control.

Morris Janowitz, a member of my department at Chicago, had pro- duced a pamphlet entitled "The Social Control of Escalated Riots"; it seemed to be the epitome of the willing involvement of top sociologists with the looming repression. As I recall it, the pamphlet advocated a strategy of massive roundup and arrest of urban rioters (defined as pref- erable to the use of deadly force). Janowitz proudly told a gathering that he had mailed this document to every police chief in America, but re- fused to engage in discussion about the morality of such an effort.

In conversations over the years, Janowitz had frequently expressed the view that sociologists had no choice but to provide systematic knowl- edge to elites; according to him, the left opposition was not interested in science. Serving as policy researchers and analysts to established elites was, at least, a way to enhance the rationality of the powerful and it was the only way, he would argue, that sociological knowledge could make a difference in the real world. It did not occur to him that his legitimacy as a scientist was weakened by his readiness to aid one side in deadly social conflict; he certainly felt no obligation to share his insights with black leaders or activists.

Janowitz's personal style and his perspective on the discipline thus provided me with daily evidence that the university in general and soci- ology in particular were on the road to becoming integrated with the control apparatus of a repressive state. At the University of Chicago, in the months following the ASA convention, this perception was brought into sharp focus in a series of what seemed to me epic events.

The first was a dinner hosted by the university in the fall of 1968 to mark the inauguration of Edward Levi as president. The dinner was held at the Conrad Hilton, just a few months after demonstrators were bloodied outside its lobby. Invited guests at the dinner included Richard J. Daley, McGeorge Bundy, and quite a few other leaders of the local and national establishment. It was, I remember remarking at the time, as if a mad director had decided to stage a guerrilla theater piece dramatizing the links between the university and the power elite. Some students picketed outside. Others, invited guests, made their displeasure known inside. These demonstrators were greeted with fury; students were kicked and slapped and spat upon by persons of considerable public renown. It was a time when almost every day you could read somebody bemoaning the ways in which student protesters were destroying civility in the university. On this particular occasion, however, a rather mild student provocation seemed to elicit quite extraordinary displays of incivility from those held to be the very pillars of civilization.

Soon after this, it was announced that Marlene Dixon had been denied contract renewal by the University of Chicago sociology department. Marlene was one of the very few women with a regular professional appointment at Chicago; she had developed a substantial student following, and the nonrenewal of her contract, after only three years, was itself unusual, since as a rule junior faculty were given six years before a final tenure decision. In a protest in February 1969, several hundred students occupied the administration building. President Levi and the faculty leadership decided that, rather than calling the police to eject the students, they would be left in the building but that disciplinary proceedings would be instituted against them.

Less than a dozen of us on the faculty supported Marlene Dixon and the student protest, while large numbers of senior faculty mobilized against the students. Almost every day, at least one distinguished faculty member would convene a press conference to "explain" events. Several émigré scholars compared the students to the Nazi SS or the Nazi invasion of their respective countries. A Nobel scientist drew headlines with the charge that the student action at Chicago was part of a global conspiracy hatched in Peking. A world-famous psychiatrist confidently diagnosed the students' neuroses. Rarely have so many famous scholars been so ready to rush forward with such egregious propaganda.

More disturbing was the readiness of faculty to participate directly in vigilante action. Faculty groups, accompanied by photographers, roamed through the sit-in, while others made themselves available to search among the photos for students they could identify. This was a university that claimed to be a haven of traditional academic values, in which faculty mentorship and student apprenticeship were at the heart of its stated mission—and yet faculty by the score were willing to participate in a process in which, inevitably, they would betray students who had trusted them deeply.

The sit-in lasted sixteen days before the students finally gave up. In the weeks that followed some 120 of them were expelled or suspended for long periods. These punishments were decided by a faculty disciplinary committee that set the penalties in relation to the students' level of remorse. Students who said they were sorry were typically not suspended; those who refused to fabricate remorse were. It was, I believe, the largest purge of student protesters at any major university. Many of the expelled students became leaders of the Weathermen—while President Edward Levi, presumed architect of this strategy of control, later became Attorney General under Gerald Ford.

The Marlene Dixon protest had a major impact within the sociology department. Graduate students engaged in an intensive, almost round-the-clock discussion of the nature of the discipline, the social role of the university, and the rights of students. Long-simmering discontents about the department's exclusion of unconventional paradigms, the authoritarian nature of faculty-student relations, and the university's role in the ghetto community surrounding it were subjected to passionate debate. The generational battle at the ASA convention the previous summer was being re-enacted, but at a far higher level of intensity and in a context that was, in a way, more meaningful.

During those weeks in the winter and spring of 1969, a significant number of the next generation of sociologists were reshaping their identities in the crucible of confrontation with some of the senior leaders of the field. Some decided to leave the field altogether; most ended up with a commitment to forge a new way of being and working, radically different from the models provided by their faculty mentors. Their discourse and their demands were virtually incomprehensible to that faculty. Some imagined they would be victims of their students' Oedipal rage. Philip Hauser made no secret of his conviction that the students were committed Maoist revolutionaries.

This mixture of fear and anger resulted in strong desires to punish students. Faculty discussions of student awards were poisoned by efforts to bias decisions against those seen as leaders of protest—all the while proclaiming that political considerations should have no part in the review process. Throughout the experience, I recall being continuously astonished by how quickly this privileged and secure faculty group could mirror a John Birch Society meeting in both temper and ideology. Lurid depictions of the student protesters' capabilities for violence and disorder—including repeated reference to their "smell" and slovenliness—

enlivened department meetings. Repeated calls for law and order, including proposals that the faculty themselves prepare to physically engage the students, were made in meetings and in public press conferences.

The climax of events for me personally occurred when a man posing as a newspaper reporter assaulted me in my office, inflicting injuries that resulted in a month-long hospital stay and many additional months of recuperation. Several of my "colleagues" immediately jumped to the conclusion that I had attempted suicide and spread this news widely in the hours after the assault. Once it was clear that I had not hit myself over the head, a member of the department commented, "Flacks finally got what was coming to him."

After these events, it was not hard for me to leave the University of Chicago; indeed, several of the more rational members of the faculty departed shortly thereafter as well. Not much in the way of reforms to meet the student demands happened in the department in the aftermath. But the experience had major effects on many of the students; I've often thought that more radical sociologists were created under the mentorship of Morris Janowitz, Philip Hauser, Edward Shils, and Donald Bogue than under the influence of all of us academic Marxists and self-avowed radicals in the years since.

A final insight into those months became available to me nearly a decade later. After several years of litigation, files of the Chicago Police's "Red (or "Subversive") Squad" were opened and made available to those of us who had been subjects of its surveillance. In my own materials, I found memoranda from the Boston police to the Chicago police, written several weeks before the Boston ASA convention in 1968, stating that they had received information that I was coming from Chicago to disrupt the ASA meeting and asking for background information about me. So, ten years after the fact, I learned that Phil Hauser had been quite serious about having me arrested, in fact had laid the groundwork well in advance.

SOME REFLECTIONS ON THE REVOLUTION

What, twenty years later, can be said about the meaning of such events? It's not an unimportant question, I think, especially now when younger people—graduate students and a new breed of undergraduate activists— seem particularly eager to learn what they can from the experience of the sixties.

Let's consider the general mission of the university and the particular issue of academic civility. The students expelled from Chicago were

charged with violating the mission of the university. Over and over, opponents of the student movement charged that its goal was the destruction of the university, or that at the very least the students by their actions
were destroying the civility without which intellectual discourse was impossible. Today, Allan Bloom's best-selling book *The Closing of the American Mind* traces the alleged collapse of our culture to the destructive-
ness of student protest; the image of Cornell blacks carrying guns on
campus symbolizes his particular nightmare.

My experience in those times was quite different. Student protests
that I witnessed were, considering the circumstances, remarkably civil in
tone and demeanor. The Marlene Dixon protest invigorated intellectual
debate across the campus; within the sit-in itself, a passionate engagement with ideas was certainly evident. Meanwhile, prevailing faculty attitudes tended to refuse the engagement that students sought, and quite a
few faculty leaders lost all semblance of civility in responding to the conflict.

University radicals in the sixties were deeply ambivalent about academic life. To a great extend the white student movement grew out of
guilt over the privileges of university existence and a desire to break
down the insulations shielding themselves from external reality. Radical
sociology was in part an effort to compel sociologists to confront these
privileges and insularities, and to bring into being a sociology for the
exploited and the powerless.

At the same time, student and faculty protest in the sixties was fueled
by betrayed hopes for the university. Much of the passion and the rhetoric of the movement grew out of the belief that the university could
maintain an autonomy from the logics of imperialism, militarism, and
capitalism, that it could be a relatively free space—indeed an arena
where the future could actually be reshaped and to some extent exemplified. In this sense, rather than destroy the university, the New Left
sought to renew its legitimacy, rescue it from impending integration into
the military-industrial complex, create within it for the first time a semblance of genuine intellectual community. In my experience, it was we
who took the mission of the university seriously and sought to preserve
it.

Whether the university could be so saved, whether its reform was in
fact a worthy political activity, or, as some came to argue by the end of
the sixties, whether such aspirations were little more than *petit bourgeois*
rationalizations for abdicating the real struggle—these issues were never
resolved within the framework of the New University Conference. Indeed, NUC as an organization never achieved a coherent identity, and

eventually died. But it helped spawn radical caucuses across the disciplines, and these networks, made up largely of those who intended to make their lives over the long pull within the academy, served for many years as symbols and centers of ferment that had great effect on the disciplines and the profession.

WHAT DID WE ACCOMPLISH?

Although many of our political comrades were driven out of university life, either by political repression or the closing down of the job market, most of our generation of academic radicals have had academic careers of some sort, and in the process have helped redefine the intellectual terrain of sociology. To a lesser extent we have helped reshape the roles and relationships that characterize the university.

Although the legitimation of the "left academy" was one of the main goals of the radical caucuses, its achievement was not what we expected in 1968 and 1969 and 1970. We thought it much more likely that the academic establishment would work to purge us from university life, while consolidating its already evident alliance with an increasingly authoritarian elite. Our choices were, we thought, less whether to work for the reshaping of the university than to define our roles in the larger society as social struggle intensified. I doubt that any of us took seriously the prospect that in a short time we would be getting coopted into leadership roles in the ASA, or that the perspectives we passionately contrasted with the established paradigms would soon become dominant rather than underground. Even more ironically, what we could not have foreseen was that the achievement of many of our hopes would be possible without the transformation of either the society or the university.

We were, it turns out, wrong to believe that there was a self-conscious and powerful "establishment" in sociology that could or would mobilize real power against us. We were, in fact, wrong to think that sociology had become a crucial vehicle for maintaining social control. Indeed, we shared with analysts like Daniel Bell and other theorists of the postindustrial society an exaggerated belief in the strategic centrality of the university for shaping the society's future—a belief that led us to think that our challenge to the discipline and to the university was more weighty than it turned out to be.

A less apocalyptic, more modest perspective in the late sixties might have enabled us to think more strategically about our relation to the university over the long term. Such a perspective, however, would have been very difficult to advance at that time, given the willingness of our elders to call the cops, and given the degree to which revolution was in the air. Because we could not, at the time, imagine the prospect of our professionalization, we did not formulate politics relevant to that situation.

Still, what we had then was the start of a community of left intellectuals that transcended the boundaries of discipline and profession, that sought links with the exploited and powerless, that embodied standards for work that were more collective and humanistic than those embodied in academia, and that encouraged us to put teaching and social responsibility ahead of career survival. Our "successes" in the last two decades have been at the cost of that community.

Intellectual collectives are relatively easily sustained as frameworks of resistance. We had not prepared to operate collectively under the conditions we've encountered in the 1970s and 1980s. Nothing in our 1960s experience had led us to expect either the tightness of the job market or the marketability of "Marxism." The result is that we have become members of the university, involved more than we ever expected with problems of personal survival, career advancement, and institutional niche making; we have accepted, more than we would have thought possible, the terms, canons, and criteria of conventional academia as unchangeable. For not a few academic radicals, the decline of the left community has been personally costly; a number of institutions that once may have been ready to accept outspoken Marxist or feminist critics instead embarked, in the late 1970s and 1980s, on "retrenchments" that included purging or punishing leftists whose presence might damage their marketing strategies. Such cases undoubtedly had chilling effects on colleagues, further reinforcing propensities toward careerism.

The political consequences of the routinization of the academic left have been largely unstudied. The most pessimistic view is that of Russell Jacoby in *The Last Intellectuals*. His claims about the failures of the academic left ought to be the subject, not of agonized hand wringing or defensive polemic, but of serious analysis and discussion. The impression he conveys—that left academics have totally abandoned our public roles—surely misses the manifold ways many of us have continued to work in community and movement contexts, and ignores the social impacts of our work as teachers and as scholars. But his challenge provides an opportunity for much-needed reflection.

If there was an establishment sociology twenty years ago, we helped do it in; and so, for good or ill, and despite rear-guard resistance in some departments, the field is to some extent ours. What we lost in the process, however, is hope for a community of radical intellectuals engaged in a collective effort to remake sociology so that it might begin to be a vehicle of human enlightenment. Such a loss was not, however, inevitable, nor is it necessarily permanent. In fact, as academic job markets change once again, along with national political climates, the time may once more be right for reconnection.

NOTE

1. See C. Wright Mills, *The Sociological Imagination* (New York: Oxford University Press, 1959); I. L. Horowitz, *The New Sociology* (New York: Oxford University Press, 1964); M. Stein and A. Vidich, *Sociology on Trial* (Englewood Cliffs, N.J.: Prentice-Hall, 1963).

Chapter 2

Steps Taken Toward Liberating Sociologists
Alfred McClung Lee

AS WE CELEBRATE here in this collection of essays the surge of efforts in the late 1960s to liberate sociologists from their apologetic, scientistic, class-bound shackles, we should not forget that their feminist, antiracist, social work, populist, and Marxist roots go back to the discipline's beginnings in this country.

From the 1870s, when sociologists began appearing on our campuses, they championed a kind of revolt against established social theorists. These new professors were led primarily by clergypeople, social workers, and occasional refugees from physical, biological, or another social science. Once ensconced within the academic structure, however, many found it expedient to disavow taints of "uplift" or even amelioration. They were soon attempting to carry this trend to the development of a more saleable and profitable, less controversial discipline.

An important part of the social work movement in the late nineteenth century was its effort, led primarily by women, to create a humanized sociology. Mary Jo Deegan (1987, 354) calls Jane Addams "the most outstanding leader, intellectually, institutionally, and politically," in this campaign. Addams cofounded the famous Hull House in Chicago in 1889. She "provided the institutional home for humanist sociology in the community and an international model for sociological pacifism." After the University of Chicago established a sociology department in 1892, Addams helped provide realistic experiences for the sociology students in Hull House, but she was not asked to be a member of the faculty. Albion W. Small, the head of the Chicago department, and his male colleagues did not want their "academic respectability" to be tainted by a "soft" or "uplift" viewpoint. The university did set up its own social work settlement in 1894 with Mary Eliza McDowell as its first head, but she was not given faculty status in the sociology department. Addams nevertheless was honored many times for her work; in 1931 she became the first

American woman to receive the Nobel Peace Prize (Addams [1910], 1960; Wade 1958).

In the late 1800s, the largest group of sociologists were the so-called social economists or practical sociologists; they were "chiefly interested in social work and amelioration" (Barnes 1948, 741). Deegan (1987) discusses two groups of female sociologists: ten she calls "pioneers," born between 1855 and 1865, and fifteen "professionals" born in the next decade. All the pioneers were members of the American Sociological Society after its formation in 1905, and eight gave papers at its meetings. Thirteen of the professionals earned doctorates in sociology. The pioneers included, in addition to Addams and McDowell, Charlotte Perkins Gilman, Emily G. Balch, Florence Kelley, Julia Lathrop, Lucy Salmon, Mary E. B. Smith, Ann G. Spencer, and Marian Talbot. The professionals had such stars of public and private welfare agencies and projects as Edith Abbott, Sophonisba Breckenridge, Leta Hollingworth, Elsie Clews Parsons, Mary Van Kleek, and Jessie Taft. These "pioneers and professionals," Deegan notes, "were oriented towards practical change emerging from an alliance between sociologists and the community" (356–57). Women before World War I may have been largely marginal to the academic sociological establishment, but through personal leadership in community and national welfare projects and through such books as Addams's *Twenty Years at Hull-House* (1910) and Mary E. Richmond's *Social Diagnosis* (1917), they did a great deal to force steps toward the liberation of the discipline in academic circles and generally.

Before World War I, dissenters from establishment thinking within academia were individual and, since there were few female professors, mostly male. Examples among sociologists include Edward Alsworth Ross and William Graham Sumner. Ross was fired in 1900 from Stanford University for his views on railroad entrepreneurs and Chinese immigration (Furner 1975). Sumner had to fight bitter attempts by members of the Yale Club of New York City to have him removed from the Yale faculty because of his attacks on plutocracy and U.S. imperialism (Sumner 1898).

The organization of the American Sociological Society (ASS) in 1905 and of the American Association of University Professors (AAUP) in 1915 did little if anything to protect dissidents. The first AAUP president, John Dewey, even went so far as to assert that politically inspired dismissals "are too rare even to suggest the formation of an association like this." The AAUP, like the ASS was dedicated to "developing professional standards"—in other words, shoring up the profession's respectability. The many creative "upstarts" who refused to conform either disguised their views or were forced out of a faculty. Historian Ellen W. Schrecker (1986, 16–17, 19) concludes, "The AAUP's preoccupation with developing principles instead of helping individuals simply reinforced the standard practice. For, despite the existence of the AAUP, academics who lost their jobs for political reasons could only rarely get them back or, in many cases, find new ones."

The 1915 firing of Scott Nearing from the University of Pennsylvania's Wharton School of Business focused attention on the utility of such an individual case to dramatize the repressive academic situation. It led the Penn trustees to make the university's decisions on tenure less arbitrary, but it did not help Nearing get his job back. The nationwide publicity from his case produced a job offer fron only one school, the labor-oriented municipal University of Toledo. He taught there for two years—until his opposition to World War I earned him another dismissal (Nearing 1972, chaps. 5 and 6).

The media hysteria of World War I nurtured an increase in academic repression similar to that of the McCarthy period after World War II. Nicholas Murray Butler, president of Columbia University, characterized wartime academic administrative policies when he told the 1917 graduating class: "What had been tolerated before becomes intolerable now. . . . There is and will be no place in Columbia University . . . for any person who opposes or counsels opposition to the effective enforcement of the laws of the United States or who acts, speaks, or writes treason (Gruber 1975, 199). He therefore fired James McKeen Cattell and Henry Wadsworth Longfellow Dana and convinced Charles A. Beard that he should resign. Schrecker (1986, 23) notes, "In almost every situation, faculty members and administrators responded to outside pressures for the dismissal of dissenting faculty members in accord with what they believed would best protect or enhance their school's reputation. The rhetoric of academic freedom obscures those concerns, as, in many instances, it was designed to."

Between the world wars, academic dissent became somewhat less an individual act and more organization-related, as student and faculty union units, social problems clubs, and socialist and communist discussion and agitation groups appeared. The world of academia was starting to include more students and faculty from the other side of the tracks. Within sociology, the struggle for secure curricular domains was making the scientism of such sociologists as Lester F. Ward (1841–1913) and Franklin Henry Giddings (1855–1931) very attractive. Aspirants to academic status found Ward's biologistic terms and Giddings's Spencerian doctrines, statistics, and antisocialism useful tools for their trade.

On the other hand, one of the most popular introductory texts of the late 1920s and the 1930s was one edited by Jerome Davis and Harry Elmer Barnes. In that book's introduction, Davis (1927, xxiv) asks, "How many Americans now see clearly . . . that we have a dualism between our ideals and practices? How many sense the aesthetic starvation in our life, the obedience to blind regimentation, the slavery to the folkways which bind us whether we will or not?" Davis is especially concerned with what he calls social reconstruction, which he believes "implies more than mere change; it involves a reshaping, a remaking, a re-forming of society, and that demands intelligence and character" (Davis and Barnes 1931, 699).

Jerome Davis, one of the coeditors of this early text, had continuing difficulties with the Yale administration from the time of his appointment to teach sociology in the divinity school in 1924 until he was fired in 1937. Despite his many contributions to sociological research, he was ignored by the university's department of sociology. His final "mistake" was the publication of his book *Capitalism and Its Culture* (1935). At the same time, the young and (for a while) somewhat insurgent Eastern Sociological Society elected him its 1937–1938 president; and he was national president of the American Federation of Teachers from 1936 to 1939 (A. Lee 1987).

However, many sociologists and social psychologists did not follow scientistic and commercialized routes to survival during the 1930s. Some wanted to help constructive social movements they saw developing. This was one motive for the formation, in 1936, of the Society for the Psychological Study of Social Issues (SPSSI). SPSSI's founders were alarmed by "the attempted silencing of political dissenters by the government, its agencies, and by conservative businessmen who controlled many colleges and universities" (Sargent and Harris 1986, 44). One SPSSI founder recalled: "Fascism was a threatening reality in Europe and an alarming possibility in the United States." SPSSI thus came into being as "a group that might seek to create more job openings, . . . to lobby in Washington for the inclusion of mental health services in the federal budget, to facilitate research on pressing social problems, and to defend colleagues who seemed to be victims of unfair treatment" (Stagner 1986, 35).

SPSSI was part of what might be called the propaganda analysis movement, which had been gaining increasing academic attention ever since the end of World War I. Such journalists as Upton Sinclair (1919), Walter Lippmann (1922, 1925), Silas Bent (1927), and George Seldes (1929) had had an impact on academic thinking through their popular books, many of which were used as texts. The scholars and teachers John Dewey

(1927), Harold D. Lasswell (1927), Peter H. Odegard (1928, 1930), Kimball Young (1927, 1930), Hornell N. Hart (1933), and F. E. Lumley (1933) concerned themselves with propaganda's impact on its consumers. There was alarm about the "merchants of death" (munitions manufacturers) and about the demagoguery of Louisiana's Huey P. Long, Detroit's Father Charles E. Coughlin, and California's Dr. Francis E. Townsend (Beard and Beard 1939). Differences between President F. D. Roosevelt's radio "fireside chats" and events as reported in the media, unemployment and the rise of new industrial trade unions, and the existence of contradictory public opinion polls, as well as social conditions generally all encouraged the propaganda analysis movement in schools, colleges, voluntary associations, and trade unions.

In 1937, coincidental with the formation of SPSSI, the interdisciplinary Institute for Propaganda Analysis was organized by an outstanding group of social scientists and educators. It published a series of widely used controversial bulletins, including "Propaganda Techniques of German Fascism," "Britain Woos America," "Mr. [Martin] Dies Goes to Town," "Propaganda in the Schools," and thirty-nine other titles. It also sponsored popular books useful as texts, such as *The Fine Art of Propaganda* (Lee and Lee 1939; see E. Lee 1986, and A. Lee 1986).

The birth of SPSSI in 1936 and of the Institute for Propaganda Analysis in 1937 reflected the attachment of many teacher-scholars to social problems. The termination of the institute in 1941 and coincidental changes in SPSSI's role, together with the temporary decline of the propaganda analysis movement, are related not only to wartime conditions but also to social pressures that encouraged the emergence of the professor-entrepreneur as an even more dominant figure. This development was led by such figures as Paul F. Lazarsfeld (1901–1976) of the Columbia University Bureau of Applied Research and Samuel A. Stouffer (1900–1960) of Harvard and the Research Branch of the Information and Education Division of the United States Army. Starting in 1941, Stouffer, with the aid of Carl I. Hovland and Leonard S. Cottrell, guided 134 psychologists, sociologists, and statisticians in a four-year study of "the attitudes of the American soldier." Stouffer "had little sympathy for the conception of 'emancipatory' social science, and little understanding of it. His conception of applied social research embraced the human engineering model that [Robert S.] Lynd and [C. Wright] Mills deplored" (Smith 1984, 194). Fortunately, that training school of servants for governmental and corporate agencies did not influence all social scientists.

At about that time, in 1938, my wife, Elizabeth, and I were asked by Frank H. Hankins, president of ASS, to organize a press relations committee. Other members, then and later, included Read Bain, Robert E. Park, Harold A. Phelps, Malcolm M. Willey, and James Woodard. In our 1939 report, the committee defensively noted that "for the theories of social scientists to gain wide acceptance, they must finally reach the columns of popular periodicals, the speeches of popular leaders, and the discussions of Everyman." The committee proved itself shortly to be too successful—from the standpoint of ASS leaders—in doing just that.

Two incidents in the work of that ASS committee highlight responses to these efforts to popularize sociology. At the 1939 ASS convention, President Edwin H. Sutherland made his celebrated speech about white-collar criminality. The media reporters, to whom we had released advance press digests, loved it and gave extensive coverage to the convention that year. Our advance account of Pitirim A. Sorokin's controversial speech at the 1940 convention in Chicago got similarly broad attention. Sorokin attacked the pretentiousness and irrelevance of much current sociological writing in a manner he later expanded into his book *Fads and Foibles in Modern Sociology* (1956). This "destructive publicity" made sociologists and the ASS come alive to the general public. Even though we were criticized for the results, we continued our publicity experiment for the ASS for a few years (Rhoades 1981, 21, 40; A. Lee 1940).

Following World War II, the repressive McCarthyite furor—attacking everything even slightly (allegedly) to the left—was rising toward the peak it was to reach in the early 1950s. Several of us wanted to organize so that we could be more effective in academic struggles. SPSSI had become more conservative and more narrowly psychological—after all, it was a section of the American Psychological Association—and it became clear that establishing a new, independent organization would be best.

After Elizabeth and I joined the Brooklyn College faculty in 1949, we continued our campaign for a new organization. The Society for the Study of Social Problems (SSSP) came formally into existence on September 6, 1951, in the faculty lounge of Roosevelt College in Chicago (A. Lee 1961). It was not, and we trust it will never be, a section or affiliate of the ASS (now the American Sociological Association, or ASA). In early numbers of the SSSP journal, *Social Problems*, the organization's objectives are described, including the "improvement of the opportunities and working conditions of social scientists" and the "protection of freedom of teaching, research, and publication." In our book *Social Problems in America*, the first edition of which appeared in 1949, we asserted: "Only through seeing and understanding actual instances of white-collar criminality, unemployment, despair, panic, and riot can the sociologist bring . . . theories into some degree of correspondence with social realities. Only by studying the accumulated generalizations of other investigators can the specific instance of crime, poverty, or panic come into some more adequate perspective" (Lee and Lee 1949, vi). At least in its early years, SSSP members shared those values.

Many times during its first four years, SSSP's viability appeared doubtful. We had dependable friends who did much to make the venture grow, but as we reached out, some alleged participants could not have cared less about the organization's future. A growing list of convinced participants such as Sidney H. Aronson, E. W. Burgess, Stanley H. Chapman, Sylvia Fleis Fava, Jerome Himelhoch, Samuel Koenig, Arnold Rose, George Simpson, and Hugh H. Smythe among others made all the difference.

The 1952 convention of SSSP was held in Atlantic City, and it well might have been its last. People who told us they were making the arrangements did not do so. Fortunately, we learned about this in time. We were denied access to meeting space in the ASS's hotel but found another nearby. Because we provided advance accounts to the press about important convention discussions, the *New York Times* gave us far more space than it did the ASS. Featured were the speeches of Florian Znaniecki, George Simpson, Erwin O. Smigel, and E. W. Burgess with such titles as "Loyalty Oath Held Threat to Sociology" and "Big Business Is Found Chiseler's Favorite."

Since our 1952 convention was very popular (more than three hundred attended), the ASS Council demanded that I come before it and give some accounting of our "fragmentation" of the discipline. It was the first of many efforts to assimilate or affiliate SSSP. I told the Council that our mission was quite deliberate: We were representing aspects of sociology they were ignoring.

After SSSP's first four difficult years, a growing and dedicated body of social scientists came to value its annual conventions and publications more and more.

What then happened among students and faculty members during the 1950s? Dean H. Hoge contends: "Beginning in about 1939 or 1940, a new era of conservatism began, and by the early 1950s college students were privatistic, conventional in attitudes and behavior, and traditional in religious views" (Hoge and others 1987, 501). He puts the peak of "traditional religious commitment" around 1952–1954: "At that time protest movements were absent from campuses."

Hoge's generalizations are not based on participant observation studies but on questionnaire surveys among undergraduate men at Dartmouth College and the University of Michigan. He and his associates do not take into consideration the role of mass media mythmaking both in the 1950s and in what they regard as a parallel time of campus quietude, the 1980s. When Alexander Cockburn recently visited academic and other intellectual groups across the country, he found that "reports of a desolate political landscape are ludicrous. So powerful, though, is the mainstream propaganda that very often activists end up believing it themselves" (Cockburn 1988, 5). (My observations on many campuses in the 1950s confirmed that this was also the situation then.)

During the 1950s, protest movements, while given little attention in the news media, were not absent from our campuses. Some joined in agitation against American participation in the Korean War. Between 1950 and 1953, a total of 5,764,143 Americans served in that war; 33,629 died in action, and 20,617 more died from other causes, almost as great a toll for Americans as that of the more memorialized Vietnam War. I remember both the protestors and those frustrated and embittered veterans who returned to school from Korea. At about the same time, some students were involved in the struggles that led to the *Brown* v. *Topeka* 1954 school desegregation decision. Also during the 1950s, SSSP steadily grew, and its conventions provided a meeting place for liberal and radical network building.

What got mass media attention during the 1950s were the allegations by McCarthy, the FBI, and other governmental investigative committees about "reds" in the universities. These attacks cost many innovative people their scholarships, fellowships, or jobs, and it drove a great many more to be conformist. McCarthyist suppression did not kill dissent, but it did drive it underground. Faculty unions were just beginning to appear. American aid to France for its wars in Algeria and in Indochina were getting faculty and student attention. Nevertheless, "The 1950s was the period when the nation's colleges and universities were becoming increasingly dependent upon and responsive toward the federal government. The academic community's collaboration with McCarthyism was part of that process" (Schrecker 1986, 340).

The spectacular sit-ins in the 1960s helped start a trend toward more open protests. By September 1961, some seventy thousand blacks and whites had participated. Soon the expanding involvement of the United States in Vietnam and growing dissatisfaction of women brought more and more people out of their closets and into the streets. At the 1967 convention of the ASA in San Francisco, the *New York Times* (September 3, 1967) reported that "the elder statesmen [of the ASA] were shocked to see younger men being photographed by the Federal Bureau of Investigation at a sociologists' peace vigil outside the . . . Hilton Hotel." The assassination of Martin Luther King, Jr., in April 1968 and the major protests against the Vietnam War at the Democratic convention that August in Chicago powerfully stimulated the formation and strengthening of antiracist and antiwar protest groups.

For sociologists in 1967–1968, these events became channeled into the Sociology Liberation Movement (SLM) and the Women's Caucus. At the 1969 and 1970 ASA conventions, the SLM had spectacular confrontations with the ASA establishment and at the same meetings the Women's Caucus presented a series of proposals. The continuing contributions of the SLM are described elsewhere in this book (see Chapters 1 and 3).

The Women's Caucus, a relatively informal organization, told the ASA business meeting in 1969 "that women were 30 percent of the doctoral students in graduate schools . . . but only 4 percent of the full-time professors in graduate departments; . . . that women were 39 percent of the research associates in the elite graduate departments but only 5 percent of the associate and 1 percent of the full professors." These facts were presented by Alice G. Rossi (Rossi and others 1970), who then asserted that it is "outrageous that a custom persists whereby a woman research associate or lecturer with a Ph.D. and ten years or more of research experience cannot apply for research funds as a sole principal investigator, while a young man with a brand new assistant professorship but no prior responsibility for conducting research can readily do so." (See Chapter 16 in this book for the full text.)

In 1970 the Women's Caucus was reorganized as Sociologists for Women in Society (SWS). Pauline B. Bart (1985, 6) outlines SWS members' principal concerns at that time: "Undergraduate women and graduate women were discriminated against in the awarding of scholarships and fellowships and in job placement, and faculty hiring, in tenure line positions, and in awarding of tenure." Joan Huber (1985) recalls how SWS functioned: "Nasty secrets that women students had typically kept to themselves could be exposed to the fresh air of collective evaluation." SWS began to provide a practical way to counter sexual harrassment and job discrimination.

At the SWS fifteenth anniversary celebration in 1985, Alice Rossi (who was president of SWS and later ASA) advised members to move on to greater participation in the general professional societies, where they could become "more visible." SWS attention, she pointed out, should concentrate "on topics of very special concern to SWS members." She wanted SWS to continue, but she predicted it would "achieve the goals for which it was established, close its books, and quietly fade into history" (Rossi 1985, 4). Gender discrimination continues, and SWS is still going strong.

The future of the SLM and its publication, *The Insurgent Sociologist* (now *Critical Sociology*), has much in common with the aspirations of the members of SWS. Even when (*if*) SWS closes its books on gender discrimination, its members and others fighting for a more egalitarian science and society will need to continue the struggle. Basic class and power problems remain to be analyzed, and sociologists must help develop strategies and movements to handle or confront them constructively. Here I will merely tell my impressions of two developments in the SLM: One is my campaign in 1972–1974 for president-elect of the ASA, and the other is the formation in 1975 of the Association for Humanist Sociology (AHS).

At the 1972 ASA business meeting, I moved that the number of signatures required on a petition for write-in nominees be reduced. The motion was made subject to a referendum and was adopted. The official 1974 candidates were announced to the ASA membership in a memorandum dated November 12, 1973; also, the memo advised members that petitions signed within thirty days by at least one hundred voting members would add names to the list of candidates for the top positions; fifty signatures would nominate candidates for the council and several committees.

A group quickly got together a list of candidates and a petition that contained this prologue:

> Several sociologists who have previously been associated with the Sociology Liberation Movement, the Union of Radical Sociologists, and *The Insurgent Sociologist* are dissatisfied with the slate of candidates for elective office in the ASA that has been presented by the Committee on Nominations. We have prepared an alternative slate, below, which we hope to be able to put on the ballot by petition.

The goal of one hundred signatures was reached by December 12, and the campaign for the election was under way. The candidates included, in addition to myself for president-elect and Carol Brown for vice-president-elect, the following: For Council: John Horton, John C. Leggett, and Sidney Willhelm. For Committee on Publications: Mimi Goldman and David Walls. For Committee on Nominations: Gail Omvedt, Clifford English, Howard Ehrlich, Richard Collins, Jack N. Porter, and Jeff Shevitz. For Committee on Committees: Harvey Molotch, Joyce Stephens, Richard Quinney, Lynda Ann Ewen, Marlene Dixon, and Ted Goertzel.

Forty-six supporters signed a campaign letter endorsing the alternative slate and describing our proposals for reorienting the ASA. The proposals and nominations appeared in such periodicals as *The Insurgent*

Sociologist and the *Newsletter* of the East Coast Conference of Socialist Sociologists. They were briefly as follows:

> 1. To widen sociological discussions by encouraging the expression and participation of the wide spectrum of sociological perspectives that exist.
> 2. To work for greater participation of regional associations and rank-and-file members in the ongoing activities of the ASA.
> 3. To encourage a greater variety of media to disseminate sociological ideas—symposia, workshops, specialized periodicals, conferences.
> 4. To promote sociology and thereby broaden occupational opportunities for sociologists.
> 5. To bring minority groups and women more prominently into the activites of the ASA.
> 6. To obtain funding for many small research grants-in-aid of $1,000 or less to be distributed by a committee of the ASA.
> 7. To help insure continued curricular supervision by sociologists of sociological specialties.
> 8. To encourage and stimulate membership and participation in the International Sociological Association.
> 9. To provide and disseminate an open ASA budget so that all members will know where the money comes from and how it is spent.
> 10. To develop ASA sponsorship for innovative social policies of breadth and action programs of foresight.

Throughout my terms as president-elect, president, and past-president of the ASA, I had to contend with persistent opposition—even sabotage—from the strongly pro-establishment Council and office staff. (The fact that I represented a majority of the ASA members did not appear to matter.) In any event, since I had a controlling vote in the program committee, those I appointed to it managed to produce a much broader and more stimulating type of program than usual. Many matters that the national office was supposed to refer to me were handled without my consultation or consent. Nevertheless the wisdom of the proposals our group made at the time was such that many of them have had an influence on ASA practices then and later.

Today the ASA is declining in membership. I believe this is partly because of the persistent and unrepresentative power that entrepreneurial sociologists hold. Fortunately, other organizations such as the more representative regional societies, SSSP, AHS, and the Sociological Practice Association, keep the discipline alive and exciting.

We need to make our friends more visible in order to counter the establishment's better access to media and its rigidifying influence in all types of sociological endeavor. The fact that the ASA still has the reputation of being the principal legitimate sociological body makes it an especially important target for liberation efforts. I trust that our 1972–1974 campaign and the subsequent modifications of some ASA practices will encourage liberation folks to mount such a campaign as often as possible to give the ASA the jolts that it needs.

The body that became the Association for Humanist Sociology arose out of exchanges in print that Elizabeth and I had in the early 1970s with John F. Glass (1971; A. Lee 1971; Glass and Staude 1972), Martin Oppenheimer (1971; A. Lee 1972), and Charles P. Flynn (1975). As I wrote in *The Insurgent Sociologist* at that time (A. Lee 1973a, 20), humanistic sociologists are numerous, and radical sociologists as humanists do not call for sociology to perfect itself before it makes itself useful to humanity. On the contrary, they look upon propaganda analysis, social diagnosis, and recommendations for social policy and action as their chief products. These contributions serve people generally rather than elite special interests because their educational efforts and publications are accessible to a broad range of social organizations.

The first AHS convention was held at Miami University in Oxford, Ohio, the weekend of October 29–31, 1976. That first meeting was a warm social event combined with candid reporting and theorizing—the model for all AHS meetings since. The founding members and early recruits all appeared to agree that such modifiers of "sociology" as "radical" and "humanist" are superfluous. A science dealing with people in their relationships has to get at the roots of those relationships. To be scientific, its practitioners cannot content themselves with superficialities, and they serve humanity as best they can rather than special, vested interests and concerns. Nevertheless it is important to use the team to help offset powerful anti-humanist influences. (A. Lee 1973b, 1988).

Through its conventions, regional meetings, and summer camps, through its publications *Humanity and Society* (for longer articles) and *The Humanist Sociologist* (for news, reports, and short opinion pieces), and sponsored books, AHS continues to thrive and to stimulate a growing membership. It is one of several alternative sociological societies that are keeping the discipline alive, relevant, and exciting for faculties and students and useful for socially constructive efforts in our communities.

Sociology may be called a science, and it has such characteristics, but it is also—because of inevitable value intrusions—an arena of social conflict. Those who do not accept this position are usually agreeing to serve as apologists for the status quo. Let us hope that there will continue to be many steps toward the liberation of sociology from scientistic and class-bound shackles.

NOTE

Acknowledgment: I am indebted for critical suggestions to Rhonda Levine, Martin Murray, Martin Oppenheimer, and especially Elizabeth Briant Lee.

REFERENCES

Addams, Jane. 1910. *Twenty Years at Hull-House*. New York: Macmillan.
———. 1960. *A Centennial Reader*. Ed. Emily C. Johnson. New York: Macmillan.
Barnes, H. E. 1948. "Introductory Note." In *An Introduction to the History of Sociology*, ed. H. E. Barnes. Chicago: University of Chicago Press.
Bart, Pauline B. 1985. "Anniversary Remarks." *SWS Network* 14, no. 2 (November): 6–7.
Beard, C. A., and Mary R. Beard. 1939. *America in Midpassage*, 2 vols. New York: Macmillan.
Bent, Silas. 1927. *Ballyhoo: The Voice of the Press*. New York: Boni & Liveright.
Cockburn, Alexander. 1988. "Live Souls." *Zeta Magazine* 1, no. 2 (February): 5–15.
Davis, Jerome. 1927. "Introduction." In *Introduction to Sociology*, ed. Davis and H. E. Barnes. Boston: D. C. Heath; rev. ed.
———. 1935. *Capitalism and Its Culture*. New York: Farrar & Rinehart.
Davis, Jerome, and H. E. Barnes, eds. 1931. *Introduction to Sociology*. Boston: D. C. Heath; rev. ed.
Deegan, Mary Jo. 1987. "An American Dream: The Historical Connections Between Women, Humanism, and Sociology, 1890–1920." *Humanity and Society* 11, no. 3 (August): 353–65.
Dewey, John. (1927) 1946. *The Public and Its Problems*. Chicago: Gateway Books.
Flynn, C. P. 1975. Letter to the editor. *ASA Footnotes* 3, no. 3 (April): 8.
Furner, Mary O. 1975. *Advocacy and Objectivity*. Lexington: University of Kentucky Press.
Glass, J. F. 1971. "Re: Action." Association for Humanistic Psychology *Newsletter* 7, no. 4 (January): 6.
Glass, J. F., and J. R. Staude, eds. 1972. *Humanistic Society: Today's Challenge to Sociology*. Pacific Palisades, Calif.: Goodyear Publishing.
Gruber, Carol S. 1975. *Mars and Minerva*. Baton Rouge: Louisiana State University Press.
Hart, H. N. 1933. "Changing Social Attitudes and Interests." Chap. 8 in *Recent Social Trends*, ed. W. F. Ogburn and others. New York: McGraw-Hill.
Hoge, D. R. 1974. *Commitment on Campus*. Philadelphia: Westminster.
Hoge, D. R., and others. 1987. "The Return of the Fifties." *Sociological Forum* 2, no. 3 (Summer): 500–519.
Huber, Joan. 1985. "Why and How I Got Involved in SWS." *SWS Network* 14, no. 2 (November): 2–4.

Lasswell, H. D. 1927. *Propaganda Techniques in the World War*. New York: Alfred A. Knopf.

Lee, Alfred McClung. 1940. "Report of the Public Relations Committee." *American Sociological Review* 5, no. 1 (February): 104–5; no. 3 (June): 413–14.

———. 1961. "To the Editor." *Social Problems* 9, no. 4 (Spring): 386–89.

———. 1971. "Re: Action." Association for Humanistic Psychology *Newsletter* 7, no. 6 (April): 11.

———. 1972. Letter to editor. *Insurgent Sociologist* 2, no. 2 (Spring): 42.

———. 1973a. "Random Notes on Radicalism in Sociology." *Insurgent Sociologist* 3, no. 2 (Winter): 20–24.

———. 1973b. *Toward Humanist Sociology*. Englewood Cliffs, N.J.: Prentice-Hall.

———. 1986. "What Ever Happened to Propaganda Analysis?" *Humanity and Society* 10, no. 1 (February): 11–24.

———. 1987. "In Memorium: Jerome Davis (1891–1979)." *Humanity and Society* 11, no. 1 (February): 131–35.

———. 1988. *Sociology for People*. Syracuse, N.Y.: Syracuse University Press.

Lee, Alfred McClung, and Elizabeth B. Lee. 1939. *The Fine Art of Propaganda*. New York: Harcourt, Brace. Reissued by Octagon Books, 1972; and San Francisco: International Society for General Semantics, 1979.

———. 1949. *Social Problems in America*. New York: Henry Holt; rev. ed., 1955.

Lee, Elizabeth B. 1986. "Coughlin and Propaganda Analysis." *Humanity and Society* 10, no. 1 (February): 25–35.

Lippmann, Walter. 1922. *Public Opinion*. New York: Harcourt Brace.

———. 1925. *The Phantom Public*. New York: Harcourt Brace.

Lumley, F. E. 1933. *The Propaganda Menace*. New York: Appleton-Century.

Nearing, Scott. 1972. *The Making of a Radical*. New York: Harper & Row.

Odegard, P. H. 1928. *Pressure Politics*. New York: Oxford University Press.

———. 1930. *The American Public Mind*. New York: Columbia University Press.

Oppenheimer, Martin. 1971. "Unity for What?" *Insurgent Sociologist* 1, no. 4 (April): 7–8.

Rhoades, L. J. 1981. *A History of the American Sociological Association: 1905–1980*. Washington: American Sociological Association. 1965.

Richmond, Mary E. (1917) 1965. *Social Diagnosis*. New York: Free Press.

Rossi, Alice G., and others. 1970. "Statement and Resolutions of the Women's Caucus." *American Sociologist* 5, no. 1 (February): 63–65.

———. 1985. "The Formation of SWS." *SWS Network* 14, no. 2 (November): 2–4.

Sargent, S. S., and Benjamin Harris. 1986. "Academic Freedom, Civil Liberties, and SPSSI." *Journal of Social Issues* 42:43–67.

Schrecker, Ellen W. 1986. *No Ivory Tower: McCarthyism and the Universities*. New York: Oxford University Press.

Seldes, George. 1929. *You Can't Print That*. New York: Payson & Clark; reissued by Scholarly Press, 1968.

Sinclair, Upton. 1919. *The Brass Check*. Pasadena, Calif.: privately published.

Smith, M. B. 1984. "*The American Soldier* and Its Critics." *Social Psychology Quarterly* 47:192–98.

Sorokin, P. A. 1956. *Fads and Foibles in Modern Sociology and Related Sciences.* Chicago: Henry Regnery.

Stagner, Ross. 1986. "Reminiscences About the Founding of SPSSI." *Journal of Social Issues* 42:35–42.

Sumner, W. G. [1898] 1911. "The Conquest of the United States by Spain." Chap. 15 in G. Keller, ed., *War and Other Essays.* New Haven, Conn.: Yale University Press.

Wade, Louise C. 1958. "Mary Eliza McDowell." *Dictionary of American Biography*, suppl. vol. 2: 407–9.

Young, Kimball, ed. 1927. *Source Book for Social Psychology.* New York: Alfred A. Knopf.

———. 1930. *Social Psychology.* New York: Crofts.

Chapter 3

The Early Years of the Sociology Liberation Movement

Carol A. Brown

I WAS PART of the silent generation of the 1950s. I had grown up feeling poor because everybody else in our town on Long Island was rich. Many years passed before I realized how much security I actually had—class, ethnic, and racial security. I would have gone on to be as conservative as the others of my generation if I had married and settled down the way I was supposed to. Instead I went to graduate school and was at Columbia in the 1960s to learn sociology and have a career.

In my classes I learned functionalism; to earn money I worked on government-supported manpower research. I recognized the social problems of the 1960s but assumed they would be solved, probably by sociologists. The War on Poverty was fought in part with social science.

Outside the classroom I was confronted with ideas and political perspectives. What was wrong about the invasion of Cuba at the Bay of Pigs? Why should Columbia students resist citywide civil defense drills? Why were my black friends so bitter despite racial progress? Without realizing it, I was becoming liberal and open to further movement left.

In 1963 an *Esquire* magazine article about crazy radicals described an organization called Students for a Democratic Society (SDS); they wanted to end racism, create economic equality, and foster participatory democracy. I remember thinking, What's so crazy about that?

But for the Columbia University student strike, I might have remained a liberal. The Columbia chapter of SDS was demanding that the university end its involvement with the Institute for Defense Analysis, a conduit for military research grants. The Black Student Association was demanding cancellation of construction of a Columbia gymnasium that turned a blank face to neighboring Harlem. Demonstrations and confrontations led to student sit-ins at five buildings, followed by a violent police raid and the arrest of more than seven hundred students. The response was a massive student strike in May 1968.

I had to become involved only because I had been elected president

43

of the Graduate Sociology Society (GSS) the previous fall. I had been president in 1964 when the first radicals had begun shaking up our department. In 1967 a core of radical students had asked, almost demanded, that I run for president again. I think they needed a popular front. If they were going to attract liberal and apolitical students, they needed a representative who was apolitical and liberal.

When about thirty graduate sociology students sat in at Fayerweather Hall, I felt morally called upon to support them personally, and was called upon by the rest of the students to hold meetings. Like many others, I was horrified by the argument of force. I became one of the strike supporters and even briefly joined a later sit-in.

The graduate sociology students were very active in the student strike, in part because so many were radical, and in part because we had an organization, including a student journal, that enabled us to act collectively, uniting the radical and the active liberal students.

I was one of the student delegates who negotiated with the sociology faculty about issues such as ending required courses, hiring Marxist professors, and sharing departmental power. Student leadership rested with a core of ten to twenty radical activists in the department. The late Al Szymanski was perhaps the most prominent. At the regular GSS election Aubrey Brown became the official convenor of the GSS, or whatever we then called ourselves.

Thus began my rapid transformation to radicalism, from "How could they?" to "Why did they?" to "What are we going to do about it?" It was an intellectual and political transformation in my way of understanding and acting on the world. I was greatly helped out by those in the department who were already Marxist. The more I took part in departmental negotiations (and later ASA negotiations), the better I understood the nature of elites and social conflict. I have felt since then that in 1968 I learned more about how society worked than I had in the previous eight years.

The more I learned the angrier I got. Professor Herbert Hyman was reported to have said, "I don't understand about that Carol Brown; she used to be such a nice sweet girl." I had realized that most of the sociology I learned had been a lie. Robert Merton had taught that society is based on consensus; Bernard Barber that there are no significant class differences in the United States. I wrote an article for GSS's journal, *The Human Factor*, entitled, as I recall, "Karl, Come Home, All Is Forgiven," which expressed my discovery of the power and basic truth of Marxian analysis.

In the next two years I was very much involved organizing the Sociology Liberation Movement. I also began attending the graduate student

SDS, which became the New University Conference. I took part as a junior faculty member in a student strike at Hunter College. My planned dissertation about allied health professions changed to a Marxist analysis of occupational structure. In 1970 I began full-time teaching at the Heller School at Brandeis.

THE SOCIOLOGY LIBERATION MOVEMENT

The conflict between left and right in sociology is as old as the profession—maybe older. The conflict of the 1960s can properly be said to have begun at the 1967 convention of the American Sociological Association (ASA) when anti-war radicals sponsored and passed an antiwar resolution at the business meeting. The ASA Council overrode it and (as required by bylaws) mailed out a ballot. The majority of voters opposed the war, but a majority also opposed the ASA taking an official stand on political issues.

The ferment continued over the year among a small number of radical members of ASA at a variety of schools. Simultaneously graduate students and some faculty at several graduate departments were struggling against the then almost monolithic hold of functional analysis and liberal ideology in their departments. The Columbia students, having had only modest success transforming their own department, concluded that the field as a whole needed to be changed.

We sent out a call to other eastern schools; the University of Chicago had a group working independently, and by August an organizing committee had formed at Harvard for the 1968 ASA convention in Boston.

We called ourselves the Sociology Liberation Movement. Our slogan was "Knowledge for Whom?" derived from Robert Lynd's question, *Knowledge for What?* Our call to action included the following analysis:

> Our "theory" exaggerates consensus, ignores conflict, and assumes that everything can be settled with a little communication . . . and a lot of good will. This is more of a prayer than a theory. . . .
> We have abstained from our moral duty to speak out against the forces of oppression in our society. The reactionary nature of our government becomes "beyond the scope of our field." . . .
> We have placed our expertise at the disposal of the establishment, letting the development of our field be guided by the needs of those who can pay for our time. . . . In the name of value-neutrality, we have failed [to help] the poor, the powerless or the unorganized. (Brown 1970a)

Our literature table at the ASA convention was swamped with buyers and browsers. Our caucus meetings had several hundred participants. I was amazed at how many gray-haired socialists emerged to tell us about the 1930s. We in our purity argued that they were sellouts. A demonstration was mounted against a speech by Wilbur Cohen, Secretary of Health, Education, and Welfare (HEW). The ASA executive council gave us fifteen minutes' rebuttal time and a cordon of police around the stage. Dick Flacks gave a critique of HEW (also see Chapter 1 of this volume), and Martin Nicolaus's speech, "Fat-Cat Sociology," was a stirring indictment of established sociology (see Chapter 15).

Because we students were more organized and more radical than faculty, leadership of the Sociology Liberation Movement stayed in our hands. The advantage was a militancy and a lack of concern with career goals that made us able to press the cultural struggle to reform sociology. We challenged functionalism's supremacy and developed radical sociology. Radical sociology evolved into several strands including Marxist sociology and conflict sociology.

The disadvantage of student leadership was a lack of organizational sophistication that defeated efforts to reform the ASA. At first we paid little attention to business-meeting resolutions, both because we could not vote and because we disdained organizational politics. In a few years we became more sophisticated and got the voting rules changed; resolutions became part of our struggle.

Another disadvantage is that we were more radical in the abstract than in the specific. I remember thirty of us sitting in a luxurious hotel room in Boston (for many, our first luxurious hotel room ever), drinking beer, planning the overthrow of established sociology, and rebelling against conformity by refusing to make our beds or throw out beer cans. The next day the hotel maids complained that they had never seen such a mess, and if we wanted to serve the people we could start out by making their lives easier. The political discussion on this subject at the next night's party was intense; Sherry Gorelick, Sue Jacobs, and other women spoke on behalf of the maids. We reluctantly cleaned up before we left.

The black sociologists organized a demonstration against guest speaker Whitney Young of the Urban League, who surprised everyone with a scathing attack on sociologists who used black subjects to further white careers. Black caucus resolutions passed the business meeting, but the issue of racism was largely ignored. For example, Nicolaus's speech was printed in *The American Sociologist* (Nicolaus 1969) with two rebuttals; Young's speech was ignored.

During 1968–1969, radical groups developed in other professions. I was "consultant" to the radical caucuses of the Modern Languages Association and the National Association of Social Workers. The Union for

Radical Political Economics (URPE) began as a separate organization around that time. In my opinion URPE is the most successful of the caucuses not only in maintaining a separate organization but also in developing Marxist economics and socialist-feminist theory. Quite a few sociologists are members. I have been on its steering committee and editorial board several times.

In that same year, radical junior faculty were fired by several sociology departments, with resultant confrontations. Columbia, Buffalo, UCLA, and Berkeley began radical sociology journals largely under graduate-student leadership. Formation of the Eastern Union of Radical Sociologists was followed by the Western Union of Radical Sociologists, who primarily planned the counterconvention to the 1969 ASA meetings in San Francisco. What was to become *The Insurgent Sociologist* began as a counterconvention newspaper.

The entire 1969 convention was tumultuous, culminating in a takeover of the ASA presidential address for a memorial to the just-deceased Ho Chi Minh. Marlene Dixon, then junior faculty at the University of Chicago, was prominent in that action. At the end of the convention, the Sociology Liberation Movement became the Radical Caucus, with the newly formed Union of Radical Sociologists as its formal organization.

The black caucus again felt itself to be ignored by the ASA. Its resolutions and demands of previous years had gone unheeded. Black sociologists announced the founding of the Black Sociologists Association.

The ASA Women's Caucus began organizing at the convention. More than two hundred attended their first meeting at Glide Memorial Church. At the time I saw the Women's Caucus as a careerist movement with no relevance to radicalism. But I and other radical women attended many meetings. The women's movement was in its early stages within the academic left and we were as affected by it as other women. We had problems understanding some of the issues. The Women's Caucus had demanded that ASA provide child care at the next convention, the men and women of the Sociology Liberation Movement wanted child care to be staffed by volunteers, to keep it free of ASA authority. We did not understand why the mothers were so adamant about *not* volunteering their time for child care at a professional convention.

Later a Chicano and then a gay caucus were formed. The caucuses made an effort to connect with each other. Each invited the other to their convention sessions and parties. For quite a few years, representatives of all the caucuses would meet for a lunch during the conventions.

The early years were very exciting ones for radical sociologists. We were part of a national, even worldwide, New Left movement. The system was wrong and we were right. We could change the world if we tried hard enough. We did change the field of sociology, and the successes whetted our appetites for more. We felt capable.

We also felt a unity among ourselves. Those who have not been part of a large social movement will have difficulty understanding the sense of "being home" that we felt as part of the national movement of the 1960s. I don't mean to imply that we were one big happy family; there were plenty of political splits and strategic disagreements, not to mention personal animosities and ego trips. Nevertheless, there was a sense of marching shoulder to shoulder to victory that I can still feel. For me and for many others I know, losing that movement and that feeling was painful indeed.

FINDING OUR WAY

Developing a coherent strategy toward the sociology profession was always difficult for the radical sociologists. Some felt the struggle should be against the power structure of the profession: the ASA and graduate schools, the journals, the government consultants and grant-getters. For some the more important struggle was "cultural," centering on the content of sociology; the task was to overthrow functionalism and develop a sociology for the people (Brown 1979). Others felt that we should not be part of the profession at all because it was inherently elitist. Instead, we should leave the academy for factory organizing or other direct action. Antiintellectualism and anarchism were aspects of radical sociology just as they were a part of the overall movement.

The uncertainty about what we should be and do made the radical sociology movement less effective than it might have been. The Radical Caucus contained activists of many political perspectives and sectarian affiliations. Unfortunately those of one persuasion or another were not content just to follow their own strategy but felt compelled to denounce the others as liberal or elitist or left-adventurist or naive or whatever. I recall refusing to be nominated for secretary of the Union of Radical Sociologists because I felt that organizing ourselves was premature, if not excessively liberal. My righteousness might have been more convincing if I had not been the person who kept the name and address file.

The Union of Radical Sociologists as an organization existed mainly at the conventions. For several years both the East and West coasts held periodic regional conferences. Ours were at Columbia University and later, under the label of East Coast Conference of Socialist Sociologists (ECCSS), at the State University of New York, Purchase campus, the Committee for Non-Violent Action camp in Voluntown, Connecticut, and other locations. These regional organizations continued into the early 1980s.

The conferences happened because someone thought they would be a good idea and a few people did the work of organizing them. That is why most of our activities happened. Evan Stark, Martin Oppenheimer, and Henry Etzkowitz were often the originators of conferences on the East Coast. The late Jay Schulman and others organized "countersessions" at the meetings of the Eastern Sociological Society. *The Insurgent Sociologist* became a journal starting in 1971 largely because Al Szymanski moved to the University of Oregon and recruited graduate students to its staff. The Radical Caucus began running candidates for ASA national office in 1972. I believe Wally Smith was behind that. Sidney Willhelm ran for president and I ran for vice-president at least once. To our surprise we actually won some of the elections, including Alfred McClung Lee's presidency in 1975–1976. Al and Elizabeth Lee have been strong supporters of left sociology for a long time. The New York City convention during Al's presidency was very radical but had a low attendance.

If anything, the Radical Caucus had more effect on the Society for the Study of Social Problems (SSSP). This group had originally formed as a social-action alternative to ASA and welcomed radicals in its ranks. Its journal, *Social Problems*, opened its pages to radical analysis much more quickly and continually than did the *American Sociological Review* (*ASR*) or the *American Journal of Sociology* (*AJS*). Radicals founded the Labor Studies Division.

Although I wrote about organizing women workers in 1970 (Brown 1970b), I was not primarily concerned with women's issues. I remember talking with Cynthia Epstein in 1968 about the National Organization for Women. I insisted I was not discriminated against. She shook her head sadly and I wondered why.

There was plenty of sexism in the Sociology Liberation Movement. I will remain silent on some personal incidents with male radicals that I would prefer had not happened. But I do not think that the Columbia group, at least, was rampantly sexist. Sherry Gorelick, Sue Jacobs, the late Sarah Eisenstein, I, and several others were fully active in the leadership, regardless of whom we slept with. In 1970 *The Human Factor* published a special issue entitled "The Liberation of American Women," probably the first special issue on women in American sociology.

Marlene Dixon, then at the University of Chicago, was a major force in the early days. The masthead in the first *Insurgent Sociologist* listed sixteen names, only three of them women (Marlene, Jetta Lees, and me). That is 19 percent, which was about the proportion of women in sociology in those years. The second issue listed ten women out of thirty-one names percent (30 percent). I was usually one of those listed (along with Marlene and Carole Andreas), and since there were always other women involved, discrimination within the organization did not seem to me to be a major problem. I only gradually became tuned into the societal discrimination that kept women out of graduate schools and kept them subject to predominantly male leadership within the movement.

For example, in 1970–1971 the late Jay Schulman, Roger Kahn, and I did a radical analysis of the Russell Sage Foundation, then funding much sociological research. We worked as equals, though Jay was ten years older than I and far more experienced a researcher. During this period, Jay confessed to me that this was the first time he had ever worked with a woman as an equal and he was not quite sure how to do it.

The radical women had an uncertain relationship with the ASA women's caucus. Many joined, but we distrusted the apparent careerism we sensed. Many of them distrusted our radicalism. During 1970–1971, Jesse Bernard made a trip to Boston to sound out some of us in the Boston Area Women Social Scientists about a proposed Association for Women in Sociology. We strenuously argued that we should not be concerned with ourselves but with women in the rest of society. She and the other organizers took our objections seriously; the new organization was named Sociologists for Women in Society.

Over the years the uncertainty had declined. The feminists became more radical, the radical women became more feminist and less identified with the male left. By the mid-1970s I was identifying myself not as a socialist but as a socialist feminist. I was founding member of Marxist Feminist Group One, an interdisciplinary group developing socialist feminist theory. We were a group of women graduate students and junior faculty who got together in response to the antiintellectualism we felt in the women's movement and the antifeminism we felt in the New Left.

Although the radical sociology organizations were egalitarian and open, the theorizing was increasingly closed. Marxism was being rediscovered and promoted as the only true radicalism. The traditional Marxist attitude that feminism is a bourgeois deviation became strong among some of the leaders. Al Szymanski was particularly adamant about this. Women had to ignore or challenge the male-led developments in order to develop socialist feminism.

Pauline Bart frequently reminds me of an East Coast Conference of Socialist Scholars (ECCSS) conference at SUNY, Purchase, in June 1974. During one session male Marxist "heavies" theorized women out of the class structure and into submission. I came in late and, not knowing I was supposed to be submissive, began suggesting the alternatives to orthodox Marxism that feminists were developing. The mere fact that I challenged the orthodox line created an excellent debate. Afterward Pauline and other women thanked me for being so brave.

The Insurgent Sociologist came to be seen as hostile to socialist feminism. Several women had feminist papers turned down by the *Insurgent* editors. They published a book review of mine that was hostile to a liberal feminist book but turned down my book reviews favorable to socialist-feminist writings. The mainstream sociology journals also did not accept socialist-feminist theory. Women published their socialist-feminist papers instead in *Socialist Revolution, Radical America, Feminist Studies,* and others.

HOLDING OUR OWN

By 1976 the Radical Caucus faced serious organizational problems. As the social movements of the 1960s died down, so did the spontaneous enthusiasm that had overcome our lack of stable organization. Although regional groups continued, the Union of Radical Sociologists hardly existed. Organizing the radical caucus at conventions was becoming more difficult. Ted Goertzel and a few others took the leadership in developing the Marxist Sociology Section of the ASA. This would assure us of regular sessions and organizational meeting space at the conventions and a newsletter during the year, all paid for by an ASA dues check-off. The two hundred signatures needed to form the section were easily obtained. The section was an immediate success and killed off the radical caucus.

I recall the meeting in which it was argued that calling ourselves "Marxist" would push out the merely radical and the liberal hangers-on. The Caucus for a New Political Science, it was reported, had been taken over by prominent liberal political scientists, thus diminishing its radical prospects. It was felt that the word "Marxist" in our section title would separate the sheep from the goats. I think that organizational goal was reached.

Marxism provided a firm theoretical basis for developing a new, challenging orientation to sociology. Unfortunately, Marxism has its own imperatives, both theoretical and political, that became more of a problem as the years went on. World Systems theory developed its own section rather than remain part of ours. Marxist sessions on women were highly critical of feminism until 1979 when I became chair. I think the problem of theoretical rigidity is now diminishing, but I think that creative thinking has not yet returned.

The Marxist Section has had the same "affirmative action" problems the radical caucus had. It is predominantly white, Anglo, heterosexual, male. The African-Americans, Hispanics, gays and lesbians, and women in sociology are more attracted to their own organizations and theoretical perspectives than they are to Marxism and the Marxist Section. Walda Katz Fishman and Robert Newby have led an effort to keep the groups in contact by organizing an all-inclusive Radical Caucus party at each ASA convention.

There have continued to be divisive repercussions from the sexual harassment case against Sid Peck, which developed while I was chair of the Marxist Section. Peck supporters saw the case as political persecution of a working-class leftist and effective political organizer, even hinting at CIA involvement. Supporters of Ximena Bunster, a Chilean refugee with a temporary appointment in the department chaired by Peck, saw the case as white male misuse of power against a Third World woman and against students and staff members who backed her accusations.

When a Peck supporter implied to me that Bunster was a menopausal spinster who imagined it all, my sympathies leaned toward Bunster. This has earned me the undying hostility of the Peck camp. At the time I was concerned with keeping the Marxist Section from polarizing and asked both sides to stifle the conflict at the upcoming ASA convention. They did so. I sometimes wonder if we would have been better off allowing a public explosion rather than letting the fires burn underground as they seem to be doing.

Despite the problems, the Marxist Section has continued. In fact, I think it has saved radical sociology. The Radical Caucus was dying anyway. The sessions on the ASA program enable us to give papers and hold political discussions. We debate and sponsor resolutions for the ASA business meeting. Our evening parties keep us in touch with each other. And some of our universities pay our ways to the ASA because we are on the program.

Having a Marxist Section has also convinced the rest of the ASA that we are not going to go away, and made us and our theories intellectually respectable. Many radicals have papers accepted in regular sessions and hold positions on ASA committees. I am now on the Committee on Freedom of Research and Teaching. SSSP continues to be an important organizational focus for radicals.

The question can be raised whether we are still radical. I am now a tenured professor with a three-family house and a daughter. My sympathy for the gray-haired socialist sellouts has increased. My sense is that the Marxist Section, the *Insurgent* (now *Critical Sociology*), our presence in

SSSP, and other efforts help us to maintain our radical identification and give young radicals entering the profession a way of connecting to the older generation and the left tradition.

REFERENCES

Brown, Carol A. 1970a. "A History and Analysis of Radical Activism in Sociology, 1967–69." *Sociological Inquiry* 40 (Winter): 27–34.

——. 1970b. "Organizing Women Workers Today." *The Human Factor* 10, no. 1: 58–73.

——. 1979. "Radicals in Sociology." *Radical Teacher* 11 (March): 23–24.

Nicolaus, Martin. 1969. "Remarks at the ASA Convention." *American Sociologist* 4 (May): 154–56.

Chapter 4

Talking Sociology: A Sixties Fragment
Evan Stark

THERE WAS an extended moment during the 1960s, with May of 1968 as its zenith, when alien ideas took root in native-born activism and reemerged in one of those rare conjunctures of theory and practice from which revolutions come. One expression of this was a style of "sociological talk" that found its metaphors for radical change in personal experience and everyday life. To me, this way of addressing the world while locating ourselves in it is the essence of "liberation sociology."

PREPARATION

My introduction to "sociological talk" started in Waltham, Massachusetts, in 1959. That summer, Frankie Lyman and the Teenagers soothed my nervous stomach with "Why Do Fools Fall in Love?" Then suddenly I was in Waltham, a million miles from *stetl* stick ball, at Brandeis, built by a great underwear king to whom my grandfather was just another Bolshie greenhorn at a machine.

Abe Sachar had been chosen as president of Brandeis over Einstein. Now he bartered radical genius in the marketplace of McCarthyism where it was cheap, a regular Captain of Erudition. Even as critical theory concentrated at Brandeis, it continued to reflect its ambiguous origins, resistance-in-hiding. These were the 1950s, and we were twenty, surrounded by sexy bohemians, avant-garde architecture, and unmade beds, things lacking in the suburbs. Yet, behind the new glass and glitter, the emotional subtext was fear. Our teachers (Herbert Marcuse, Philip Rahv, Abraham Maslow, Louis Coser, Kurt Wolff, and the younger Americans, Alan Grossman and Maurice Stein) talked (and dressed) as if the Führer and Joe McCarthy had personally run them out of their homes.

Coser was typical. Although he seemed less introspective than the rest and his run-on sociobabble was a bit more aimless, he conveyed the same aura of perpetual distraction. Even as he smiled down at you through the stub of a Raleigh cigarette, he was pivoting, preparing to leave, as if called away to a forgotten appointment. After I asked about Merton's early link to the Communist party, Coser stopped our personal seminar together. Yet he continued to greet me in the halls with a broad smile. Only once did I sense his deeper feelings about Brandeis. It was my first American Sociological Association convention, Montreal in 1964, and I had presented a rather dense critique of sociology's nonresponse to the Harlem riots ("Radicals, Revisionists and Clowns") on a graduate-student panel. Suddenly Coser was on his feet, shouting, "That's how Maurice Stein would write, if Maurice Stein could write." He followed this with a stream of invectives, aimed over my head at "red" colleagues in Waltham who treated him a bit like the simple son in the Passover Haggadah. Finally, Irving Louis Horowitz reminded Coser I was a student, not a representative of the Fourth International, and Coser collapsed back into his chair.

Brandeis was a surreal travel agency. Our assignments converged into one: We were to negate the negation, make the return trip to the places our émigré faculty were afraid to go, and root out the big *F* (for fascism) that had been planted everywhere around us. And yet, there were no trustworthy paths for us to follow, no shortcuts, outlines, or codes of entry. Behind a barrage of broken meanings the faculty attacked each practical proposal, exposed every pleasure as a seducer's ploy, until eventually the best of times seemed the worst of times and our affluence felt like a thin veneer for the nuclear umbrella.

We would have gone anywhere for these men, except back to our own homes, of course. But what were we to say or do, what baggage should we carry, when we lacked a "historical address"? So we took to the streets of our mind, guided by the same desperate eye for survival that had gotten us through childhood.

The members of the radical generation-to-be came to Waltham in the early 1960s to play Sancho to the Harvard dons. For me, the best were Norman Mailer, Malcolm X, James Baldwin, and Paul Goodman. Each had made personal estrangement the center of his identity and improvised a spoken sociology that was as rich as anything he wrote.

Mailer stumbled out onto the stage and sat, a pint bottle of vodka in hand, and read half-heartedly from some note cards about a visit to Iowa. Then he stopped and asked for questions. This was to be a lecture in reverse in which we made his points by negative example. We had come to worship ourselves in his epiphanal presence; instead he forced us to engage him through our anger, hoping to touch the hurt underneath. Where our fathers dodged our wise-ass curves, Mailer took them in his gut. "Why did you let *Naked and the Dead* become a grade B movie?" someone shouted. "That's like asking me about my wife's twat," he mumbled, head lowered. By refusing to respond, he made us listen, first to his obscenities, then to ours. As if called to some magic ritual, we went at it, crack after crack, until our precociousness came back to us as an incantation, a kind of manic zen. Here we were again, tough little Jewboys in *cheder*. But this time, instead of mere jibes at the rabbi, our nasty questions were points of intimacy, moments of alienation suspended in front of us. Mailer invited us to see terror maul and mold his mind-in-the-making. Unlike our faculty, he struggled with his fear and trembling, in the open, like a street fighter. Like he too was an exile in the wrong place at the wrong time. Yet for him, exile was a powerful point of contact.

Goodman was less complicated, though more elusive. I was reading *Growing Up Absurd* on a bench in New York's Bryant Park, having come early for a fallout-shelter protest. "Have you seen this?" blurted a man in a seedy tweed jacket. Without waiting for a reply, he read aloud from the *New York Times* for what seemed like an hour. When I tried to get away, he smiled, extended his hand and announced, "I'm Paul Goodman." For Goodman, everything was like this. Politics, architecture, poetry, philosophy, sex were all part of a single, ongoing conversation about love and power, and it made no difference whether a teenage boy, a college dean, or Robert Moses was at the other end. However long it had been between our meetings, I always felt comfortable stepping into his stream of talk. Frank Lloyd Wright ridiculed a decade of urban design by setting the Guggenheim Museum in the middle of New York. In the same way, by making the utopian seem obvious and accessible, Goodman made everyday compromises like Kool-Whip and Arthur Schlesinger, Jr., seem stupid.

This was heady stuff. And I should have been more cautious. But I'd learned my "sex, sin, and society" in an Admiral TV box from Helen, a hefty goyish groupie for the toughs, who exorcised my fantasies while she amused the big kids by holding my ten-year-old body down. I saw myself only in passing, the way you glimpse a defaced subway poster from a speeding train. I went to bed with many women, offering to exchange my self-denying empathy for sex. Meanwhile, I slept alone, like some Puritan bookkeeper, thinking sex was part of my work, making distraction my real job. At P.S. 34, Mrs. Byrne explained that our dog tags would survive the A-bomb blasts our bodies couldn't. Now I wore my identity like this, wondering whether it could survive if my self dissolved.

In class and in bed, I practiced readying my private spaces for inspection. "You use happiness," pronounced my émigré psychiatrist, "to avoid facing yourself." Oy america! Is this your problem too? In my first class in graduate school at the University of Wisconsin, sociology professor Hans Gerth sat quietly until well after the starting bell. Then, as if responding to a private signal, he rose from his chair and started in midthought: "Your playground directors train ten-year-old girls for the competitive pursuit of appearance values by writing on the blackboard 'Gina [the daughter of an Italian innkeeper] is the best-dressed girl in the playground.'"

Gerth was close to our mark. But if Gina hid behind her appearance, we hid *through* ours, deriving a strange power from our confessional repertoire. Success in the bedrooms and classrooms of the early 1960s was unthinkable without a pat vocabulary of self-exposure. Still, the "identity crisis" (circa 1960) and "playing it cool" (circa 1965), so different as styles, were united by the feeling of being perpetually absent. Goffman coined the phrase "nonperson." And Clark Kerr affectionately termed us the "walking wounded," recalling Ernst Toller's reference to his post–World War I generation as "corpses on furlough." But Gerth saw something else in us as well: a new subjectivity without the Oedipal underpinning of guilt and repression. Again, Gerth put us straight:

> The rebelliousness of our most highly educated youth seems readily understandable. It is an expression of the profound agony of youngsters taught to consider what Freud called the superego as superfluous overhead. Under the universal atmosphere of drift and aimlessness, in a world of "operators," they strive for "success" (whatever it may be) and one man is the other man's wolf (as Hobbes had it).

We turned out more like a pop-left collage (with bits of Mao, Marx, Marcuse, and Marlon Brando) than Yankee symbols of the American dream. This was less because we rejected success than because, having cultivated our image of success secretly and in isolation from the mainstream, we had a picture that was distorted and uncompromising. As Marcuse quipped after the 1967 May Day demonstrations in Washington, D.C., we were the first radical generation to measure victory by the number arrested or beaten by the police. We wanted to sell out. But we expected a price so high the bank would collapse.

Our elitist feeling that nothing was good enough found its intellectual rationale in critical theory where everything that felt right paled against its ideal form—sex against Eros, politics against Revolution. We simply had no idea the style we worked so hard to perfect in the early 1960s would leave us pursuing failure like a windup doll pointed at a wall.

Our politics were no less stylized than our personal lives. We were hardly refuseniks. In the winter of 1961 we presented ourselves cordially to John F. Kennedy for a peace tea at the White House, and I remember modeling my tie and Eisenhower jacket in the mirror that same year before going to Woolworth's to be arrested at a civil rights sit-in. The bohemian interior and the respectable exterior of the yuppie; the conventional morality of the peacenik and the beard and T-shirt of the yippie—these were alternate facets of a new psychological type for whom alienation was less a cross to be borne (as it had been for the beats) than essential baggage for prospering without an address. As had Marcuse, Mailer, and Goodman, Gerth recognized us as compatriots in exile.

> It is the age of the Superman and Batman on TV and of "the Fugitive" as the neurotic personality of our time which these hundreds of thousands of academic youth feel "alienated from." They are driven into exile by "adults" and learn to think of themselves as voluntary expatriots and lost generations . . . and they protest in their agony against the insensitivity and hard rubber callousness with which the victors of World War II tighten their helmets and prepare for the eternal peace without resurrection.

But, Hans, I want to tell him now, there was ecstasy in our exile as well. With reverence, I followed the fixed agenda of cultural rebellion, seeking out Joan Baez at the "Golden Vanity," feasting on early-morning home fries at Hayes-Bickford's in Cambridge, suffering hours of prep school talk about motorcycles and dope, going on the road and sharing my horniness with Korean vets in Boulder and Berkeley. I dropped college and chirped pacifist slogans at scared sailor boys in Groton who beat our knuckles bloody for trying to hold their atomic sub at bay. I went to work in the post office, like my father and uncle during the Depression, hung out in the Village with folksy communists like Will Geer and the Weavers, got crabs at Sarah Lawrence from the daughter of an upstate bowling alley king, wrote and then destroyed my *Moby Dick* . . . carousing in homosexual bars till late-night almost-sex orgies led to sunrise drives back wherever it was we stayed. I hid other people's marijuana in my accordion and waited for the big bust that never came. The orchestrated protests and the emotional agenda tasted the same, like lovemaking with a stranger the morning after.

INITIATION

Since college had been my bohemian interlude, I went directly to grad school. Maurice Stein told me he'd learned more listening to Hans Gerth for an hour than he had in all his years at Columbia. "And he was Mills's teacher," he added. I set out for the University of Wisconsin expecting to apprentice to a radical guru at a Midwest *studium generalis*.

When I arrived in Madison in 1963, the civil rights movement was passing into a phase of creative militancy. Nationally, the New Left was still confined mainly to political Holden Caulfields, an elite strata of tight-ass crewcut jacket-and-tie "leaders" who had formed SDS and thought (and still think) their own shock of recognition should be heard 'round the world. To me the Port Huron Statement seemed saccharin, patronizing, and unbearably social-democratic. In Madison, the statement attracted the *Studies-on-the-Left* crowd, Marxist academics whose search for a new revolutionary class could not be interrupted for leafletting and the like. The women who were the mainstay of SNCC (the Student Non-violent Coordinating Committee) and the old left front groups (like Fair Play for Cuba) took little notice of SDS (Students for a Democratic Society), and the great mass of blonds were not active at all. There were only inklings of another level of political activity among those for whom college poverty was no brief interlude. Less ambitious to start than the elite students, this group was more angry than disillusioned.

In defiance of Prohibition, "Fighting Bob" LaFollette's German constituents had built the student Rathskeller at the university in the 1920s. Outside on the patio overlooking Lake Mendota, huge depressed graduate students in English sat like elephant seals, sipping beer and staring longingly while hefty coeds skillfully maneuvered their sailboats. There I met Gerald Marwell, my first "real" sociologist. "You'll like it here, Stark," he promised with a contempt transplanted from the East. "We'll bust your ass, but it'll do you good." The football lingo was apt. During the next three years, Ed Borgatta, statistician, player-coach of this, the largest sociology department in the world, communicated with us twice: to remind us to join the departmental football team and to offer us team T-shirts at a discount subsidized by the same National Institute of Mental Health (NIMH) grants that paid the way to games (i.e., conventions).

When Gerth extended a Fulbright stay in Tokyo, I called Al Gouldner, chair of sociology at Washington University and a former teacher of Maurice Stein's, and he invited me to come to St. Louis to help start *Trans-action*, a new popular sociology journal.

If the Madison department seemed anonymous and bureaucratic, the department in St. Louis was a primal horde. Seven of the ten senior faculty were from Stuyvesant High School in the Bronx. Gouldner was an amateur photographer and lined the halls with blowups of little-seen heroes of the profession. "At Brandeis," he greeted me, "they are concerned about the purity of purpose. Here we're concerned with the clarity of thought. What do you think of that, Stark?"

My supervisor at *Trans-action* was Mary Strong, widow of Chicago sociologist Sam Strong, a magnificently astute and gentle optimist who survived a decade of infighting—including the magazine's move to Rutgers. She introduced me to Irving Louis Horowitz at lunch. Big as a gorilla, he ate like a watchmaker, afraid to get food on his lap. "Why don't you say something brilliant?" he snapped, looking up from his bagel. I could help him correct the galleys for Mills's book on pragmatism, he said. "If you make any mistakes," he warned, "I'll lash you with a whip."

He asked what music I liked.

"Jazz," I replied.

"Who?" he asked.

"Getz," I said, retrieving a name from somewhere.

He asked why, then supplied the words I would never have found. "You want to know why you like Stan Getz? I'll tell you why. The metronomic line, that's why. He uses the metronomic line better than anyone in the business. Now you know why you like Stan Getz."

It wasn't over. I'd come to grad school, I said, because I was ignorant of many things. "Don't you think your teachers are ignorant?" he snorted. He was convincing me, I finally jabbed. This was what he'd been waiting for. He rose, looking like Charles Laughton after his first interrogation of the Winslow boy, and shook my hand—or me really, lifting me off the floor. "Stay away from my class," he said when I returned to earth, "and I'll give you an *A*." Like Gouldner, he needed intellectual combat to relax. It made the insulated success of academic reputation feel significant and gave vicarious substance to Mills's cowboy dictum, "Ride and shoot."

My job at *Trans-action* was to locate significant social science articles to translate for a lay audience. However, without jargon there was little substance to most of what I read. One *American Journal of Sociology* article, for instance, ended: "In short, the evidence indicates that the dirtier the household, the less white girls will be instigated to make a delinquent adaptation." Horowitz quickly nailed the other problem. When our article-length translations were published, the original authors were listed only as "main source," as if we had done the major work, not they. This was plagiarism, Horowitz announced. So Gouldner threw him out. The next day, a huge photo of Mills appeared mysteriously in the hall. With his flattened Texas nose and small bright eyes, Mills was the waterfront priest for Gouldner's rogues gallery.

A split with Gouldner was inevitable. To Gouldner, I was the hapless ward entrusted to him by a naive and unsuccessful younger brother

(Maurice Stein), to be instructed in the essentials, taught manners, and disabused of my principles. Gouldner thought I knew, though at the time I didn't, that Stein—not he—had done the major field work for *Patterns of Industrial Bureaucracy* and that he had not actually been down into the gypsum mine, about which he wrote with such authority, more than once. The blowup occurred after I'd spent several weeks in jail for a civil rights action. Although I'd completed my assignments for *Trans-action* in solitary, Gouldner begged an argument, insulted me somewhat more directly than usual, pushed me, and when I retaliated, informed me: "You can get A's up the ass, but you'll never get a degree here."

I turned to the neo-Freudian anthropologist Jules Henry. Henry, Lee Rainwater, and Gouldner were studying the Pruit-Igo housing project, and I had been consoling Boone Hammond and several other black graduate assistants whom Henry had ordered to find the "death instinct" among the families they interviewed. Henry had offered a sympathetic ear when I got caught in the wars between Gouldner and Horowitz. After listening patiently, he explained that the real trouble was my "radical lifestyle." So I returned to Madison.

EDUCATION

In 1964, student activism in Madison centered on Cuba and supporting civil rights in the South through SNCC. To me, this was too removed from everyday travail. So, as in St. Louis, I worked with CORE (the Congress of Racial Equality), struggling for our economic agenda against the black nationalists. We forced Sears to integrate with a series of sit-ins and "shop-ins"—customers would simply leave merchandise on the counters after "discovering" Sears' employment policy. This made them fearful of any black, woman, or white hippie who used the store. While picketing the Republican state convention in Milwaukee, Madison activist Lea Zeldin was pushed down. She refused to rise until the offending guard apologized, and we surrounded her for safety. In Madison, the *Capital Times* headline was "CORE Stages Sit-In." I was shaken. History, it seemed, knew us better than we knew ourselves.

I spent the summer of 1964 in New York, with a woman who literally bit through my lips to touch the pain she needed to know I felt. Then Harlem. With another white, I was locked for safety in the back room of East Harlem CORE headquarters (home of "The River Rats") running off "WANTED: Gilligan" leaflets when the cops entered the front room and simply shot several black men working there. Then Chaney, Goodman, and Schwerner disappeared. Goodman's family was old CP and close to my cousins. Mickey Schwerner and my woman friend worked in the same Brooklyn settlement. The news was catching up. The blacks who gathered at the Federal Building to protest the murders in Mississippi refused to mourn in silence. They got us to sing and shout instead.

Before the summer ended, I went to the Democatic convention in Atlantic City and vigiled in the rain against the Vietnam War. Inside the hall, the Mississippi Freedom Democratic party was avenging the deaths in Mississippi by trading their seats with Americans for Democratic Action (ADA) head Joe Rauh ("Don't make trouble this year and we'll let you stay next time") so a real liberal (Hubert Humphrey) could get into the White House. I remember thinking on the bus back to New York that I had done my job to stop that war. During the ASA convention in Montreal, I tried in vain to convince a clandestine meeting of Quebec nationalists that LBJ was as likely as Goldwater to escalate in Vietnam.

Back in graduate school that fall, I became sidekick to Ken Knudson, Madison's anarcho-pacifist loner. The Peace Center, which he and Clark Kissinger had maintained to do antidraft education (a popular pamphlet was their "Advice to Young Men on How to Get into the Army"), suddenly emerged as the major stimulus for civil disobedience in Madison, presenting a program of "direct action" that evoked the enthusiasm, if not the participation, of large numbers of students. In October 1965, in an effort to directly confront federal lawmakers, we presented a "citizen's arrest" warrant for the commander of Truax Air Base, Colonel Arasmith, and blocked the entrance to the base with the help of dozens of assembled newspeople. Then there was our annual Anti-Military Ball, started by Kissinger and Knudson in a small classroom as a parody of the fancy-dress military ball run by ROTC. By 1965 (a year after we "kidnapped" the military honor guard) it was the event of the radical social season, attended by thousands, many in costume, highlighting radical skits, Bo Diddley (records), and asking, with a prefeminist naiveté, "Do Anti-Militarists Have Balls?"

All this was oddball to the social democrats and sectarian groups like the Socialist Workers party (SWP) and the Communist party (CP). CORE was not politically correct because civil disobedience supposedly alienated the masses and because the majority of CORE's members were older blacks (many of whom had come to Truax from Alabama and Mississippi) and older women ("townies"). And we had fun, which threatened the sects most.

Throughout 1964–1966, the campus Committee to End the War in Vietnam (CEWV) provided a loose but important framework for antiwar protest. A coalition of campus groups dominated alternatively by the CP and SWP, the CEWV organized the campus teach-ins, maintained antiwar booths, aggressively recruited in the dorms for "classes" on Vietnamese history, held periodic soapboxes and rallies, and maintained contact with the national antiwar movement. When the State Department "Truth Team" came to campus in May 1965, 132 faculty signed an ad of greeting and gave them a reception. That evening, however, about 300 of us quickly ended the Truth Team presentation, an action which, thanks to a report in *Time* magazine, prompted competitive protests by antiwar groups wherever the team appeared.

Those we recruited became increasingly frustrated with endless wrangling in the CEWV about which line to promote through leaflets and rallies. My own differences focused on the opposition of the SWP and particularly the CP to direct action and civil disobedience. When we proposed the Truax action for the International Days of Protest, for example, the CEWV refused support. A comment from my FBI files by the attending informer (an employee of the student union) suggests the reasons students were bored with left politics. "Civil disobedience was voted down, some discussion was held with nothing specific coming out, except possibly to hold some seminars and speeches or wander about the streets in some sort of demonstration form."

Whatever the formal status of my activity may prove to have been on the long march to socialism, it had tremendous personal importance. My new friends aggressively demanded that program and tactics grow from need and imagination. Because of this, in a speech to a peace rally on Hiroshima Day 1965, I felt I could talk sociology the way it had been talked to me. As I saw it, the problem was neither to stir liberal guilt and appeal to principle nor, as my social democratic and sectarian comrades insisted, to pull together every "interest" into "coalitions." The problem was to comically correct alienation so that it became a point of connection rather than isolation. Putting Hiroshima (and Vietnam) in context meant not merely linking it to the violence of the Cold War through which we'd been raised but to a more fundamental hurt,

> a violence which reaches the heart of my generation like the headlines of the newspapers no longer can, a violence that forces us to choose again and again between our need for personal freedom and integrity and loyalty to our government, a choice no man should be forced to make, between a death of courage, truth and dignity—giving up the need to be whole—and isolation from the social and political community.

Of course, by this time Berkeley had erupted. SDS had brought thirty thousand of the five million U.S. students to Washington to protest Vietnam. But these events were less important to me than the sense that I too could use my imagination as a springboard for generalizing. In a world of exiles, I was no longer an outsider on good behavior.

Hofmannstahl said of the German youth movement in the 1920s, "They seek not freedom but connection." Things were a bit more complicated for us. There was no way I could return to the Bronx, where patient arthritic elders waited for rumors that their grandchildren had risen from the *cheder* to become surgeons. But I felt equally far from Westchester, where my Catholic buddies worked on construction gangs building edifices for children they quickly forgot they had once wanted to have. Nor could I fathom the populist myth of a native-born "community" promoted by William Appleman Williams and eagerly devoured by Madison's "red diaper" graduate students searching for a tradition in which to lose the immigrants (their parents) and locate themselves. But what if, rather than agonize in the abyss of our fragmentation or build a political movement whose utter conventionality was an extended defense mechanism, we actually *chose* alienation and declared negativity the most positive basis for communion we owned. I concluded the speech:

> America's community has become 80 million isolated TV viewers, sipping cocktails and Cokes and watching, with their aspirin bottles nearby, as those to whom they pay their taxes bring them closer to nuclear death. Indeed, as Mr. Bayer assures us after each exhausting newcast, "relief is just minutes away." . . . Disloyalty not community is the basis of our society; it is the basis of our market; of our international relations . . . our heroes, our weapons, like our cars, our women—all are dynamically obsolescent. So we have learned our lesson well—too well, some say— and made disloyalty our creed.

POLITICS

Among my fellow sociology graduate students in Madison were: one sole black man, polite, street-wise but aloof; a cynical Brooklyn Jew who studied "deviance" and worked every sexual angle; a comical, clumsy, and overweight gentleman from India who wanted us all to be his friend; a North Dakota preacher's girl hoping to enjoy sin without knowing it; a beautiful genius whose mother tortured her by long-distance telephone; an overambitious creep we knew would make it, and an eager nice-guy we knew wouldn't. Alone or somewhere else, all might have felt good about whatever it was they did well. Here (making allowances for the few women), with the eternal waiting for care packages or letters from home, each with a private dream about life "after this was over," we were an army platoon from a third-rate 1940s film. We learned to take whatever was dished out. And it was plenty. My first semester, I sent my advisor a proposal to study the civil rights volunteers being trained to do voter registration in Mississippi. He shared the proposal with two other assistant professors; they passed it off as their own, got funding, hired another graduate student pledged to secrecy, and then produced their prestigious "original" work.

My Virgil in this comic inferno was Hans Gerth. I can picture him in his armchair, a loose undershirt under his elegant Japanese bathrobe, following his fingers across the page, cigarette dangling, eyeglasses almost off. If the up-and-coming faculty lured their graduate students with money, Gerth got me with talk, constant and unrelenting. I felt like a medieval scholar. Books were the background, the "official version" to which Gerth offered a living counterpoint. History was here, in illustration after illustration, in the dramatic weight of events that Gerth seemed to bear physically and of which he spoke with intimate knowledge.

But I hadn't bargained on being his sidekick. Once with him, it was hard to get away. He feigned almost total helplessness in everyday matters and played the benevolent patriarch with whom one must constantly travel so that nothing important will get lost, including car keys.

Soon after he returned from Japan, he invited me to help him "get it straight" for a paper on Sorge and the American wing of the First International. We worked through till morning. In class, although I was often hypnotized by his incantations, I kept my distance by taking notes. Alone with him at his house, however, I became a party in his ritual. He knew I spoke no German. But he talked it at me incessantly, punctuating his monologues with bursts of rage and poetry reading from ancient books piled up everywhere in his house. As chorus to his Greek tragedy, I searched through my past for countermetaphors to the historical motifs Gerth represented: being driven out by the Nazis in 1938, neglect and harassment by Midwest colleagues, the suicide of "the countess" (his first wife), and his sense of betrayal by Mills and other students. It seemed only a matter of time before he discovered my inadequacy.

I felt compelled to close the distance between us and could do so only by reaching down for my own hidden hurt and estrangement. He was a living newspaper, moving with studied melodrama from theory to memory to the latest headline, then to the story behind the news. Often we ended the night with the single line with which he had begun. "Write this up, Stark," he would say, and it was time for me to go. At first, I took his instructions literally, painfully trying to link the evening's talk to some coherent picture of Sorge or the Claflin sisters, for instance. But I finally got the more general meaning of his parting words. Gerth intended "writing it up" to be my life's assignment.

Franz Neumann says university life under Bismarck "excluded the study of social and political reality." So did Madison sociology from the mid-1950s on. But if "speculation and book learning" dominated the Second Reich, the fetish in Madison was data. The department was hardly conservative politically. Besides the well-known radicals like Alford and Zeitlin, a number of the senior people had been Communists in the 1940s or had pioneered the study of race and class. But a healthy suspicion of the "unproven"—often linked to the disillusionment with Soviet Marxism—had degenerated into a virtual veto on speculative thought. Despite potentially sharp divisions about politics, a concensus had been reached, which included the radicals, that the importance of a work lay not in its bearing on the central questions of the day but in the techniques used to gather, interpret, and display information. As the orgy of trivia became less shame-faced, the younger faculty took the initiative: The course in theory became a rote lesson on theorems; the language requirement for the Ph.D. was dropped (with Gerth the sole dissenter); the old-fashioned M.A. essay became a "publishable empirical paper"; and required classics were replaced by current readings on "the controversy in functionalism."

Even as these developments ensured our isolation, Gerth's colleagues developed a strange, if distant, respect for him. Neither a team player nor a conduit for research dollars, he nevertheless lent intellectual credibility to the lackluster pursuit of careers. Or perhaps Gerth was respected by his colleagues because he was unable to be like them, though they could not fathom why.

So, even as it sought recognition as an arbiter of public policy, academic sociology was retreating from the historical comprehension Gerth represented. Intellectual passion in Madison was treated as something that needed to be controlled, like flatulence. During the Free Speech Movement, the president of the university, Fred Harrington, confided in us that what was wrong in Berkeley was "they got all the kooks and brains." He meant Jews, that became clear when he promptly proposed a "metropolitan quota" on admissions. The department's big guns took Gerth's social isolation as an object lesson in courage and kept their distance, though remaining formally friendly.

Efforts to make Gerth popular were fruitless. He needed real companionship too badly to mince words on its behalf. I tried introducing Zeitlin. "Hans," I began, "Professor Zeitlin wrote *Cuba: Tragedy in Our Hemisphere*."

Zeitlin, who smiled at everything, smiled.

"Tragedy?" groaned Gerth, already pivoting to walk away. "There was nothing tragic about it!" And that was that.

During his initial job interview by E. A. Ross, Gerth was grilled about Veblen. Afterward, the American muckraker took Gerth to his office and pointed to the single shelf of books. "All Ross," he announced, with a sweep of his hand. Such populist chutzpah was nothing compared to the next two decades when Gerth was kept from promotion by chairs from McCormack and Howard Becker through the upstart Karl Taeuber. When Mills took to Oxford Press the Weber essays that Gerth had translated as class handouts, Gerth asked that Mills be listed as his "research assistant." Although he could not read German, Mills was furious and threatened a lawsuit. Oxford turned to McCormack—the southern gentlemen reminded Gerth of his status as a registered alien in 1945—and Gerth bowed low. Still, however much Mills's behavior offended Gerth's social democratic puritanism, he would quickly point out that Mills "died of a failure of heart, not of nerve." In the 1950s, after the publication of his collaborative volume with Mills in social psychology, *Character and Social Structure*, with McCarthyism spreading faster than pollen in the August air, even Merton's introduction could not stop Madison's empiricists from relieving Gerth of the social psychology course. And so on into the 1960s, when the class we designed called "Sociology of Film" (we concentrated on the historical basis of aesthetic imagery) was taken from us by Jay Demerath and rotated among the younger men as "Sociology *Through* Film."

Madison's radical historians, and particularly William Appleman Williams and Harvey Goldberg, presented history as a great allegory woven from models (Goldberg) and moral lessons (Williams) for us to emulate. It is hard to appreciate the impact of an orator like Goldberg, entering a hall packed to the rafters with five hundred radical students, hour after hour reconstructing the world of the French Revolution or the Commune, a world inverted, in which radicals are heroes and sectarian quarrels are debates of universal moment. Yet ultimately I found this history ephemeral, almost patronizing in its appeal to myth over lived experience.

Gerth painted a picture that was closer to Hegel's "great slaughterhouse" than Granville Hicks's "great tradition." And beneath every paradox he detected the same compelling contradiction, the absolute need to break with the terms of the present and the absence of any means to do so that was not either illusory or barbarous. Although (perhaps because) Gerth had looked the devil in the face, he sustained his sanity with a stunningly naive faith in nuclear deterrence, a faith parodied in the anti-left (and pro-NATO) diatribes of Gerth students like Arthur Vidich and, more recently, Jeff Herf. But what distinguished Gerth most from his students was his ear. He had almost perfect sociological pitch and could hear the national agony as much in the "unwept tears" secretly shed by the suburban housewife at the shopping-center cinema as in Secretary Forrestal's scream "The Russians are coming," before throwing himself from a Pentagon window. Gerth directed attention to the layers of human significance beneath the seemingly banal and evasive features of everyday experience. Critical thought was neither a weapon nor a morale booster for him. It was simply a way to pose reality in its full complexity as a problem to be solved by our collective self-invention.

DEPARTURE

Early in 1966, the university offered to share student grades with local draft boards. In response, defying the pleas of radical student leaders, about one hundred of us occupied the administration building. Our act was to be exemplary and limited. But by evening, as if they had simply been waiting in the wings for their cue, about two thousand students had joined us, and the administration abandoned any thought of removing us with force. During the next few days, Williams, Goldberg, Zeitlin, American historian William Taylor, and other faculty talked to us, then left, promising they would win faculty support for our demands. When the faculty refused to meet under this "duress," we agreed to leave. As the crowd moved tiredly home, I noticed the old-line social democrat Gerth chatting with some students in a stairwell. He was the only professor who actually sat in. Perhaps he was there because he too was treated as a student, alternately patronized and bullied, or perhaps he felt he wanted to be there when *his* students got the trouble he was always expecting. Perhaps he believed his memories had a secret power to protect us. Or maybe he simply wanted the company.

The inevitable faculty turndown brought thousands of students into the night looking for a spot to rest their anger. With scouts hunting for a building to seize, I held the crowd at bay with a talk on the medieval university. But my leadership had less to do with speech making than with standing at the center of huge ballrooms and facilitating a mass conversation among thousands sitting on the floor. As so often happens during spring at college when sit-ins and sexual exuberance coincide, my heart had been broken by the collapse of a love I'd finally learned to trust. My public fury surrendered to the child in me and I spoke with a sense of serenity that felt religious, helping others transgress their emotional boundaries by doing so myself.

We seized Bascom Hall, the symbolic center of the campus. At night, faculty climbed through the windows to join us, recognizing a need to talk to their students in a new way. A prominent economic historian confessed to being a "brown shirt" during the war. The campus police chief asked for help with a paper on student demonstrations for his national convention. In exchange, he gave us his crowd-control equipment. Since everyone was somewhere else, classes stopped, and schooling simply shifted to our little space. Initially, talk focused on overcoming differences: a sorority girl exposing her fear of Jews, a Commie confessing he loved the Mets. From here, talk became utopian. What would life be like if this "moment of autonomy" was extended outward? This too was a type of sociological talk it would never have occurred to us to have in class.

We left Bascom Hall when the discussion was done, several days after founding our "walking university." But we had been closely watched. When we sat in again a year later, they broke heads within minutes of the occupation. This was less because they feared what we would do *to* their buildings than because, by becoming our own kinds of adults *in* their buildings, we put their obsolescence on public view.

By 1967, I was a "student leader," one of a rare breed of postadolescent gun fighters whose artillery combined rhetorical flamboyance, Jewish humor (even for the non-Jews), and an inhuman capacity for all-night meetings. I was reified like a campus queen (and felt as isolated), doing radio and TV spots, talking at "bagel breakfasts" and Unitarian services, and getting anonymous love notes ("I was holding the candle when you read 'Howl' at Hillel"). In 1966, the FBI elevated my security rating to "dangerous subversive" and officially targeted me for harassment as a potential "terrorist" under its clandestine Cointelpro operation. I was followed to dinner and reports of my activity were provided by reporters on the Wisconsin *Daily Cardinal*, the manager of the student union, and by several patriots in the sociology department.

The relative peacefulness of our draft sit-ins had sent Chancellor Robin Fleming to the University of Michigan as president. Sociology professor William Sewell was now chancellor, picked largely for his progressive reputation—his son had been arrested at Berkeley and he had chaired an early antiwar rally. A kind methodologist without a whit of administrative skill or experience, he lacked even his predecessor's patronizing aura. Sewell remained incredulous when we documented plans between the dean of students and city police to plan a possible campus "occupation." Just days before Dow Chemical came to campus to recruit,

Sewell personally assured me police would not be called if we refrained from violence.

At a school where 90 percent opposed the war, students saw little point in symbolic protest. But when "concerned black people" pulled out of the planned Dow protest, the Trotskyist leadership of CEWV opposed direct action, calling instead for "peaceful and educative" leafletting. A parallel leadership had developed outside the sectarian groups by this time, partially rooted in the new SDS chapter we founded to offset the Communist party's influence in CEWV and partially in the increasing numbers of students drawn to direct action and antidraft work. When SDS proposed that Dow be blocked, the planning meeting of three hundred was split, but by midnight the one hundred remaining agreed to my compromise proposal—peaceful picketing on Tuesday and civil disobedience on Wednesday—and ten of us were appointed ad hoc leaders. I oriented the flier to the growing number who saw the official campus left as the antithesis of direct action.

> We must move from protest to resistance. Before we talked. Now we must act. We must stop what we oppose.
>
> We must enter the arena of action to make the kind of history we want.
>
> We will enter a building in which Dow is recruiting and stop them.

The first day more than five hundred students met to picket at Bascom Hall. Soon after the peaceful rally began, about one hundred "jocks" approached and began tearing signs and pushing through the crowd. I took the bullhorn and spoke extemporaneously about "why the football team is losing," drawing a parallel between spoon-fed education and plays spoon fed from the bench. In each case, energy was wasted and potential lost. I told the story of a young black player from Galveston who had come to the university despite an ACT score of only 18. After an outstanding first year, he had in the second year been one day late for practice, thus missing the team photograph. Kicked off the team, and so out of school, he had returned to a street world from which he was suddenly totally alienated. Not realizing the impact of what I was saying on young athletes, I promised that tomorrow we would have a real chance to moblize our energy to smash this "spectacle."

Shortly after we entered the commerce building the next morning, the police arrived. After the dean (wielding an ax) led an abortive charge, the campus chief urged me to meet with Sewell, and my two bodyguards (they are now both prominent sociologists) kept the police from grabbing me as we moved through the crowd. The chief and I begged Sewell to avoid a "bloodbath." But the man who began his career by "disproving" the influence of early child rearing on adult behavior had frozen stiff in his role; his face was pasty like the heart attack victim he would become shortly after. When the beatings escalated, Marc Sticgold, a law school dean, rushed into Sewell's office and asked to phone an ambulance. Sewell was sitting in the same spot, riveted. Staring at the wall, he shook his head, no.

When the police broke through, they met a cordon of athletes who had been counterdemonstrators just hours before. I remember watching Kim Wood, a 250-pound varsity fullback, urging the cop vainly trying to beat him to calm down.

One episode encapsulates my experience of sociology in Madison. While we were fighting the gas in the courtyard, I did an odd thing. Having gone into the social science building to wash out my eyes, I thought, "Why not check my mail?" The hall in the sociology department upstairs was empty. But there was the department faculty, clustered at the windows, watching the melee through soundproof glass, strangely silent, as if they were in a movie theater, then suddenly cheering if they saw a student they recognized. I slipped in next to them for a few minutes, enjoying the irony of my participant observation. Then I returned to the street.

After things settled, I visited the wounded in the hospital, feeling a bit like Napoleon after Waterloo. Then I left the city, resigning from graduate school just hours before we were officially suspended. For years, I had a recurrent nightmare that left me in a cold sweat: Police were coming up the stairs to my bedroom at home, beating my friends bloody on the way.

After the letter inviting Gerth to Frankurt sat unopened on his desk for a year, he finally agreed to go, as he put it, "to show them what it had once been like." In Frankfurt, left-wing students insisted he make history a footnote to Marxology. When he refused, the left students "turned off the lights" (as they say in Germany) and he retired. Soon after, he died.

SOCIOLOGICAL TALK

The varieties of experience I encountered in the Midwest bore little external resemblance to the world portrayed by the sociologists at Brandeis. What resonated was Marcuse's vision of a repressed and potentially explosive energy just beneath the surface of everyday life and the sense—modeled for us by Mailer, Goodman, James Baldwin, Malcolm X, and others—that alienation was the essence of a positive subjectivity. In the anonymity and conformity of the urban masses in mid-nineteenth-century Manchester, Engels recognized the core of a new class identity. Similarly, humanists and critical theorists believed that alienation was the tragic consequence as traditional bonds to occupation, class, community, and family collapsed. But for us, freedom from these bonds became a point of contact and the basis of political strategy. Alienation allowed us to move through the world without being fixed by its structures or institutions, to reflect on, develop, and manage ourselves, and most important, to become immersed in "the data" of everyday life without being consumed by it (as had the empiricists) or frightened away, as had the critical theorists. Living out one's exile strategically—that was the essence of sociological talk.

In the "one-dimensional" society pictured by Marcuse, mainstream resistance merely reinforced domination. Disenfranchised peasants might revolt, but the laboring classes and their affluent children had clearly been bought off. Yet, oddly, it was precisely where critical theory was so wrong, in its depiction of the mainstream political terrain as closed, that it had its greatest influence, converging with our need to feel our alienation in as full and as uncompromising a way as possible. The sense that American liberalism was fascism in disguise was utterly paranoid. Yet, it defined an oppositional project that broke decisively with the boring machinations of Communists and Trots as well as with social democratic gradualism, a total opposition, pushed to creativity by its very unpredictability. Neither the war in Vietnam nor anything about our background, socialization, or experience was sufficient to evoke the imagination and energy we put into protest. Born to affluence, we mistakenly thought we had to take the world to which our birthright entitled us.

Our legacy, then, is to have played a larger part than economics assigned. This was necessary, not to end the war in Asia perhaps, but to exorcise the political spectre that had overtaken the left since Stalinism and World War II, to divorce idealism from pessimism, rid it of the anonymity of the Gulag and the death camps and root it once again in subjective imagination.

I would like to believe that the conjuncture between critical theory, sociological talk, and direct action bore political fruit. By once again showing that the outcomes of confrontations with the state are always a question of "We shall see," the protests that circled the globe between 1966 and 1970 rescued the Marxian dialectic from the idealist heights to which it had been chased by the Nazi war machine, as well as from the prevalent sectarian view of history as a footnote to economic necessity. The current surge of popular democracy in Eastern Europe is the direct legacy of these protests, capturing their enthusiasm as well as their ambiguity.

Whenever we travel—from Lordstown, Ohio, to a convention of district attorneys in Disney World—I meet veterans of the sit-ins. A sense of recognition binds us, however much we have grown apart in other respects. It is a sense of once having been so filled with collective imagination and personal possibility in a space from which authority had been cleared that inventing the future came almost as an afterthought. The memory of these moments of autonomy can easily dissolve into nostalgia. But having experienced this sense of my capacities, I always know when I am settling for less. And whether I respond by lapsing into sociological talk with my students, clients, or children by muttering loudly at the back of a lecture hall, tapping the hidden courage of teenagers, students, battered women, or the like, or with an angry public refusal that leads others to call us "subversive" once again, I feel my alienation authenticated and know that we can keep them guessing for another day.

Chapter 5

The Contradictions of Radical Sociology: Ideological Purity and Dissensus at Washington University

Henry Etzkowitz

> *If somebody wrote it all down, that would be something.*
> George Rawick, 1972

THE MOST AMBITIOUS effort in the United States to build a radical sociology program at a major university took place in the department of sociology at Washington University, St. Louis, in the late 1960s. For a brief period it appeared that a unique program had been created, a department comprising a broad range of radical scholars. However, by 1972 almost all the radical faculty either had been expelled or had left of their own accord. Similarly, within the American Sociological Association a broad-based radical caucus eventually was reduced to the more narrowly based Section on Marxist Sociology.

The critical mass of radical sociologists brought together in St. Louis during that era imploded, destroying the first radical department in the history of American sociology. Of course, part of the very nature of radical sociology, a critique of the sociological establishment and a self-critique of radical ideas and practice, makes its institutionalization a difficult enterprise. Nevertheless, a major contributing factor to the purge of radical sociologists at Washington University was their constant attacks on each other's work and lifestyles, revealing their disunity and lack of political bonds. The absence of solidarity among radicals opened the way for old-guard faculty members to reconstitute themselves as the dominant political force within the sociology department, where they used their unified strength to remove radicals from their jobs. Thus, at Washington University radical sociology was repressed not only by its opponents but by the actions of radical sociologists themselves.

The failure to institutionalize radical sociology can be explained, in part, by the internal dynamic of radical movements as well as by the opposition they engender. Radical social movements typically contain an inner tension between advocates of ideological purity and advocates of diversity. Purists wish to narrow the base of a movement to those who are committed to a particular vision, believing with Lenin that a small coherent group is the most effective form of revolutionary praxis. Proponents of inclusiveness believe that a broad coalition of persons and groups with related goals is the key to achieving social change through attaining a majority position. Historically, such tensions have torn apart radical and revolutionary movements in late eighteenth-century France and early twentieth-century Russia, among others. These same tensions characterized debates in the radical caucus of the American Sociological Association and among radical sociologists in academic departments in the late 1960s and early 1970s.

THE UNIVERSITY AND THE COMMUNITY

Until the late 1960s there existed a belief that private universities, by virtue of being private, had considerably greater autonomy, more free space in American society, than public universities. This view of the academic sphere was reinforced by the loyalty-oath hearings of the 1950s: Some of the great private universities such as Harvard and Chicago protected their faculty from outside interference, while the University of California, a great public university, was forced to insist that faculty sign loyalty oaths.

Earlier writers did not share the vision of the "independence" of private institutions. Thorstein Veblen (1918), Upton Sinclair (1922), and others in the post–World War I era excorciated business trustees who forced university policy and faculties to conform to the contemporary reactionary waves of their time, often with the willing acquiescence of university administrations and even sometimes under their leadership (Hofstadter and Metzger 1955). Recent critics of the university such as Paul Goodman (1962) and James Ridgeway (1968) have revived this analysis as an explanation of contemporary developments. They argue that today's major universities are as much under the control of a corporate and academic elite as any of the pre–World War I universities, despite the emergence of an ideology of academic freedom and societal liberalism with respect to institutions of higher learning.

Until the 1950s Washington University was largely a streetcar school, attracting an undergraduate clientele from the local area. In the early postwar era the university began a bid for intellectual distinction with the appointment of Arthur Holly Compton, a distinguished physicist, as chancellor. The subsequent appointment of Thomas Eliot, a political scientist who had helped establish the Social Security system in the 1930s, solidified an emerging tradition of distinguished academic leadership drawn from a national pool. By the early 1960s, with foundation and government support, Washington University had built its academic reputation up to the bottom of the top twenty U.S. research universities and was attracting a braoder undergraduate population from the Chicago and New York regions.

The dominant ethos of Washington University was value-free scholarship. Most departments attempted to achieve excellence by conforming to received academic standards and theoretical frameworks within their disciplines, trying only to *do better* at Washington University what was done similarly elsewhere. On this basis most departments reached second- or third-level rankings in their fields during the postwar era. One of the few departments to achieve first-rank status was sociology, through its independent radical stance under the leadership of Alvin Gouldner during the 1960s.[1]

The chairman of the board of trustees, James McDonnell, head of the McDonnell Aircraft Corporation, supported the university's stance of independence from outside governmental controls. Through the trusteeship of leaders from private enterprise, these acts of liberalism (in the face of heavy pressure to the contrary) helped renew the theme of the affinity of private universities to academic freedom at Washington University and elsewhere.

With the decline in federal funding of higher education in the late 1960s, Washington University became more dependent on the local St. Louis corporate elite. The largest single contribution in those years, a $13 million gift, was from the Danforth Family Foundation. Less than a year later, the board of trustees made William Danforth, then dean of the medical school, chancellor of the university. The university community accepted the appointment, with a few wry comments about renaming the school Danforth University. Danforth saw his task as strengthening the relationship between the university and its prime potential donors in the St. Louis business community.

THE ORIGINS OF RADICAL SOCIOLOGY AT WASHINGTON UNIVERSITY

The formation of a department composed mainly of radical scholars had its origins both in the general intellectual history of radical sociology and in the specific institutional history of the department at Washington University. Alvin Gouldner set forth the theoretical framework for the first stage of radical sociology at Washington University in his classic article

"Anti-Minotaur: The Myth of Value Free Sociology" (1962). The article challenged the prevailing interpretations of Max Weber's precepts for social scientists detailed in "Science as a Vocation" (1958). Weber had long been used as an authority to legitimate only neutral and passive observation techniques in researching controversial issues. "Anti-Minotaur" calls upon social scientists not only to start their research from a position of value commitment but also to take value positions in analyzing and drawing conclusions from their research. Gouldner warns social scientists that even if they do not take explicitly political positions in their writings, they are doing so implicitly because their silence lends support to the status quo. "Anti-Minotaur" brought back into sociology the fundamental Marxist principle that intellectual productions are conditioned by concrete social relations. To ignore the social base of social science, Gouldner argues, is to hold to a false ideology of scientistic self-deception.

Earlier, Robert Lynd, in *Knowledge for What?* (1939), had expressed much the same critique of sociology for almost totally ignoring the effects of the Depression on American society. *Knowledge for What?* did not at the time become the basis of a social movement in the discipline (Etzkowitz 1979). Nevertheless, Lynd can be located within a group of revisionists who broke with an earlier sociological generation's "ban on values" (Bramson 1961, 144). In those years sociology itself was a much smaller enterprise, and sociological radicals so inclined participated in contemporary movements without creating analogues within the discipline. It was not until C. Wright Mills echoed Lynd's concerns and developed his own critique twenty years later (in *The Sociological Imagination*, 1959) that this dissent became clearly voiced within the discipline. Even so, although his critical perspective was taken up by individual scholars elsewhere, Mills was not able to create a body of colleagues in his own department (Horowitz 1983).

With the possible exception of John Seeley at Brandeis University, Alvin Gouldner in his capacity as chair of the department of sociology-anthropology brought together at Washington University a group of scholars who were critical of American institutions for producing inequality and oppression both in the United States and in the Third World.[2] Anthropological research techniques were brought home from the "underdeveloped world" to expose the assumptions of American culture. In a series of participant-observation studies conducted in the St. Louis area, Jules Henry and his students showed how schools and family structures stifled the self-realization of parents and children (1963). The Pruitt Igoe research project under Lee Rainwater exposed the bankruptcy of urban renewal housing policies and the exploitive conditions that they fostered

(1970). Irving Louis Horowitz and his students analyzed the dependence of underdeveloped upon developed countries (1972). Alvin Gouldner first investigated the roots of contemporary social theories in their classical Greek predecessors (1963) and later identified the sources of contemporary theorists' assumptions within current political ideologies (1970).

The formation of *Trans-action* magazine created a new public for this innovative research both inside and outside sociology. *Trans-action* broke the bounds of academia by attracting a readership that included nonacademics and nonprofessionals. Within the social science disciplines it made socially relevant research legitimate by providing an outlet for its publication.

From my vantage point at the New School for Social Research in the mid-1960s, Washington University was the seat of radical scholarship. Rather than primarily being concerned with either exegesis of theory, as at the New School, or refining methodological tools as an end in itself, St. Louis sociologists derived research questions from contemporary political and social issues and took a critical stance toward received perspectives. This distinctive approach to the discipline attracted an increasing number of highly motivated graduate students from the United States and other countries. One of these students recalled, "The atmosphere was one of constant intellectual challenge and stimulation, very rough and tumble. Everything developed in conflict. One *had* to defend his own views, long before he knew what they really were. We were expected to be original, imaginative and controversial" (Glazer 1971, 113).

The first stage of sociological radicalism at Washington University carried out the conclusions of Gouldner's "Anti-Minotaur" through the creation of a value-engaged social science department. This stage came to a close when a series of disputes split the faculty that Gouldner had attracted to St. Louis. Perhaps the most bitter was the struggle between Gouldner and Horowitz for control of *Trans-action* magazine. Gouldner had turned the journal over to Horowitz while he was on sabbatical in Europe, but when he returned, Horowitz refused to relinquish editorship. Horowitz was supported by the university administration, the owner of the journal. There was also a dispute about the ethics of the research methodology used by Laud Humphreys, a graduate student of Rainwater's, in his study of homosexual practices in public places (1970). Remarks posted on bulletin boards led to further conflict within the department. Gouldner and Humphreys came to blows in the departmental hallway and in print (see Gouldner 1968).[3]

While the faculty was fissioning, the graduate students were organizing to increase their power within the department. The graduate student organization began with an intellectual focus on the discipline of sociology, with members reporting back on talks they had heard at American Sociological Association meetings. The emergence of the student antiwar movement, together with calls by Gouldner for a critical intellectual stance toward sociology and by Horowitz for an activist involvement in the issues of the times, encouraged the graduate students to move in a more radical direction. Most faculty took a passive stance toward the students, neither encouraging nor discouraging their antiwar activities or their critique of sociology.

By the late 1960s graduate-student demands for participation in departmental governance caused still another split in the faculty, between those who believed that the students should have more authority and those who wished to maintain students in their traditional subservient position. The intrafaculty and faculty-student disputes, combined with the lure of attractive offers elsewhere, led to the departure of several of the department's most eminent members. Irving Louis Horowitz went to Rutgers and took *Trans-action* with him. Lee Rainwater went to Harvard. Joseph Kahl, theorist of social class, went to Cornell. Jules Henry, preeminent anthropological scholar of American culture, became seriously ill. By the end of the 1969 academic year, the department was all but gutted. Alvin Gouldner, the most prestigious senior person remaining in the department, and perhaps the only individual with the authority to reconstitute the department under stable leadership despite a tumultuous past, was banished to an independent chair. (As part of the resolution of the controversy with Humphreys that had culminated in a lawsuit, Gouldner became Max Weber Professor of Social Theory and moved out of the department both organizationally and physically.) Excluded from department meetings, Gouldner could exercise his influence on the department only through friendly faculty and graduate student emissaries. In the institutional madness that ensued, he stood in relation to the department like an exiled Trotsky.

With the department severely weakened, the remaining faculty acquiesced to graduate-student demands for equal membership on departmental committees and veto power on the hiring of new faculty. The graduate students used their new powers with vigor, greatly influencing the selection of faculty by the fall of 1969. Those hired had two things in common: radical credentials and the approval of the graduate students. Several were in fact drawn to Washington University partly because the position of graduate students was so different from what they had recently experienced as graduate students themselves. Ironically, the junior faculty soon found themselves reduced to the traditional status of graduate students since power in the department was shared by senior faculty and graduate students.

The sociologists recruited in 1969 constituted the largest group of radical scholars brought together in a contemporary American sociology department.[4] Even though they were a relatively large group, they did not constitute a majority of the department. The others, those who had remained after the disputes, received their new colleagues with varying degrees of sympathy or antipathy.[5] The department chair encouraged us all to attend the American Sociological Association meetings in San Francisco in late August of 1969 to show the sociological world that Washington University was still an active center of the discipline.

A personal note: Academic departments, through their interaction with the university and the community, provide the material conditions within which we labor, and influence what is possible for us to do or say in our work. To publicly discuss a department's internal conflicts is to break an unstated but strongly held academic norm, but if the call for reflexivity in sociology is to be taken seriously, we must be willing to critically examine our own social bases (Gouldner 1970).

RADICAL DICHOTOMIES

American radical sociology contains conflicting positions on several basic issues of theory and practice:

> ■ Should Marxism be the sole theoretical framework of radical sociology?
> ■ Is Marxism to be taken as a *given* theoretical framework of world historical social development, or is it to be used as a *methodology* for further sociological work?
> ■ Is sociological radicalism exclusively a *theoretical* enterprise or should it include an *activist* political engagement with social issues as well?
> ■ If activism is accepted, what form should it take? Are reform and revolutionary approaches mutually exclusive, or can they exist in a complementary relationship?

The different positions taken on these issues explain, in part, why radical sociologists have been unable to act as a unified force within American sociology—even within a particular department.

	Revolution	*Reform*
Theory	Marxist academic	Phenomenology/ethnomethodology
Practice	Marxist activist	Institution formation

FIGURE 5.1   Typology of Radical Sociology

A typology of radical sociologists (and radical sociology) can be developed by considering their stand on questions of theory versus practice and revolution versus reform; see Figure 5.1. On a theoretical level, Marxism and phenomenology/ethnomethodology provided frameworks for change, challenging the relatively static structural-functionalist paradigm. But whereas Marxism concentrated on discontinuous change of large-scale social formations, phenomenology and ethnomethodology tended to focus on the individual and on small-scale, interpersonal levels. On issues of practice, Marxist activism looked toward raising consciousness as a precursor to revolutionary activity, while institution-formation was concerned with inventing and implementing models of social reform. The tenuous link among these diverse approaches to sociology was a rejection of value-free social analysis.

Although structural functionalism never achieved the status of a unitary paradigm within American sociology since various schools of symbolic interactionism (principally Chicago and Iowa) provided a significant alternative approach, many internal critics of the discipline acted on the premise that it had (see Foss 1963). Sociological radicalism of the 1960s evolved from the critique of functionalism into a search for alternative grounds (see Etzkowitz and Glassman 1991).

Although a range of perspectives, from Jungian to Marxian, were represented in the Washington University sociology department during the late 1960s and early 1970s, the primary conflicts were among academic Marxists, activist Marxists, and institution-forming sociologists. The tensions among these positions, which could have been fruitfully pursued in collegial sociological debate and analysis, through the opportunity presented by the contiguity of their proponents in the same department, were instead translated into personal and political vendettas in St. Louis.

Academic Marxists

Academic Marxists represented an earlier generation who, remembering the past, thought of a time when it was personally and politically dangerous to discuss or write from a Marxist standpoint. Academic Marxists who had courageously expressed their views during the 1950s had

seen their careers suffer for their politics. Some had encountered Mc-
Carthyism and had been blacklisted from American universities. So Marxist academics believed that the theories they held were potentially dangerous. The steps taken during the 1950s to forbid the teaching of
Marxism in secondary schools dramatically reinforced this belief. Indeed,
such teachers were treated no less harshly than their predecessors who
had tried to teach about natural selection in the 1920s.

Then in the late 1960s Marxism underwent an intellectual revival as
McCarthyism receded and as social sciences became receptive to conflict
and class models to explain persisting stratification and social inequity.
Scholars who had been relegated to minor academic institutions now
found themselves desired by first-rate universities. The irony was that
after waiting for so long, they found their position in the forefront of
radical thought jeopardized not by those to the right of them but by
those to the left: the proponents of the new radicalism. Not satisfied with
Marxist analysis, the new radical left demanded concerted action to bring
about Marxist consciousness and revolutionary potential. The academic
Marxists could neither tolerate nor understand this position.

The academic Marxists believed that consciousness came first and that
action would naturally follow. They wanted to create in the university an
intellectual climate where the finer points of Marxism could be openly
debated within the context of a common theoretical framework. They
believed that by this intellectual tradition they were standing fast and
against all odds keeping alive the revolutionary tradition. Thus, the
model Marxist was a scholar, not an activist. The academic Marxists believed their influence would be felt through the graduate students they
trained, who would in turn go forth to train undergraduates in Marxism,
and presumably the undergraduates would then become the primary and
secondary schoolteachers of the next generation, and thus Marxist theory
would eventually percolate downward to the masses.

Activist Marxists

Beginning in the early 1960s, certain university professors came to
perceive themselves as working-class intellectuals. Some donned boots,
work shirts, and blue jeans—the "uniform" that represented a working-
class consciousness. These scholars viewed the university as a bureaucratic factory, an analysis that had emerged from the Berkeley student
movement of the early 1960s. They hoped to achieve two objectives: to
transmit their own revolutionary working-class consciousness to their
colleagues and students, and to contribute to social movements.

It became apparent in the mid 1960s that factory workers were, by and large, not interested in the tenets of working-class consciousness. Attempts made by New Left intellectuals in this area gained few adherents. The new working-class scholars, encouraged by their successes in engendering radical consciousness in their students and colleagues, now thought it might be possible to expand this movement to intellectuals who worked under factory conditions as scientists and technologists in the corporations of the military-industrial complex. For example, Jeff Schevitz, as a graduate student at Berkeley, helped organize an antiwar group of technical people from the weapons industry.

Marxist activists also believed in the possibility of engendering a revolutionary consciousness among those who had not yet been drawn into the factory system, such as the unemployed, women on welfare, the members of the underclass. For example, Dave Colfax, while a faculty member in St. Louis, helped organize a radical group of poor blacks and social workers. Implicit in Marxist activism was the premise that participation in the factory system tended to prevent people from attaining revolutionary consciousness. These neo-Marxists realized that the contradictions of capitalism were not taking what Marx had predicted would be their inevitable course. Therefore, they now believed that if the revolution was to occur, they would have to look to groups outside the capitalist system or to those who, because of their intellectual background, could attain a revolutionary consciousness in spite of the system in which they were enmeshed.

Theory Versus Practice. There were irreconcilable differences among Marxist sociologists at Washington University over both the theory and the practice of social change. The activist Marxists did not believe in waiting for the revolution in the ivory tower. Viewing the community as their laboratory, they attempted to introduce a catalyst to energize a reaction that would bring forth working-class consciousness in the St. Louis area. The activists believed that creating working-class consciousness as a way of attaining revolutionary action was in accordance with Marxist theory. The Marxist academics responded that undertaking action was the province of the working class. If the Marxist activists did so, they were neither proper Marxists nor proper sociologists. The activists then charged the academics with improper revolutionary lifestyle—living in large houses more befitting of the *haute bourgeoisie*. The academics responded that, relative to academic rank, the activist's lifestyle (in middle-class homes) was just as elegant.

The academic Marxists expected to be respected by their radical colleagues for having kept alive Marxist studies; they felt insulted that their Marxist credentials were being challenged by those who had come to

Marxism at a time when it was in academic fashion. The academics felt that this new generation was careerist, building upon the very views that an earlier generation had suffered such difficulties for holding. When the academics did not respond to the call to cover their typewriters and go into the community, the activists attacked them for not being willing to put Marxist principles into practice.

Revolution Versus Reform. A question among those who favored action was the form the action had to take in order to be considered radical. At issue was the purpose of the action: Could the action be considered radical as a demonstration project in creating new social forms in opposition to the status quo according to a theoretical framework of social change occurring through reform, or was the primary purpose of action in the community the raising of revolutionary consciousness? Nonradical sociologists in St. Louis found the distinction between revolutionary and reformist intent irrelevant; they could not countenance involvement in controversial community issues as a sociological methodology in *any* form.

Radical Action for People. Radical Action for People (RAP) was a Marxist activist group founded by Professors David Colfax and Jeffrey Schevitz of the Washington University sociology department, along with social workers and community activists, to investigate and expose repressive institutions. Viewing total institutions as reactionary, RAP focused on Missouri Hills, a reformatory predominantly for black inner-city youth. Missouri Hills had already been under attack by conservatives because of its inability to control its inmates, high rate of recidivism, and costliness. The St. Louis *Post Dispatch* and other liberal forces had also censured Missouri Hills for its lack of programs, characterizing the institution as a way station for delinquents who would eventually end up in the state prison. RAP found itself in the position of attempting to raise consciousness on an issue on which consciousness had already been raised. RAP was not interested in either reforming Missouri Hills or constructing an alternative to it. Both strategies were antithetical to its founders' theoretical framework of delegitimating existing institutions, thus creating a radical consciousness as a precursor to revolutionary acts.

RAP confronted the Missouri Hill governing board with objections to the way the reformatory was run and demanded representation on the board. RAP's leaders were stunned when this demand was met and they were invited to join the board. They had expected to be turned down and even forcibly removed from the meeting. The purpose of the action had been to demonstrate the nonresponsiveness of the governing board. Thus, without a negative response to react against, RAP considered the action a failure and dropped the project.

In another action, RAP transported a group of mothers on welfare to the St. Louis hotel where the annual banquet of the Midwestern Sociological Society was to take place. RAP's plan was to demand that the sociologists give their dinners to the women, expecting that they would refuse and call the police to have the women thrown out. This would show that the sociologists were part of a repressive establishment and the women would presumably be radicalized by this confrontation. However, when confronted with the demand sufficient sociologists gave up their meals so that all the women could be seated. The women concluded that, although the meal was fine, they were more interested in seeing conditions improved in their neighborhood.

RAP and the women were at cross purposes. RAP hoped to use the incident to raise the consciousness of the St. Louis black community. The women went not to get a meal or embarrass the sociologists but to express their desire for improvement of conditions in the black community to a group that they believed had influence in American society. RAP's theoretical framework of social change proceeding from consciousness raising to revolution led them to misread the desires of the women and the reaction of the Midwestern sociologists.

Institution-Formation Sociologists

The theory of institution formation (Etzkowitz and Schaflander 1968; Etzkowitz 1970a) holds that incremental reforms can lead to qualitative social change. The role of the sociologist in testing and developing this theory includes inventing and organizing new institutions as a method of both examining and solving social problems. The new institutions serve as demonstration projects to motivate people who desire change but are often restrained from taking action because of lack of an alternative model. The new institutions also serve as a research tool, drawing out the response of existing institutions through negotiation and conflict rather than interviews or participant observation.

By their very existence, public-interest law firms, free medical clinics, infant and child care centers, and free schools demonstrate that more humane social institutions are possible. As they proliferate, incremental social change takes place that holds within it the potential that institutions of an inhumane bureaucratic society will wither away. For when new institutions work, old institutions are challenged. When the old institutions begin to perform tasks that people demand because they have seen them happen in new institutions, then a co-optation from below has occurred.

Institution formation often leads to the techniques of "legal offense." An example from our work in St. Louis occurred when the social welfare authorities attempted to close down an infant care center, the Infant Growth Environment (IGE).[6] IGE had been organized by a coalition of young mothers, Washington University sociology students and professors, and teachers and professors from a summer program at the Graduate Institute of Education designed to link inner-city and suburban schools. IGE established itself in a space that an inner-city church had been using for child care on Sundays. In St. Louis there were no legal provisions for group day care of children under two years of age. The social welfare authorities called on the city building department to close down the IGE on the grounds that it did not meet the building code, even though IGE supporters made the suggested improvement. The denial of an occupancy permit is a common bureaucratic technique to impede the establishment of a new institution.

The infant care center decided to remain open without a permit. This act of "institutional civil disobedience" brought the attention of the media to IGE, which had been operating in relative obscurity until then. There was more. A student support group sued to force the issuance of an occupancy permit. Others organized a demonstration in front of the Spanish Pavilion that drew the attention of the news media. Students in a class on urban sociology organized a class-action suit against the mayor.[7] The publicity from these actions brought new sources of support. The IGE was soon invited to move to space that had already been approved for day care in a major black church.

Some old-guard members of the sociology department were perturbed by the publicity, but by making news IGE was able to communicate its ideology to a wider audience than could be obtained through the underground or radical press. The new institution was a small-scale model of day care for infants and a practicum site for a course entitled Childhood and Society. Through the controversy over its existence, the IGE also became a means of raising consciousness about child care, a nascent social issue.

The Contradictions of Radical Sociology

RAP's activist Marxist framework was irreconcilably opposed to the institution-formation position of incremental change. Reform was viewed as counterproductive since it was believed that conditions must worsen in order for dissatisfaction to erupt into a revolutionary explosion. Institution formation was perhaps the most precarious position in the Washington University sociology department since it departed from the norms of both academic and activist Marxism as well as the tradition of value-free sociology. These differences came to the fore at the meetings of the

Sociology Liberation Movement (caucus of radical sociologists) at the 1970 meetings of the American Sociological Association in Washington, D.C., where faculty and graduate students from Washington University were among the key participants.

The caucus meetings provided a reprise of the St. Louis debates. The central issue was whether radical sociology would take an academic or activist Marxist turn. Marxist activists attacked Marxist academics on a broad range of issues from tactics to lifestyles. The academics walked out, and the activists gained control of the caucus. They quickly obtained permission from the ASA leadership to make a statement in response to Reinhard Bendix's presidential address. (To my surprise, I was selected as one of two persons to make a statement, even though I had made it clear that I would represent my own position [Etzkowitz 1971a].) However, those who were most outspoken in attacking the academics chose not to speak. At first the reason was not clear. It became evident the next day, when David Colfax, the leading Marxist activist, and three colleagues issued a statement calling for the end of radical sociology, denouncing it as just another career hustle.[8]

The experience of RAP and the Radical Caucus illuminate the inner dynamic of activist Marxist practice. When a movement is gaining widespread support, as the Sociology Liberation Movement had within sociology or as Radical Action for People did when its demand was accepted by the board of Missouri Hills, the movement becomes suspect *because* of its success. The success of a radical organization or movement is viewed as proof that it is not truly radical. Success is interpreted as de facto evidence of cooptation. Instead of accepting victories, the action is given up or the group broken up. Thus, RAP withdrew from Missouri Hills and the activist Marxists split the Sociology Liberation Movement. Radical practice becomes a "lefter than thou" game in which the holder of the most extreme position is viewed as the only true radical. When the objective is to take the ideological high ground at all costs, the building of an effective movement suffers.

PRAXIS DISMISSED: THE REPRESSION OF RADICAL SOCIOLOGY AT WASHINGTON UNIVERSITY

The result of these efforts to arrive at a single "correct" position was that radical sociologists would not accept one another's credentials as radicals. Increasing energy was spent in attacking other people's positions. The sociology department at Washington University, like the Sociology

Liberation Movement, seemed to the outside world a unified body of radicals; when viewed from within, both more resembled a fragmented regime. Upset by what they viewed as constant turmoil within and without the university, most of the tenured faculty wished to return the department to the practice of value-free sociology and to governance without student participation. In short, although they had, under pressure from the graduate students and for lack of an alternative approach of their own, acquiesced to the reconstitution of the department as a center of radical sociology, they did not want the department taken over by radical sociologists.

Perhaps the first indicator was the failure, by one vote, to restore Alvin Gouldner to membership in the department. The vote took place in fall 1969 before the radicals split and was thus a good measure of the underlying fault line in the department. A later example of the ambivalence of the senior department members was their reaction to Jeffrey Schevitz's response to the My Lai atrocities. He announced to the sociology department and to the university community his intention to reorganize the Introduction to Sociology course to focus on sociological analysis of issues underlying the Vietnam War. Schevitz also offered his students the opportunity to organize local antiwar activities as class field projects. Professor Levi, a senior member of the philosophy department, strongly objected. The senior sociology faculty, in an attempt to improve the department's standing within the university, insisted that Schevitz accept an accommodation with Levi. This maneuver backfired when the administration viewed the department's injunction to Schevitz as further evidence of lack of internal unity. Ironically, by the end of the spring semester, other courses would be reorganized to work against the war. After Cambodia and Kent State such activities became a commonplace and even acceptable nonviolent alternative to such acts as burning down the campus ROTC building.

When the senior faculty realized that they had not mollified the university community, they met to discuss which members of the junior faculty should be terminated. In the course of this discussion someone suggested checking the contract terms of the junior faculty in question. Finding that several were on three-year contracts, they temporarily postponed the purge.

Among the teaching activities found unacceptable were: field work in the inner city for a research methods course; street theater performances as part of a political sociology course; use of T-group techniques in the classroom; and a proposal of a joint student-faculty curriculum committee to revise the undergraduate curriculum to allow faculty to teach collectively and incorporate field work in the degree program. The senior faculty were also embarrassed by the radical faculty's work with members of the community on such issues as lead paint poisoning, day care, and juvenile detention facilities. The widespread publicity arising from such activities as the class-action lawsuit over the Spanish Pavilion and an analysis of the misguided priorities of the United Fund led senior faculty to conclude that engagement in the community was too disturbing not only to the administration but to their own notion of what sociology was about.

The presence of radical sociology was acceptable as a marketing strategy to distinguish the department from its academic competitors. But when it became more than an academic rubric for distinguishing among theoretical positions, when radical sociologists went beyond the walls of the university to pursue action-research methodologies of whatever stripe, radical sociology was found to be too controversial. Of course, making taken-for-granted activities and views into controversial issues was the heart of radical sociology practice and the analysis of such social controversies the core of its research design.

Activist radical sociology was basically incompatible with the department's strategy of seeking an accommodation with the administration. But since the department did not wish to give up its radical identification, the obvious choice was made: Emphasize the theoretical side of radical sociology. This strategy was at least formally compatible with prevailing academic mores as to the proper role of the academic. In early 1971 an observer of the academic scene predicted "It is likely that within the next year there will be crucial test cases regarding tenure and promotion which will do much to determine the tolerable limits of dissent in the academy" (Hitchcock 1971). At Washington University the purge was already under way: All the radical activist professors hired in fall 1969 were fired.

The Colfax tenure case in 1971 was a watershed event. David Colfax believed he had been assured when he was appointed associate professor in 1969 that his imminent tenure would be a formality. However, when it came to a vote the senior faculty split almost evenly; when one senior faculty member who had initially voted for Colfax saw the depth of the split he changed his vote from positive to neutral. A group of students rallied to support Colfax during the appeals process. At the same time Alvin Gouldner, with whom Colfax had been engaged in a bitter dispute over the leadership of the radical sociology movement, issued a leaflet reminding the department that at the national sociology meetings Colfax had participated in a call for the elimination of radical sociology, contradicting his claim to tenure based partly on the prominent role he had played in creating a radical sociology. Not surprisingly, the administration rejected Colfax's tenure and the appeals process sustained the administration.

Washington University had assembled a group of radicals who could not agree on a strategy to act as a unified force within the department. Even on issues on which some of us were perceived as sharing a common framework, such as accepting the sociologist as an active participant in organizations and movements for social change, our differences were far more important to us than what we held in common. The key issue among the activists was the meaning of cooptation. If a demand is accepted should it be taken as evidence of a victory or as a potential sign of cooptation? If short-term gains cannot be accepted for fear of cooptation, then refusal can be achieved by escalating to a more extreme position. Both revolutionaries and reformers are needed to achieve social change. If reformers and revolutionaries do not coordinate their efforts they leave themselves open to divide-and-conquer tactics by those who wish to thwart any change, whether incremental or revolutionary. Both elements were present at Washington University but we worked at cross purposes and facilitated our dismissal.

In *Theory and Theory Groups in American Sociology* (1973) Nicholas Mullins found that the department at Washington University constituted a center of radical sociology that would be a training ground for graduate students in coming years. "Three (roughly) radical training centers have recently materialized; one at Santa Barbara around Richard Flacks; one at Washington University, St. Louis (with David Colfax and Henry Etzkowitz); and a third at Rutgers (with Irving L. Horowitz, Martin Oppenheimer, and John Leggett). All three centers are still quite small; but they are starting to train students and are working hard on theoretical issues" (280). By the time the book was published the St. Louis group had dispersed.

The next generation of radical sociologists hired at Washington University was also fired as the administration made it clear that any form of radicalism in sociology was unacceptable. In subsequent years the department, with negligible exceptions, lost the ability to tenure its junior faculty and was not allowed to accept new students into its Ph.D. program. The history of intradepartmental conflict had taken a toll, with the department losing its credibility both in the discipline and the university.

EPILOGUE

In the October 1987 *Employment Bulletin* of the American Sociological Association the department of sociology at Washington University advertised for a new chair to rebuild the department. The search was coordinated by a member of the political science department, suggesting the sociology department's loss of control of its future course. In 1989, rather than rebuild, Washington University announced plans to close its sociology department. Tenured members were to be relocated to other departments and untenured faculty given two years' notice. Thus, the failure to institutionalize radical sociology led also to the demise of sociology in this academic setting. Washington University became, along with the University of Rochester, the second major university to deny an institutional base for the discipline in recent years.

Despite the sociology department's ability to attract significant research grants and large numbers of students, the administration soon viewed it with disfavor because of its iconoclastic stance. During the 1960s, given the department's ability to sustain a national reputation and the reliance of the university on national sources of support, sociology could be reluctantly tolerated as an anomalous, disruptive, yet prestigious presence on the campus. But when the university returned to a local orientation for financial support in the early 1970s, after more than two decades of maintaining a national stance, the department found itself in a precarious position. A succession of sociology students and faculty members were involved in research and action projects that were critical of the local business community. As late as the mid-1970s an anti-redlining research and action project organized by Professor Richard Ratcliffe drew the ire of the St. Louis banking community (they were using research data to contest bank charters before regulatory authorities). With the decline of its national reputation and inability to reconstitute itself during the late 1970s and early 1980s, the sociology department became more of a liability than an asset to the university. In the increasing financial stringency of the late 1980s the decision was made to terminate the discipline, despite the quietude that had overcome the department by that time.

In a reversal of the usual process whereby scientific societies in a new area of scholarship are formed to bring practitioners together for occasional meetings leading to the formation of departments and centers of research, radical sociology became deinstitutionalized and devolved into looser forms during the 1970s. Regional groups such as the East Coast Conference of Socialist Sociologists and the Marxist Sociology Section of ASA organized sessions and panels for the presentation of papers. No sociology department during that decade attempted to emulate Washington University's attempt to encompass in a single setting the various strands of radical sociology, although certain aspects were well ensconced at SUNY Binghamton, Livingston College at Rutgers, the University of California at Santa Barbara, University of Oregon, and elsewhere. Not until the 1980s, with the revival of the department at the University of

California at Berkeley, has a many-faceted radical sociology found a single home. The irony, of course, is that there is no longer a self-conscious radical sociology. The oppositional tendencies that came together in the late 1960s have gone their separate ways and a historical Marxism has subsumed the central place of radical sociology on the academic left.

NOTES

An earlier version of this chapter was presented at the annual meetings of the Southwestern Social Science Association in Dallas, 1972.

1. The other great iconoclast at Washington University, Barry Commoner, was never able to reorient his department, botany, along the lines of the environmental paradigm that he was so influential in creating. Although Commoner attracted considerable funds to the Center for the Biology of Natural Systems, he was allowed only his personal office in the department. The rest of his operation was located in a house trailer, provided by the Teamsters Union, that was parked behind the botany building.

2. A small group of critical sociologists was also constituted in a single location under the leadership of John Seeley at Brandeis University.

3. The issues at hand were addressed on a more theoretical level in the Becker–Gouldner exchange; see Becker 1967.

4. The group included: Pedro Cavalcanti, Warsaw Ph.D., Marxist theorist and Latin American scholar in political exile; David Colfax, Chicago Ph.D., a leader of the emerging radical movement in sociology, denied tenure at the University of Connecticut after leading an insurgent movement in the university and neighboring community; Henry Etzkowitz, New School Ph.D., formulater of the Institution-Formation action research methodology and organizer of a community cooperative in Bedford-Stuyvesant; George Rawick, Wisconsin Ph.D. in history, Marxist theorist and civil rights activist, formulater of a revisionist approach to slavery studies; Jeffrey Schevitz, Berkeley A.B.D., antiwar organizer, researcher, and film maker of engineers in the San Francisco Bay area military-industrial complex; Fred Schiff, U.S.C.A. A.B.D. counterculture participant and researcher of public attitudes toward the war using phenomenological methods; John Raphael Staude, Berkeley Ph.D. in history, biographer of philosopher-sociologist Max Scheler, phenomenologist and psychotherapist, an innovator in using therapy techniques in classroom teaching; and Irving Zeitlin, Princeton Ph.D., Marxist theorist and student of the ideological origins of sociological theory.

5. Senior faculty members included: Robert Boguslaw, New York University Ph.D., formerly a researcher at the RAND corporation and author of *The New Utopians*, an award-winning study of systems analysis ideology; David Carpenter, University of Washington Ph.D., department chair, former dean, coauthor of classic text in urban sociology; Nicholas Demerath, Harvard Ph.D., an expert on the sociology of population control in India; Helen Gouldner, UCLA Ph.D., director of

the Black Education research project after the death of its founder, Jules Henry; Robert Hamblin, University of Michigan Ph.D., organizer and director of an innovative behavior-modification project for autistic children; and David Pittman, a leading expert on the sociology of alcoholism and director of the Social Science Institute, the research arm of the department. Wolf Heydebrand, University of Chicago Ph.D., a specialist in the sociology of organizations with an interest in critical sociology, had recently received tenure. He participated in the caucus of radicals that was called together in 1971. There were also two other junior faculty members: John Goering, Brown Ph.D., urban sociologist; and James Swift, Washington University Ph.D.

6. Supported by small grants and parents' fees, the St. Louis IGE cared for eight to ten children from six weeks to two years of age. Open Monday through Friday from 8:00 A.M. to 5:30 P.M., the center combined a paid staff with student volunteers. For more about the IGE see Etzkowitz 1971b and Etzkowitz and Zeffert 1970. The model for the IGE had been developed at the Bedford-Stuyvesant Community Center in New York in 1967. For more about the Community Co-op Center, see Etzkowitz and Schaflander 1968.

7. As part of a strategy to revive a declining downtown, city officials had solicited money from citizens to move the Spanish Pavilion restaurant and exhibition complex from the 1964 New York World's Fair to St. Louis. The enterprise failed, and the mayor had announced that the complex would be turned over to a hotel developer. IGE supporters mounted a demonstration outside the complex, demanding that the Pavilion be turned into a day care center instead. Remodeling plans developed by Washington University architecture students were displayed as a visual backdrop during a television commentary. On another front, the urban sociology class members formed themselves into a group called Pavilion for Children and Youth and filed a lawsuit against the city on behalf of the original contributors, charging that transferring the property to the hotel developer was misuse of their funds for a private purpose. They searched newspaper files to identify contributors and contacted them to participate in the class-action suit.

8. See "Seize the Time" and "More on Washington University," *Insurgent Sociologist* 2, no. 4 (Fall 1972): 49, 44–51.

REFERENCES

Becker, Howard. 1967. "Whose Side Are We On?" *Social Problems* 14, no. 3 (Winter): 230–47.
Bramson, Leon. 1961. *The Political Context of Sociology*. Princeton, N.J.: Princeton University Press.
Colfax, David, and Jack Roach. 1971. *Radical Sociology*. New York: Basic Books.
Daniels, Lee. 1989. "Some Top Universities in Squeeze Between Research and Academics." *New York Times*, May 10, sec. B.
Etzkowitz, Henry. 1970a. "Institution-Formation Sociology." *American Sociologist* 5, no. 2 (May): 120–25.

————. 1970b. "Legal Offense: A Radical Strategy." *Focus Midwest* 8, no. 52: 11.

————. 1971a. "Reply to Bendix." *The Insurgent Sociologist* 1, no. 4 (April): 5.

————. 1971b. "Sociology and Praxis." *Social Theory and Practice*, Spring, 1–8.

————. 1979. "The Americanization of Marx: Middletown and Middletown in Transition." *Journal of the History of Sociology* 1 (Fall).

Etzkowitz, Henry, and Gerald Schaflander. 1968. "A Manifesto for Sociologists." *Social Problems* 15, no. 4 (Spring): 399–407.

————. 1969. *Ghetto Crisis*. Boston: Little, Brown.

Etzkowitz, Henry, and Robert Zeffert. 1970. "Strategy and Tactics of Institution Formation: Organization of the Infant Growth Environment." Paper prepared for the Center for Institution Formation, Washington University, St. Louis.

Etzkowitz, Henry, and Ronald Glassman. 1991. *The Renascence of Sociological Theory*. Itasca, Ill.: Peacock.

Foss, Daniel. 1963. "The World View of Talcott Parsons." In Maurice Stein and Arthur Vidich, eds., *Sociology on Trial*. Englewood Cliffs, N.J.: Prentice Hall.

Glazer, Myron, ed. 1971. *The Research Adventure*. New York: Random House.

Goodman, Paul. 1962. *The Community of Scholars*. New York: Random House.

Gouldner, Alvin. 1962. "Anti-Minotaur: The Myth of Value Free Sociology." *Social Problems* 9, no. 3 (Winter): 199–213.

————. 1963. *Enter Plato*. New York: Basic Books.

————. 1968 "Sociology as Partisan." *American Sociologist* 3, no. 2 (May): 103–16.

————. 1970. *The Coming Crisis of Western Sociology*. New York: Basic Books.

Henry, Jules. 1963. *Culture Against Man*. New York: Random House.

Hitchcock, James. 1971. "The Radical Professors." *New York Times Magazine*, February 21.

Hofstadter, Richard, and Walter Metzger. 1955. *The Development of Academic Freedom in the United States*. New York: Columbia University Press.

Horowitz, Irving Louis. 1972. *The Three Worlds of Development*. New York: Oxford University Press.

————. 1983. *C. Wright Mills: An American Utopian*. New York: Free Press.

Humphreys, Laud. 1970. *Tearoom Trade*. Chicago: Aldine.

Lynd, Robert. 1939. *Knowledge for What?* Princeton, N.J.: Princeton University Press.

Mills, C. Wright. 1959. *The Sociological Imagination*. New York: Oxford University Press.

Mullins, Nicholas. 1973. *Theory and Theory Groups in American Sociology*. New York: Harper & Row.

Rainwater, Lee. 1970. *Behind Ghetto Walls*. Hawthorne, N.Y.: Aldine de Gruyter.

Ridgeway, James. 1968. *The Closed Corporation*. New York: Random House.

Sinclair, Upton. 1922. *The Goose Step: A Study of American Education*. New York: The Cornwall Press.

Staude, John. 1967. *Max Scheler: An Intellectual Portrait*. New York: Free Press.

Veblen, Thorstein. 1918. *The Higher Learning in America*. New York: B. W. Huebsch.

Weber, Max. 1958. "Science as a Vocation." In Hans Gerth and C. W. Mills, eds., *From Max Weber*. New York: Oxford University Press.

Zeitlin, Irving. 1968. *Ideology and the Development of Sociological Theory*. Englewood Cliffs, N.J.: Prentice-Hall.

Chapter 6

Building Fires on the Prairie
Martin J. Murray

IT IS DIFFICULT if not impossible to pinpoint a single event that marked my personal transition from naive working-class kid growing up in the 1950s and early 1960s outside Oakland, California, to professor of sociology, State University of New York at Binghamton. The fact that I both commuted thirty miles away from home and attended a Catholic high school in Berkeley certainly made a difference. While my college experience at the Jesuit-controlled University of San Francisco arrested my intellectual development, the fact that I lived in the San Francisco Bay area (rather than a less "radical" environment) influenced the way I interpreted the emergence of the civil rights movement, the antiwar movement, and the broader political-cultural explosion that now is loosely, and nostalgically, called "the sixties." My political awareness came in graduated stages, a series of building blocks that eventually led me away from my "safety-first," sheltered environment of the suburban working-class areas of Walnut Creek, California.

During my high school and early college years, my class aspirations were not particularly ambitious. Neither of my parents had attended college. In the back of my mind, I suspected that I would probably become a high-school mathematics teacher. I was astounded when my twin brother announced that he planned to enter a pre-med track when we started college in 1963. Becoming a doctor, or even a Ph.D., seemed so far beyond my grasp that I had never considered any profession like medicine, the law, or higher education as a real career option.

I registered for the Reserve Officer Training Corps (ROTC) program during the first two years of college. Participation in ROTC was mandatory for all male students. During the 1963–1964 and 1964–1965 academic years, the issue of growing U.S. military involvement in Vietnam emerged as a topic of discussion in ROTC classes. The instructors, all full-time U.S. Army personnel, emphasized duty to God and country along with anti-Communism in their protracted ideological warfare with stu-

dents. They hoped that by instilling a combination of patriotism and ma-
chismo within the largely lethargic first- and second-year students, they
could attract sufficient numbers to register for two more years. On the
material side, they dangled full-tuition scholarships and an eventual commission as a second lieutenant in the U.S. Army.

I refused the bait. I was compelled to make an appointment with
Colonel So-and-so. I marched into his office in my military uniform and
smartly saluted and stood at attention. I refused his offer to "go upper
division" (as the next two years were called) because, as I told him, I had
moral reservations about the war in Vietnam. He jumped up from behind
his desk, yelling red-faced that he would make sure that I was drafted. I
was dumbfounded. Initially, I interpreted his reaction as an affront to the
inviolability of following my own conscience, a dictum hammered away
in my moral philosophy courses in college. The response of the university administration to the pathetically small group of students that
emerged in 1965 to oppose mandatory ROTC on campus brought me to
the abrupt realization that questioning the wisdom of the Vietnam adventure was more than an issue involving a moral choice. To grapple even at
a personal level with the moral dilemma of Vietnam was tantamount to
challenging the entire institutional apparatus that sustained the war machine. University administrations appealed to doctrines of a just war and
the totally unconvincing "if we don't stop Them there we'll have to fight
Them on the Mexican border" arguments. Failing to win the war of
words, the administrators expelled the students and fired their faculty
advisor.

During the summers of 1965 and 1967, I worked on community-de-
velopment projects in central Mexico. Through this invaluable experience, I learned firsthand that poverty is not the product of laziness, the
squandering of talent, poor judgment, or even bad luck. I came to realize
that the relationship between rich and poor is structural and that those
who have little can rely only on the power of their numbers and their
willingness to struggle together against those who have money, power,
and influence. Intellectually, I possessed a sort of C. Wright Mills understanding of power elites. Class analysis came later.

During my last two years of college, my friends (who remained in
ROTC for the duration of college) fondly called me the "pasty-faced white
peace creep," a moniker coined by George Lincoln Rockwell, a neo-Nazi
who was later assassinated. When I graduated in 1967, I applied for conscientious objector (C.O.) status. I pleaded my case before my local draft
board in Martinez, California. I knew that I would never submit to induction into the armed forces if I were drafted. I also knew that I would not

use the "Canada option," as increasing numbers of draft-age young men were.

I submitted to two preinduction physical examinations (one at the Oakland Army Induction Center and the other at Fort Sam Houston in San Antonio, Texas). After spending a day in each place, I learned that the overwhelming numbers of those sent as "cannon fodder" for Vietnam were black or Hispanic and poor. U.S. Army physicians behaved like bored cattle inspectors. Middle-class whites obtained attestations of physical disabilities from their personal physicians. Army doctors were to medicine what military music is to music.

During the summer of 1968, I finally received my C.O. draft status. I remember the day distinctly because my father brought the registered letter from the draft board to the place where I was working. I am really grateful for my parents' moral support for what at the time were rather unpopular political views.

In 1967, I entered graduate school at the University of Texas at Austin in the department of philosophy. My choice of Texas was not rationally decided. Unlike those students who attended elite undergraduate schools and calculated their selection of graduate program on the basis of future occupational opportunities, I more or less blindly made a choice.

I had attended rallies against the Vietnam War in San Francisco and had been involved in the small anti-ROTC group. Within the first month in Austin, I came across a sit-in demanding the expulsion of Marine recruiters from campus. I joined the protest. It was the first of many demonstrations organized by Students for a Democratic Society (SDS) as part of a "fall offensive" designed to confront the university's complicity in the war effort. I began attending SDS meetings on a regular basis. When the head of the local "Red Squad" section of the Austin police department greeted me one day on campus with a hearty, "Hi, Martin, so you've joined SDS," I knew that my presence had been noticed.

What distinguished Austin SDS (and the growing political movement in the Southwest in general) was a visceral rejection of national politics. The original Austin SDS chapter was one of the first in the country. The early years were particularly lean. The university, with about forty-five thousand students, had what was called the "free speech area," a small patio the size of a classroom for one hundred students, completely surrounded by buildings. The chair of the board of trustees for the University of Texas was an oil multimillionaire, Frank Erwin, who ran the university like a personal fiefdom.[1] Fraternities and sororities were gigantic. Football was king. About 99 percent of the enrolled student body was white. There was only one black scholarship player on all university athletic teams. The Ku Klux Klan was quite active locally. Public facilities, like movie theaters and restaurants, had only been integrated since about 1966.

Yet in the midst of this confusing situation, new forms of cultural and political expression took root and grew. SDS veterans from the formative years pointed with pride to a 1964 sit-in at the LBJ ranch outside of town, a demonstration that received national media attention. The 1966 SDS national secretary, Bob Pardun, and the 1967 national secretary, Greg Calvert, both lived in Austin. Both had developed a healthy disregard for internecine power struggles in the Chicago headquarters. Each in his own peculiar way preached a populist gospel that elevated themes like "all power to the provinces" to the level of political principle. Almost overnight, Austin became the hub of a regional political-cultural movement spreading east to Houston and north to Dallas, and including Oklahoma and Arkansas. This "prairie fire" message that resonated throughout the region mixed decentralized organizational structures with a plainly anarchistic disrespect for authority of all types.

Texas populism has a long independent history, and the peculiar brand of 1960s radical populism that germinated in Austin was both a blessing and a curse. Austin SDS never succumbed to Weatherman madness. The local Progressive Labor party stalwarts never amounted to more than a shrill, vocal minority singing their "class-purity" chorus with a unanimous voice. Antiimperialist and Marxist study groups and "action caucuses" of various sorts formed and reformed without the permanent fixtures of disciplined sect groups that seemed to plague the movement elsewhere. However, there was also a negative side to the deep-seated anarchism and populism. Antiintellectualism was rampant. Most hardcore activists failed to understand the relevance of theorizing about strategy and tactics. They tended to worship action for its own sake and had little patience for thinking about how to build our base beyond alienated youth.

Until its demise at the 1969 SDS national convention in Chicago, SDS functioned as the focal point of movement activities in Austin. Thursday night organizational meetings ranged from fifteen or twenty of us during lull periods to three hundred participants during periods of heightened, frenzied action. We organized annual Armed Farces Days and disrupted ROTC events. We demonstrated against corporate recruiters like Dow Chemical, against the CIA and military recruiters, and against prowar speakers. SDS spearheaded the drive to push our message out from the confines of the campus, spawning a Movement for a Democratic Society (MDS) chapter, a left-wing law office that handled the growing number of political court cases, an informal caucus among local social workers, and a host of other grouplets. We mimicked each and every national trend or spectacular event: We had our own Stop the Draft Week, our own People's Park, our own anti-ROTC demonstrations.

In the spring of 1969, SDS held its last national council in Austin. It was immediately obvious from the nature of the debate that the seeds of self-destruction had already been sown. The posturing and back-door maneuvering were a dress rehearsal for the sectarian in-fighting that eventually marked the demise of SDS. The one image that has remained fixed in my mind is Bernardine Dohrn striding around in a short skirt, with expensive high-heeled black leather boots and huge quantities of makeup. Less than six months later, she had emerged as the self-proclaimed leader of the Weather vanguard promising to "smash the state by any means necessary."

The *coup de grâce* took place in June 1969 in Chicago. Todd Gitlin provides a brief summary of the Chicago fiasco.[2] Curiously, he provides no explanation why the National (Office) Collective, which for all intents and purposes represented a temporary alliance between the Revolutionary Youth Movement I (RYM I) and Revolutionary Youth Movement II (RYM II), orchestrated the walkout of the main convention hall and the eventual decision to "expell PL" (Progressive League). My personal recollections of the Chicago SDS convention differ from all accounts I have read. The litmus test was the vote in which Tim McCarthy, the perennial chair of SDS gatherings, lost the vote of the assembled participants to chair the proceedings. This vote indicated that the PL forces would be able to muster sufficient votes on all key issues to at least block decisions that were not favorable to the Worker-Student Alliance position. Realizing that PL had outflanked them, the anti-PL faction stole the march on their opponents by staging a walkout to an adjoining hall and an eventual return to the main hall to denounce PL. The four of us from Austin who went to the convention as official delegates remained more or less neutral during the ensuing blood letting.

Ironically, the collapse of SDS recharged an increasingly hydra-headed political movement that was too large and too diverse to be confined within a single organizational focal point. Crippled by factionalism and beset by political posturing, SDS increasingly lost touch with its mass base and thereby relinquished its leading role as the main national coordinating body for national protests. SDS had certainly outlived its usefulness to a movement that was still growing by leaps and bounds. At least initially, SDS chapters nationwide tended to side with one or the other of the two main factions, each proclaiming to hold the mantle of the "real"

SDS. Yet in time, the release of the accumulated pressure occasioned by the SDS fiasco gave the movement a much-needed face life, contrary to the general view that it marked the beginning of the end of the movement.

The downward spiral of increasingly sectarian sloganeering and debilitating factionalism largely bypassed the Austin movement. We held meetings under the banner for SDS for a few months and then quietly abandoned the idea of keeping the SDS name alive. The small PL contingent disappeared. An occasional escapee from the Weather Underground surreptitiously slipped into Austin to live incognito among the rural communes that seemed to sprout everywhere in rural hideaways outside Austin's city limits. But the politics of Weathermen never achieved a following.

For the next several years, numerous organizations emerged, grew, reached a highpoint (usually around a major demonstration or protest march in the fall or spring), withered, and eventually disappeared. While those of us who generally shared a similar political perspective thought differently at the time, it was clear that no single organization could have been capable of leading, or even channeling, the huge outpouring of hostility directed against the vast machinery of war, institutionalized racism, and entrenched authoritarianism in the schools, workplaces, and elsewhere. Certainly after 1969 if not before, we were engaged in coalition building, reaching out to the local Black Panther-type "Breakfast for Children" group, a fledging Chicano grouping, emergent women's and gay caucuses, the GI movement, the skyrocketing countercultural communes, and so on.

Those of us who worked closely together politically did our best to exploit available cracks in the system that opposed us. At the university, we formed campus-approved groups, accumulated huge bills for posters, paper, mimeographing, and other services, and then abandoned the organization. On the legal front, we aggressively countered the increasingly sophisticated efforts of the police to use the courts to keep us off balance. We filed class-action suits; we organized "group-defense" strategies for common offenses, and we used nonviolent resistance tactics to fill the jails on several occasions.

In 1968, I was charged with violating university rules restricting commercial sales on campus property. (I and another SDS member, Allan Locklear, were selling books and pamphlets at a literature table.) We made use of the *pro bono* services of an American Civil Liberties Union attorney, challenging the university's inconsistent enforcement of regulations and its sloppy detective work. I faced expulsion. After a marathon eight-hour closed-door disciplinary hearing, I was acquitted of all charges of wrongdoing.

Soon after, the Austin movement forged a long-term working relationship with lawyers associated with the Center for Constitutional Rights in New York. A local legal collective (modeled after Bar Sinister in Los Angeles) came into being. Police regularly used the tactic of arresting people at rallies and demonstrations on charges of disorderly conduct, refusal to obey a lawful order, failure to disperse, and so forth. As the number, size, and militance of demonstrations increased, the numbers of those arrested (and charged with felonies) escalated dramatically. The lawyers and legal aides in the local radical law collective worked tirelessly and for free. Despite the myriad felony charges leveled against us over the years, very few people were actually convicted. Jail time in Austin was to be avoided at all costs. Local police frequently placed our people in overcrowded cells with redneck thugs. One long-haired philosophy graduate student, Bill Meacham, had his nose and a few ribs broken. Some were raped.

Spring 1970 was a watershed for the Austin movement. The killings at Kent State in May galvanized the movement. (The murders of black students at Jackson State were largely ignored.) Previously apathetic or hostile students and community people joined the seemingly endless round of marches, rallies, and demonstrations. The huge outpouring of support for antiwar politics was unprecedented in terms of sheer numbers. Those of us who assumed leadership of the mass movement were jubilant with our success. Day after day increasingly larger crowds ignored the refusal of the city administration to grant our request for parade permits, marching from the campus stronghold to the state capitol building located in the heart of downtown about three miles away. The capitol building itself was tear-gassed, innocent onlookers and bystanders were harassed and arrested, cars were overturned and burned. Eventually, the National Guard was called in to occupy the campus. The high point was a peaceful march and rally at the state capitol building involving about twenty-five thousand people.

In a sense, we had achieved the impossible. The counterculture served as a bridge linking varius subgroups in a common albeit temporary bond. Longhairs and rednecks mixed freely and cordially in Austin's country-and-western bars. In 1968, Lee Otis Johnson, a black community activist in Houston, was convicted of selling marijuana and sentenced to twenty years for passing a joint to an undercover police officer. After 1970, "Texas torpedoes" (foot-long joints) were everywhere, and the feared "drug bust" for users and small-time dealers became extinct. Also seemingly overnight, the majority had turned against the war in Vietnam. Alternative lifestyles flourished; communal living arrangements were the norm; sharing, being "mellow," and "doing your own thing" were honored values to be emulated and praised.

Those of us who saw ourselves primarily as political activists were confronted with a novel situation. We were no longer preoccupied with finding creative ways to convince ever-greater numbers to accept our antiwar message. Within the broad community and youth movement, we faced what in the end proved to be a losing battle. While we were able to mobilize consistently large numbers for rallies and demonstrations for particular events, we were unable to engage counterculturalists in the kind of sustained day-to-day preparation required to reach out, and win over, new constituencies, particularly working-class communities. Large numbers of alienated youth simply chose to withdraw from political struggle.

Within the political left, we also came face to face with our own ideological differences, stylistic preferences, and accumulated contradictions. In Austin, the leadership core remained relatively stable from around 1968 to 1973. Anywhere from thirty to sixty people took turns serving as leaders of the myriad organizations, caucuses, and groups that emerged, developed, and collapsed. Ideologically, there were at least three separate currents. One tendency argued for building a broad antiimperialist prosocialist front that would both reach out to nonstudent, nonyouth working-class constituencies and maintain a high level of militance. I gravitated toward this position. We turned toward strategic thinking for a time, attempting to evaluate how other movements had confronted our dilemmas and pushed forward. The visceral antiintellectualism of the New Left was too strong, and this political perspective never amounted to anything but a nagging minority.

Another tendency promoted a sort of consciously naive radicalism, measuring its success in its ability to manipulate the liberals who flocked to the movement after 1970. The individuals who were attracted to this position tended to be the egomaniacs, those who wished to share the spotlight with such liberal luminaries as John Kenneth Galbraith, local Austin politicians who coveted the youth vote, and big-shot professors who gave speeches but did little else to build the movement. These self-conscious radicals privately declared their solidarity with Southern Vietnam's National Liberation Front (NLF) and the Democratic Republic of Vietnam (DRV) in the north, claimed to be socialists and even Marxist-Leninists, and called for "the revolution." In their view, the "greater good" of bringing the war to an end meant that we should downplay antiimperialism and socialism, and substitute instead a sort of populist radicalism.

The third major current demanded action, and action for its own sake. This political tendency won the ideological battles of 1971–1972 but was unable to sustain momentum after the Paris Peace Accords in 1973.

Despite the gravity of the issues that bound it together, the Austin movement was also internally divided along a number of other lines. The contradictions of racism and sexism divided the movement from the beginning. In Austin, very few black, Chicano, or other minority people participated fully and actively in the student, youth, and community movements. The Austin movement failed miserably here. By 1968, some SDS women had formed consciousness-raising groups. By 1970, the full-fledged women's movement had ballooned to enormous proportions. By 1971, small affinity groups like the Women's International Conspiracy from Hell (WITCH) were engineering their own independent actions, like painting graffiti such as FREE FOOD TODAY on supermarket walls. Gay and lesbian groups developed. I remember being informed that my presence at a particular party was mandatory and that I was required to wear a dress.

In retrospect, I can locate the lack of political unity of the Austin movement in a historical perspective that at the time I was not privileged to fully comprehend. We developed a sufficiently sophisticated critique of U.S. imperialism and offered a naive, yet workable, understanding of socialism as an alternative to monopoly capitalism. We were totally unprepared for the social issues of racism, sexism, and homophobia.

In my judgment, the high point of antiwar protest in the United States was the April–May 1971 demonstrations in Washington, D.C. The Vietnam Veterans Against the War held its Winter Soldier Investigation in Detroit in early 1971. Here former soldiers exposed the atrocities of the war machine in Vietnam. The anger, frustration, and guilt of returning soldiers culminated in Operation Dewey Canyon III, a so-called limited incursion into the Congress of the United States in late April 1971. The high point of this series of events was the well-publicized rally on the steps of the U.S. Capitol, when shaggy-haired, disheveled Vietnam veterans tossed their military medals over eight-foot-high police barricades.

Washington swirled with activities. The "Give Peace a Chance" moratorium liberal-radical coalition orchestrated another of its high-profile "babies-and-balloons" marches around the same time. This annual spring "peace march" was followed by what seemed to me the most significant and provocative mass demonstrations of the entire antiwar period, the

May Day protests. Organized around the (utterly utopian) slogan "If the Government Won't Stop the War, We'll Stop the Government," the national leadership targeted twenty-one sites in Washington to be shut down through disruptive tactics beginning the morning of May 3 and continuing for three days.

The action-oriented folks in Austin were captivated by this proposed "national action" and feverishly began making plans to participate under the aegis of still-another organization aptly named the May Day Tribe. The undertones of anarchism, adventurism, and antiintellectualism that accompanied the long process of building toward this demonstration once again split the Austin movement. The militant rhetoric frightened many away. Some objected to the putatively antiworking-class tactics of disrupting traffic and generally causing havoc in a largely black city. The firmly entrenched hippie wing of the movement declared that this event was just another national demonstration that would not accomplish anything anyway.

I understood the objections to this sort of national extravaganza demonstration, but decided that the potential gains outweighed the drawbacks. I participated wholeheartedly in building a Southwest regional contingent for the May Day demonstrations. We organized groups from dozens of cities and college towns throughout Texas, Oklahoma, and Arkansas. All in all, we gathered together more than 250 people to make the trek in Volkswagen vans, rented buses, and overstuffed automobiles. Our designated target was Scott Circle, a strategic point along major routes into the heart of Washington, where Massachusetts Avenue, 16th Street, and Rhode Island Avenue crossed.

Preparation clearly resembled an army planning for battle. In our efforts to maximize efficiency in the field and to minimize the need for centralized coordination, we divided into about fifteen to twenty self-sufficient "traveling groups" who were responsible, logistically speaking, for getting back and forth from Washington. I traveled with a ragtag squad of eleven, which was further subdivided into three "affinity groups." Our uniforms consisted of jeans, heavy jackets, and work boots. We carried food, bail money, at least one piece of positive identification, and the telephone number (written on our arms) of the *ad hoc* legal assistance group established in Washington to handle the anticipated mass arrests. We also carried molotov cocktails, stink and smoke bombs, three-pronged nails, and sand (for dumping in gas tanks of stalled cars). We were prepared for battle.

Washington was an armed camp. To maintain order, the city deployed more than 4,000 active-duty troops (some of whom had just returned

from Vietnam) with another 4,000 in reserve, 1,400 D.C. National Guards-
men, and the bulk of Washington's 5,100-person police force, in addition
to park and capital police. Despite this unprecedented display of force,
protestors managed to disrupt the normal functioning of government for
three days. Streets were littered with abandoned cars, their tires flattened
and distributor caps removed. Some roadways were blocked with makeshift barricades of burning trash bins, bricks and large stones, and whatever else could be lifted and piled high. Tear gas blanketed the city. Brief
skirmishes erupted everywhere. Small knots of protestors stood their
ground, trading rocks and bottles for tear gas cannisters. Roving bands
carried the message of protest throughout the downtown areas. As police
cars whisked away the arrested, ambulances carted off the wounded and
injured. On May 3, the first day of the demonstrations, about 8,000 people were arrested, the largest number for any single day in U.S. history. A
total of about 13,000 were arrested during the three-day protests.

The forces of law and order were clearly surprised by the endurance,
level of militance, and ingenuity of the protestors. They were certainly
not prepared to handle the number of arrests. When the jails were filled
to capacity, those arrested were held in makeshift detention centers, such
as a huge practice field near RFK Stadium on the outskirts of the city. On
the second day, the police abandoned their initial plan of making sweeping arrests of anyone they could lay their hands on, shifting to the macabre tactic of forcibly removing and beating protestors but not making
arrests. I distinctly remember two undercover police officers (one white
and the other black), dressed in army fatigues festooned with political
buttons and slogans and driving around in a yellow Volkswagen. They
would approach small groups of protestors, hailing them with the appropriate "Power to the People" and clenched-fist salutes. Once within strik-
ing distance, they pulled out short clubs concealed in their clothing and
proceeded to beat people mercilessly before strolling off to their car.
Once the thin veneer of legality was stripped away, the ugly core of po-
lice-state tactics emerged with a vengeance.

The May Day Tribe returned home weary but virtually unscathed. No
one was seriously injured. A few people were charged with felonies (re-
sisting arrest, grand theft, assault) but in the hopeless confusion of the
overburdened judicial system these charges were eventually dropped. In
Austin, the May Day Tribe coordinated a massive protest against the dedi-
cation of the LBJ Library on the campus of the University of Texas, an
event that received maximum exposure because it was nationally tele-
vised. The militance, inventiveness, and sheer determination of the antiwar movement was matched by a qualitative shift in police strategy and
tactics.

On the eve of this particular demonstration, a combined police task force (involving the local criminal intelligence division, the Secret Service, and the statewide Texas Department of Public Safety) issued temporary restraining orders to protest leaders, including myself, as a way of dampening the enthusiasm for carrying out a protest action that was bound to result in confrontation, street fighting, and numerous arrests. Undercover police camera operators, posing as news reporters, took hundreds of pictures later used to identify individuals engaging in illegal activities. The police carried out early-morning arrests, usually around 4:00 A.M. This tactic certainly achieved one of its goals of spreading maximum fear amongst the antiwar movement. After 1971, I always stayed away from home for a few days following demonstrations.

The police had clearly infiltrated our ranks very early. The example of "Nick the Cop" illustrates how the police operated. Nick was a man in his early thirties who turned up in Austin around 1969. He enrolled as a student yet never managed to complete his courses. He dropped out every semester, saying that "political work was more important." To explain why he had money yet never worked, he claimed that he had inherited money from his grandparents. He said he had lived in Mexico for the previous decade, which provided a convenient yet difficult-to-contradict alibi explaining his whereabouts and why he had not been drafted. He used the rhetoric but had no clear understanding of capitalism, imperialism, Marxism, and socialism. He came to every meeting, took copious notes, and always volunteered to handle mailing lists and phone numbers. He and his camera were inseparable. He disappeared for days and even weeks at a time, offering only vague answers in accounting for his unexplained absences. He owned a pistol and kept extensive records on demonstrations, groups, and individuals in a locked file cabinet.

Nick was only too obvious. There were others. Barbara R., the best chairperson we ever had for raucous SDS meetings, turned up ten years later working for the former head of the Austin Red Squad. The local Vietnam Veterans Against the War (VVAW) chapter had a few undercover police agents. By 1971, VVAW was propelled to center stage in the antiwar movement. The respect that antiwar veterans had gained provided legitimate cover for military intelligence. Various agents provocateurs regularly attended planning meetings for demonstrations. Their encouragement for "trashing" (breaking windows, setting fires, throwing rocks and bottles at police, and so on) found a ready audience among the growing numbers of impatient, anarchistic, antiintellectual, and youthful hippies who urged us to escalate the struggle "to smash the state."

The seemingly endless round of demonstrations continued. Nixon's decision to renew bombing of northern Vietnam and mine Haiphong

Harbor in the spring of 1972 became a focal point for nighttime demonstrations. The police cordoned off university grounds, tear-gassed the whole area, and called on the National Guard to occupy the campus once again. The 1972 Christmas carpet bombing of Hanoi marked the bitter end of organized public demonstrations against the Vietnam War.

The numbers of active participants in antiwar activities declined significantly after May and June 1971. What we called movement fatigue took its toll. Bitter and often rancorous debate about how to revive a movement that seemed inexorably bent on mindlessly escalating "trashing" to an art form produced casualties. Those long-time political activists who called for a multipronged strategy of low-profile political organizing and coalition building were accused of being Marxist-Lenininists, of talking about the revolution but being unwilling to make the revolution, and of failing to understand the urgency of the moment. Moral appeals of this sort did not succeed in winning very many converts from among those not already committed to this political position.

Many veterans of the Austin movement showed little tolerance for what they regarded as rhetorical harangues that questioned their commitment. They no longer participated in events, making concerted efforts to develop and perfect their personal relations and to building small, manageable collectives (such as food co-ops, communal living arrangements, and forms of entertainment). Women's collectives, in particular, proliferated. Frustrated with male-dominated organizations and the prevailing male chauvinistic approach to politics, many women turned their attention to sisterhood, abandoning the male movement to its own self-destructive impulses. Some of the best and brightest activists gravitated toward existing Marxist-Leninist groups as well toward inchoate preparty formations. The personal and the political gaps widened.

I had entered graduate school as a Ph.D. student in the department of philosophy. I was disappointed and dissatisfied with the lack of connection between the prevailing philosophical discourse and my growing political consciousness and activism. In September 1969, I abruptly dropped my philosophy courses and, without too much forethought, transferred to the department of sociology. The department was conventional in every sense, but there was a handful of professors who were somewhat sympathetic to the New Left. The subject matter of what constituted sociology was sufficiently diverse, ill formed, and fluid that I could pursue my intellectual interests without fear of reprisal.

Radical and Marxist graduate students formed a political group called the Gerrard Winstanley Memorial Caucus (named after the English anarchist Digger) to proselytize our views. Within a year of so, we had a core group of about twenty to twenty-five graduate students, almost one-fifth the total number enrolled in the Ph.D. program. During the May 1970 national student strike, we transformed the sociology department into one vast study group, linking ourselves to a network of caucuses that had formed in other university departments. The intellectual ferment that we created in the department provided me with a creative environment within which to learn, and to learn quickly. We investigated Marxist theory together, we formed study groups, and we debated revolutionary strategy and tactics handed down from the masters like Lenin, Trotsky, Mao, Luxemburg, Gramsci, Guevara, Ho Chi Minh, and Vo Nguyen Giap.

There was, however, an unbridgeable gap between the way I satisfied my intellectual curiosity and how I behaved as a political activist. My friends in the department of sociology were my intellectual comrades. With a few exceptions, these people were somewhat appalled by what they regarded as the crudely reductionist ideas of the political activists with whom I worked closely. Without exception, these political activists were not students and were bored with what they saw as scholastic, arcane intellectual debates that led nowhere in their estimation. Until 1971 or so, juggling these two dimensions of my life was really no more than a nagging inconvenience. In time, however, maintaining a proper balance between these separate spheres became more difficult. After 1970, the Austin political movement was no longer student based or even student oriented. Organizational meetings were rarely if ever held on university grounds. The campus played virtually no part in social life or socializing activities. The attractions of country-and-western music, public parks, swimming holes, and off-campus communal living arrangements pulled me into the community. My political activist friends gradually developed a sort of visceral contempt for the university and the authoritarian power mongering that its main representatives exhibited. The movement had been germinated on the university campus. But once the movement abandoned its confines, it was impossible to return.

I wrote my Ph.D. dissertation in virtual isolation. I left Austin during the summer of 1973 to take an academic job at the University of Missouri at Kansas City. I hated leaving. I returned periodically over the next academic year. A New American Movement (NAM) chapter filled in the political space on the margins of university life. My militant action-oriented friends bemoaned its intellectualism, its lack of confrontational politics, and its caution. The counterculture flourished, eventually consuming the remnants of the vibrant political movement that had grown in tandem with it. Private entrepreneurship reared its ugly head. Small-scale capitalists recognized the growing market potential for the food, clothing, paraphernalia, and music that had at the time symbolized opposition to the "imperialist and capitalist system."

I returned to Austin for a few days in 1986. It seemed hotter, dustier, and dirtier than I remembered. Like a disturbed octopus, the campus had spread its tentacles in every direction. The once-quiet, tree-lined student and youth neighborhoods were gone, replaced by high-rise apartment buildings. The formerly "outlaw" music was now big business, a veritable tourist attraction. "Austin is second only to Nashville in its country music," local advertisements proclaimed proudly. Perhaps I had supressed the reality of the long ribbons of fast-food restaurants, gas stations, and used car lots leading in and out of town. I carefully scrutinized every aging hippie and longhair I saw, hoping to recognize a face, to meet by happenstance an old acquaintance.

As I watched youthful, smiling, and well-dressed students lounging in the sun beneath the tower from where an ex-Marine had shot and killed so many innocent people in 1966, I wanted to scream, "This is where we fought the war machine. This is where the police beat us and tear-gassed us. This is where the National Guard set up their temporary communications headquarters." I refrained. I gazed up at the slogan emblazoned on the tower: "You shall know the truth and the truth shall make you free." I am convinced that those of us who participated in the Austin movement contributed to curbing military excesses in Indochina and bringing the Vietnam War to a close earlier than might otherwise might have been. I'm less convinced about what enduring legacy we left behind with respect to building a durable movement for peace, social justice, and equality at home.

NOTES

1. Around 1969, Erwin was responsible for firing John Silber, the dean of arts and sciences. Silber moved to Boston University, where he instilled his own peculiar brand of autocratic rule.

2. Todd Gitlin, *The Sixties: Years of Hope, Days of Rage* (New York: Bantam Books, 1987).

PART II

Becoming a Sociologist

The essays in this part give insight on how history and biography inter-sect to produce radical sociologists. Martin Oppenheimer describes how his personal experience as a German-Jewish refugee in the 1930s, his family murdered by the Nazis, gave him the desire to learn about the causes of war. Becoming a socialist while an undergraduate, he went to graduate school in sociology to study social movements. Involved in socialist, civil rights, and antiwar movements, Oppenheimer became a radical sociologist through his political experiences. For him, one of the major purposes of radical sociology is to undermine authoritarian structures.

Norma Stoltz Chinchilla and Lynda Ann Ewen discuss their experi-ences as women graduate students at the University of Wisconsin at Madison. Chinchilla, influenced by the work of C. Wright Mills while an undergraduate, became interested in student politics and the civil rights movement. Living in Guatemala in 1965–1966, she experienced first-hand the plight of the Third World and decided to go to graduate school in sociology. Her discontent with graduate school and its lack of a feminist perspective only strengthened her desire to develop a radical theme within her sociological work. Ewen was excited and challenged by sociology as an undergraduate and in 1965 went to graduate school at Wisconsin, where she, like Chinchilla, became disturbed with the treatment of women graduate students. While at Wisconsin, Ewen became involved with student politics, but it was her first job in Detroit and her affiliation with a left political base in the working class that di-rected her analysis in a distinctly Marxist direction.

Robert G. Newby and Hardy T. Frye discuss the significance of race and their particular involvement in the civil rights movement as the ma-jor stimulants in their aspirations to become sociologists. For Newby, race played a significant role in shaping his social construction of real-ity. For Frye, sociology provided the arena to study race relations in the

United States. Both men came to sociology after becoming involved in movements to end racism.

Robert J. S. Ross recalls his involvement in the New Left and within sociology. Influenced by C. Wright Mills's call for a social science suffused simultaneously with the values of reason and freedom, Ross went on to become active in Students for a Democratic Society while an undergraduate at the University of Michigan at Ann Arbor. When he became a graduate student at the University of Chicago, he joined SDS's local community-organization project and became a founding organizer of the New University Conference. Ross provides us with a case study from which to examine what Mills meant by the intersection of history and biography. Ross concedes that the theoretical heritage of the movements of the 1960s is not without its complications. Nevertheless, new perspectives were developed, and democracy was well served.

Chapter 7

Pages from a Journal of the Middle Left
Martin Oppenheimer

I WAS BORN in a town in Westfalia, Germany, two and a half years before Hitler came to power. My father, a lawyer, quickly recognized the shape of things to come (especially after a brief arrest and his disbarment because of his "non-Aryan" ancestry). He visited what was then the British mandate of Palestine with a view to moving there (he was a lifelong Zionist), but Arab-Jewish riots were going on then and my mother vetoed going from one frying pan into another. So we came to the United States in 1937. The Spanish Civil War was under way, Japan had invaded Manchuria, and Hitler was about to annex Austria. The world was an ominous place and would soon become worse.

Like many other German-Jewish refugees, we ended up owning and operating a chicken farm in New Jersey. I was the only Jew on our school bus route, an unpleasant experience around Eastertime. I had few friends and was pretty bookish. When some black kids were introduced onto the school bus, they were harassed. I told the other kids to leave them alone. This made me not only a Christ killer but also a nigger lover. Even worse, the teachers liked me because I appeared to be somewhat interested in learning.

Sometime in the spring of 1945 we got a phone call from the International Red Cross. There was a cable from my father's brother and his wife: "We are alive and well. Where are our children?" We had not heard from them, or any other relatives who had remained behind in Germany, for around four years. These two were the sole survivors. I, and one other, were the only survivors out of our Jewish kindergarten class of six.

My uncle had been gassed in World War I and permanently disabled. This event earned him two Iron Crosses, which paradoxically saved his life. The Nazis, with their odd German sense of honor, sent such people to Theresienstadt concentration camp, where only some of the inmates were periodically, apparently on whim, weeded out and sent to be gassed, and only some died of starvation.

These tragic events, and their impact on my parents, sharpened my desire to discover the causes of wars. I ran across *Days of Our Years* (1941), a muckraking account of the interwar years by a Dutch journalist named Pierre van Paassen, and learned about Sacco and Vanzetti. I stumbled onto Harry Elmer Barnes's revisionist history of World War I (*Genesis of the World War*) and soon concluded that war was rooted in imperialism. I didn't know it yet, but I had become, vaguely, a socialist.

Probably many of us began our political journeys in high school. I learned early on that history was far from objective. In the late 1940s history still consisted of the accepted Anglocentric version of world events. I was a Zionist, which was as natural for me as mazzohs at Passover. At that time, when the Jews were fighting an underground war against the British Empire, Zionism was, for me, synonymous with antiimperialism. My European history teacher was an apologist for the British, and I was a troublemaker. In American history Bobby B. and I together seemed to know more than the fresh-out-of-Teachers' College instructor. We threw fact after fact at her, gleaned in part from such works as Charles and Mary Beard's *The Rise of American Civilization* (1933) and James Oneal's *The Workers in American History* (1912). She got pregnant and quit because, as we saw it, she couldn't handle us any more.

Many students regarded our high school as a prison. You needed a pass to go to the bathroom. For a while we chalked "P.W." (for prisoner of war) on the backs of our shirts. I wrote a column for the school paper and got called on the principal's carpet for questioning why our Saturday-night dances were all white. I resigned, and we put out an underground mimeographed newspaper called "Cousin Al's Gazette" (somebody had a cousin Al). It was my first contact with a mimeo machine, a critical moment in my vocational-technical preparation for socialist organizational affairs.

I cried when Roosevelt died, rooted for Henry Wallace, and went off to the adventure and freedom of college. I chose Temple University over the University of Pennsylvania because there was a feel to it that was somehow real and exciting and not standoffish and snobbish.

In the fall of 1948 I went door to door (in the white working-class neighborhood that surrounded Temple University in those days) for the Progressive party and attended classes and drank beer with World War II vets. I hated fraternities and the ROTC passionately. I soon came to despise Young Progressives of America (YPA), the Communist party front group that had replaced Students for Wallace, because of its one-sided apologetics for the Soviet Union. YPA did have good music and pretty girls, as is well known among our age cohort. As a civil libertarian, I defended YPA's right to a campus charter, which is more than some of the socialists in student government did (these were the ones who would later support the Korean War).

In class we fought the professors more often than not. We argued with an Anglocentrist historian in a class on Africa, and with a Menshevik sympathizer in one on Russian history (our private text was *The Ten Days That Shook the World*, and he finally, despairingly, ordered us to shut up). In a sociology class on minorities, the professor announced that cuisine was all that was left of ethnic culture, and the Communist faction walked out. We, the radicals around the Socialist Club, all studied philosophy with Barrows Dunham, who was later fired by Temple University after he refused to cooperate with the House Un-American Activities Committee. This landed Temple on the AAUPs' blacklist for many years.

Dunham was a debonair type, a Philadelphia aristocrat cut from the same social cloth, but holding quite different politics, as Digby Baltzell (the conservative author of numerous sociological treatises on the Philadelphia and national Protestant establishments). Dunham had been in an automobile accident that had left him with a permanent, some thought supercilious, smile. He smoked English oval cigarettes, and so did his groupies. One of his disciples taught us Greek dialectical theory and led the local chapter of the Labor Youth League (youth section of the Communist Party–U.S.A. then). "Oppenheimer," this graduate student once intoned, shoving his finger into my chest, "when the revolution comes you'd better be on the right side or I'll have you shot." He wasn't kidding, either. I met him years later, considerably mellowed. "We've taken over the First Unitarian Church in Los Angeles," he chortled proudly. "We *are* the first unitarian church, anywhere," I sneered back. He knew I was Jewish.

We had organized a socialist club that would split over the Korean War. In the library we read George Seldes's newsletter *In Fact*, and later *I. F. Stone's Weekly*. We attended lectures organized by the Socialist Labor party, the DeLeonists, in a rundown hotel downtown, our first real exposure to serious (if antiquated) Marxist ideas. We drank half-and-halfs and ate hot roast beef sandwiches in an Irish bar on Columbia Avenue, and learned dirty limericks from a seedy, cynical, wonderful old English prof. We also learned not to ask some of our drinking buddies, guys whose previous schooling had been Guadalcanal or Anzio, questions about World War II.

The Korean War broke out in June 1950. A tiny handful of antiwar leafleters near the campus was mobbed and rescued by the police just before I got there. The Cold War atmosphere became translated into something more real: the draft. I didn't know much about conscientious objectors, though I was against the war. Besides, I wasn't a pacifist. I decided to go to graduate school, switching from journalism to sociology because I thought sociology would provide a good way to make a living while continuing to study social movements, my main academic interest.

There was no such thing as radical sociology at Columbia in 1952. We jeered at Adlai Stevenson, took courses with Seymour Martin Lipset, Robert K. Merton, Herbert Marcuse, and Bernhard Stern. C. Wright Mills was on leave the year I was there. I liked Lipset best because at least he was talking about real issues (unions). I read Michels's *Political Parties*, which gave me more ammunition for my critical outlook on social democracy. Marcuse was exciting because of his incredible historical erudition. Stern, who was editor of *Science & Society* then, taught evening courses but was not particularly radical, I thought. Merton was, almost needless to say, pretty abstract and I understood little of what he said although I dutifully plowed through *Social Theory and Social Structure*.

By that time I considered myself a socialist. Someone handed me the program of a new group called the Libertarian Socialist League; I agreed with its anti–social-democratic, anti-Stalinist, and pro-workers' power line, and joined. It was a tiny group, with probably never more than 150 members, but, unlike other left sects, it was actually headed by a real worker, a printer. In addition to a worker wing, there was a bohemian wing, one of the members of which occasionally dragged her boyfriend, Maxwell Bodenheim, the once-famous poet, to meetings. He seemed on drugs most of the time. I finally quit when the organization got mired in the problem of whether, after the revolution, you should have workers' councils and unions, or only workers' councils.

I got drafted into the army in the spring of 1953 right after getting my M.A. The shooting war stopped while I was still in basic training; that was the summer of the Rosenbergs' execution. I spent nine months learning about southern culture in Alabama, and most of the rest of my time in England. Early in 1954 the CIA engineered the overthrow of the Guatemalan government. My FBI files, obtained years later via the Freedom of Information Act (FOI), reveal that I voiced disapproval of this action. They also reveal that I spent a lot of time in the local library. I had by then been classified a security risk because of my student socialist activities.

When my two years were up I was discharged. While waiting for "the character of my discharge" to be straightened out (there was a continuing investigation of my "loyalty"), I went to work for the Temple University library. From that base I reorganized the Temple Socialist Club. One day our chairman naively told us that the FBI had asked him for our membership list and he'd supplied it. It was the only time I ever actually participated in a formal expulsion proceeding (it was in absentia: He had meanwhile resigned, never really comprehending what had happened).

I finally got an "honorable," and went back to graduate school in 1956. I rented a shabby room that came with a tiny walk-in kitchen and bath, and one very tall grimy window looking out onto a dank alley. It cost $40 per month. I loved it. The GI Bill paid for tuition, and I went to work part time for the Central Committee for C.O.'s for rent and food money. I still had not met a radical sociologist.

At the University of Pennsylvania I found one other radical graduate student (in the anthropology department; the sociology department was so conservative that I ended up taking a lot of anthropology), and we became the Philadelphia chapter of the Young Socialist League (YSL), the unofficial youth group of Max Shachtman's Independent Socialist League. This was the former Workers party, a group that had split from the Socialist Workers party many years earlier. They'd changed the name because the WP had been put on the U.S. Attorney General's list of subversive organizations.

The YSL in Philadelphia had five members, one of whom was an informer, as my FOI files reveal. I believe he had also been a member of the Temple Socialist Club. Our chapter met in my dingy little room on Pine Street every other Sunday evening and held educationals with titles ranging from "Negro History" to, of course, "The Russian Question." We drank cheap beer, collected 25 cents per can, and used the profit to pay for postage.

In collaboration with local members of the Socialist party we occasionally picketed the Spanish consulate and once even leafleted visiting Spanish sailors. We were deeply immersed in the romance and the tragedy, as well as the political lessons, of the Spanish Civil War. People of our particular political tradition had read Orwell's *Homage to Catalonia* and knew about the civil war within the civil war.

Every New Year's Eve our YSL group headed for 114 West 14th Street, New York, headquarters of Max Shachtman's organization. Hal and Anne Draper would lead us all in folk dancing, and at midnight we'd sing the "Internationale." (Hal Draper would later write *Berkeley: The New Student Revolt*, and the classic pamphlet *The Mind of Clark Kerr*, plus three very important volumes on Karl Marx's theory of revolution. Anne Draper died some years ago. Hal died just recently, of pneumonia, in his apartment in Berkeley, among the books he loved so much.)

Every August, we'd have a retreat near Washington, New Jersey, borrowing a Socialist Workers' party camp. Carl Skoglund, a retired sailor who had been one of Trotsky's entourage in the 1930s, made martinis. They were fifty cents. There were long romantic walks in the country, nude swims, and many discussions. And despite our many (actually relatively minor) disagreements, there was comradeship.

The Cold War was still on, but somehow we felt a change coming. The Montgomery bus boycott had already started to shatter all that end of ideology mythology; Hungary and Suez came soon after. Suez made it crystal clear to me that even if Zionism had once been a component of antiimperialism, the Zionist state was now an outpost of the West.

It was the era of coffeehouses. Elsa B. had a "salon" in Powelton Village, and there we once argued until 3:00 A.M. on a name for a coffeehouse that never got off the ground. We went to Boswell's, and we were able borrow it for larger meetings. Max Shachtman spoke to a packed house there, once going on for two hours on American exceptionalism. You could hear a pin drop, he was that good. We read Ginsberg and Ferlinghetti and went to endless meetings organizing socialist, peace, civil rights, and other activities.

The chair of the graduate department of sociology at the University of Pennsylvania in 1956–1957 was Thorstein Sellin, a famous criminologist. He invited a French penologist in for a lecture. I went, armed with International Red Cross data about concentration camps and torture in Algeria, still part of France then. After the speaker had completed his discourse (mostly pleasantries about prison architecture), I raised my hand and described some of the more gruesome aspects of the French prison system, focusing on Algeria. Although the speaker actually agreed with me, I had broken the code and was finished as far as any hope for a fellowship was concerned. My dissertation advisor, Jeremiah Shalloo, who looked and talked like an Irish private eye, told me in a nice way to finish as fast as I could and get out.

In 1958 four of us took a leaf from Jack Kerouac's book *On the Road* (1957) and drove to Mexico City to spend the summer. I read Trotsky's *History of the Russian Revolution*, interviewed his widow, Natalia Sedova, at Coyoacán, enthusiastically toured from mural to mural, visited Zapata's home village, and drank tequila. By the time I got back, Shachtman had successfully maneuvered us into the Socialist party–Social Democratic Federation. The aging, still imposingly evangelical Norman Thomas was now our leader.

On February 1, 1960, the sit-ins began in Greensboro, North Carolina. I knew at once that this movement would be the material for my doctoral dissertation. Life was getting hectic. I was now teaching at a community college, writing, organizing for the Student Peace Union, and was soon to be married.

I did two stints for the CIA during these years. The CIA, through a conduit foundation (as we later found out, thanks to *Ramparts* magazine), funded various student groups to go to the Vienna and Helsinki Youth Festivals (in 1959 and 1962) to do counter-communist propaganda work. I was at both festivals. My Vienna room and board were paid for by the International Union of Socialist Youth (IUSY). My group, now the merged Young People's Socialist League, was affiliated with IUSY, which was the youth section of the Second International. The Socialist party belonged to that. My second trip, to Helsinki in 1962, was paid for by an outfit called the Independent Research Service, which was loosely hooked up with the U.S. National Student Association. Michael Harrington was there. Gloria Steinem was there. Etc. We had a lot of fun in Vienna and in Helsinki, and met some very fine people from many other countries. We got tear-gassed in Helsinki because local people didn't like the festival and the cops had to keep gassing the area to keep things under control. (Footnote: A sauna is very good to get the stuff out of your pores.) The CIA, in addition to funding the conduit foundation, was putting money into the Socialist International, its youth affiliate the IUSY, the Independent Research Service, and the International Secretariat of the U.S. National Student Association. What the heck, we thought later. Lenin took a free train ride from the Kaiser, too.

It was after the Vienna Youth Festival that I learned about class at the gut level. An old buddy of mine and I took a third-class overnight train from Vienna to Rijeka, Yugoslavia. We were feeling and looking pretty ghastly when we got out near the border the next morning to a breakfast of ham, eggs, and slivovitza. In the same compartment with us were two members of the Yale Russian Chorus (sent to Vienna to sing Russian songs; probably also funded by the CIA), one of whom was Sam Bowles, now a well-known radical economist. They emerged from our compartment looking ready for a day at a Wall Street brokerage house, clean and cool. I then understood: those people don't sweat.

The southern sit-ins of 1960 had generated numerous support groups in the North, not only on college campuses but in many communities, both black and while. I had become an active member of the Philadelphia chapter of the Congress of Racial Equality (CORE) right after the sit-ins in the South began. Soon CORE in the North shifted its strategy from support of the southern students to tackling tough local issues: police brutality, poor housing, poor schools, unemployment. In Philadelphia we conducted sit-ins on the issue of employment on city construction projects and learned (once again) that liberals and trade unionists might be part of the problem rather than part of the solution. On one occasion, when a group of us were sitting in all night at the city manager's office, the air conditioning was turned up and we learned another definition of cold war. We all got mug shot by a police photographer on our way to the bathroom, too. The CORE chapter soon abandoned nonviolent actions in support of integration. It became more of a black proletarian, rather than an integrated middle-stratum group. A handful of us white socialists were about the only whites who stayed for a few more years.

The black leadership of CORE in Philadelphia was in no way antiwhite, and I felt fully part of the scene even though I was living on the Haverford campus by then. I volunteered to teach a course on the history of black protest, which was well attended by chapter members and officers. I was a delegate to the CORE national convention in 1964 and remember hearing there the chilling news of the murders in Mississippi. It was not until the summer of 1965, at its Durham, North Carolina, convention, where I was also a delegate, that CORE moved in a distinctly black nationalist direction and whites began to be excluded. White socialists felt that black nationalism was a bad strategy, and would have dropped out anyway, as did many of the more socialist-oriented blacks.

After completing my dissertation I spent a year working for the Peace Education program of the American Friends Service Committee (AFSC). My "boss," actually more my partner, was Paul Lauter, who later helped organize the radical caucus within the Modern Language Association. I think we both felt a bit out of place in this nest of Quakers since we were both secular radical Jews. Our assignment was to organize faculty groups around peace issues; it boiled down to helping a network of antiwar faculty get started on some of the early teach-ins against the Vietnam War. This was exciting. But there was a negative side to working with AFSC. As a sociologist somewhat familiar with propaganda research, I found it irksome that this particular group of Quakers was studiously unwilling to evaluate the effectiveness of its educational work so long as the message seemed to meet its standards of morality. The AFSC bureaucracy was, it seemed, as locked in to its vested interest (in this case, the religious purity of its output) as any other organization.

Thankfully, the overall division head believed in connecting with union people. It was in that connection that I arranged a meeting with Stanley Aronowitz, who was still with the Oil and Chemical Workers. We met in his New York office moments after the news of President Kennedy's assassination was broadcast. We both instantly assumed it was a conspiracy, possibly the forerunner of a fascist coup. I was prepared to rush back to Philadelphia to destroy the Socialist party files. I think I was chair of the local then.

AFSC and I parted ways after the year was over, and I got my first full-time teaching job, a fill-in at Haverford College. It was the only place where I found myself a moderate among the faculty: there was a sizable faction of direct-action pacifists to my left. About that time I resigned from the Socialist party national committee and dropped out of active participation in the party as it became clearer to me that its internal divisions would keep it from playing any significant role either in militant civil rights or in antiwar activities.

A year later, in the summer of 1965, Allan Brick, a long-time peace activist and educational innovator, recruited a team of people including Paul Lauter, Florence Howe, myself, my wife, and several others to staff an institute for inner-city teachers at Goucher College in the suburbs of Baltimore. This experience exposed me to the radical critique of the educational process (a component of what is sometimes called the reproduction of social relations) and to a variety of innovative teaching techniques designed to overcome student resistance to the conventional structures of learning. Some of these techniques had been used during Mississippi Summer, and we tried them in our little institute. It was very new and very exciting, and I plunged into reading Paul Goodman, Paolo Freire, A. S. Neill, Abraham Maslow, and Carl Rogers. Later I attended sessions run by the National Training Laboratories in Bethel, Maine, and for a number of years (at least while my classes in sociology were relatively small) experimented with these antiauthoritarian methods.

Participatory or student-centered education was, for me, simply another dimension of the old socialist idea of workers' power, or "worker-centered management." I was excited by the rapid development of collectives and affinity groups within the New Left. My particular brand of socialism was entirely congruent with the idea of participatory democracy as it was developed in those years by Students for a Democratic Society (SDS). I considered myself a follower of Rosa Luxemburg in her critique of both social democracy and Leninist vanguardism, the former for its betrayals and the latter for its inherent oligarchic tendencies. So I joined SDS, as probably its oldest card-carrying member. I was hardly a student by then, and therefore didn't play a direct role in SDS. I was technically faculty advisor to the Vassar College chapter in 1967–1968.

Vassar was my first regular faculty appointment. I quickly located the local CORE people and the tiny handful of peace activists in Poughkeepsie. The War on Poverty was underway and we did our best to keep it honest, and out of the hands of the social-work establishment. G. Gordon Liddy was Assistant D.A., and as riots racked the country he promised to keep law and order in Poughkeepsie by means of heavy investment in police armaments. One day, in the course of a political discussion, my Italian-American barber invited me to join the local Liberal party, of which he was a leader. Several of us quickly realized we could take over the party in that entire congressional district and did so, together with the barber's faction. We ran a peace candidate, an aging hippie poet who had been a bomber pilot in World War II, for Congress in 1968 against a hawk Democrat. The result was a Republican victory, which was, under the circumstances, no big tragedy. However, I made the classic organizer's mistake of not training successors; soon after the 1968 election, the intellectuals went back to their books and the Liberal party old guard came back in.

Antiwar activity was continuing to build up. In October 1967, we all went to the big Pentagon demonstration, the one in which the yippies "levitated" the building, and Norman Mailer, Benjamin Spock, and Robert Lowell, plus many others, got arrested, and almost everybody got a whiff of tear gas. There would be many, many more demonstrations, much larger ones, in the next years, but that was probably one of the more memorable ones. There were many rallies and meetings; one big one (in the Vassar College chapel) was monitored by an FBI informant who sent in a page of names of those in attendance. In April 1968, Columbia University students struck and seized several buildings. The police moved in; many students were hurt. Vassar students and faculty held a support demonstration. Then came the assassination of Martin Luther King, Jr. My eight-month-old daughter went to her first demonstration on that occasion.

We left Vassar that long, hot summer and moved to Lincoln University, an old, predominantly black college in rural Pennsylvania, just four miles north of the Mason-Dixon line and KKK territory. I had been recruited by a white liberal president who had managed to pull the place back from the edge of bankruptcy. The university community was an enclave of academic culture in some pretty hostile territory. In that year's Presidential election, George Wallace ran first in our township, Nixon ran second.

Most of the white faculty at Lincoln were progressives; some of the older ones had been purged from other institutions during the McCarthy era. A handful of us radicals constituted the New University Conference chapter. From the moment I arrived at Lincoln I realized that the time for white presidents of black colleges, and white chairs of black departments, was over. When I succeeded to the chair a year later I made it a priority to hire my black replacement and prepared to debark. A number of us had read Barbara and Al Haber's *Getting by with a Little Help from Our Friends*, which discussed the strategy of radicals in the professions, a version of the idea of a "Long March Through the Institutions," and I had concluded that my place ought to be in a large state university system, preferably one with a significant working-class constituency.

In addition, it gradually became clear to us at Lincoln that we were standing in the way of a basic and necessary confrontation, that between the black students and their black faculty and administration. The students saw us as allies in their increasingly militant actions to try to create a more "relevant" (pro-movement, pro-black) curriculum. The faculty saw us as irresponsible outside agitators. Some of them had been there through many difficult years. They had barely managed, by a shrewd combination of accommodation (Uncle Tomism) and careful reform, to assure the survival of the school. Who were we to threaten that survival?

In fact, our role was often to calm the students down while trying to explain their demands to a paternalistic faculty shocked at the rebellion of "their" youngsters. We concluded that we were not helping the situation, and that a correct strategy called for getting out of the way. Most of our group eventually left. To my surprise, that faculty later organized a union (against their new paternalistic president), once again proving Saul Alinsky's point that it isn't union organizers that organize unions—it's management.

It was through New University Conference that I first came in contact with radical sociologists. In June 1969, Carol Brown and others convened a conference in Middlefield, Connecticut, and formed the Eastern Union of Radical Sociologists. They organized a wider conference at Columbia University that October, a forerunner of the regular gatherings later run by the East Coast Conference of Socialist Sociologists (ECCSS) until 1980. These conferences, plus "countersessions" that we organized at the Eastern Sociological Society (ESS) meetings, made more sense to me than the circuses I heard about at the ASA meetings—the famous memorial service to Ho Chi Minh in San Francisco in 1969, the eight-foot-high plastic penis painted with red, white, and blue stars and stripes in Denver in 1972. The idea was to communicate and change people, not turn them off by giving them the finger (no matter how much they deserved it). My style, learned in my years with the Young Socialist League (YSA) and the Socialist party, was to push literature. Selling two hundred copies of *The Insurgent Sociologist* in an hour at an ESS cocktail party seemed a better educational tactic than theatrics at business meetings.

At that time I took participatory democracy, with its emphasis on undermining authoritarian structure (including in the classroom), very seriously. When Sid Willhelm read (actually read!) a long paper, an early version of his *Who Needs the Negro?* at that Columbia conference, I inter(dis)rupted him, attacking him for replicating the style of bourgeois sociology. He stomped off in disgust. It was not a comradely thing for me to do, and I hereby apologize to Sid.

In 1970 Irving Louis Horowitz, the charter chair of the department at the new Livingston College of Rutgers University, invited me to join his group. It was the first (and I am afraid the last) time I was to be part of a radical sociology department.

There had been a series of urban uprisings in New Jersey. Rutgers University, in April 1968, had only two hundred black students. The university was headed, at that time, by a fairly liberal guy, Mason Gross, who very well understood the concept of cooptation and the need to reform in order to preserve. Livingston College was the result. Livingston was intended to be innovative, serving minority as well as more radical white students. Cynics called it a benign concentration camp for reds and blacks.

Irving had already hired Dale Johnson and Lee Weiner (of the Chicago Eight) by the time I arrived, and soon John Leggett, Jim Cockcroft, and Sherry Gorelick would join us. It was a fabulous time for a few years. We attracted some highly political graduate students from a number of Third World countries. Then, as the conservative backlash began, around 1975, our (rather diverse) brand of radical sociology became an embarrassment to the larger universitywide department, indeed to the university as a whole. The new president, Edward Blaustein, a mild version of John Silber, President of Boston University, a notorious reactionary, was bending every effort to sell the university out to corporate interests, break our unions, and otherwise purge the place of serious dissent. Irving drifted away from our group. Weiner had been red-baited out of his job by then, and soon Livingston (and the departments located there) lost autonomy. At present, of eight or so radicals associated with Livingston sociology in that decade, only John, Sherry, and I remain.

The early 1970s were exciting. I joined the collective that published the local alternative newspaper, *All You Can Eat*, just as it was repulsing a takeover by a faction affiliated to the National Caucus of Labor Committees (later the U.S. Labor party, the "Larouchies"). The faction came to a meeting, read a long statement charging us with petty-bourgeois anarchism (which was not far wrong), the rest of us broke up laughing, and they left.

In May 1972, following Nixon's blockade and bombing of the dikes in northern Vietnam, Rutgers students seized the ROTC building and Old Queens, the administration building. There, students "liberated" correspondence describing university dealings with the CIA and police surveillance of campus political groups. We published it. We also published photographs of local "narcs." We managed to get out 25,000 copies of a fairly good, politically and culturally radical paper on a monthly basis. It was distributed free to all college campuses and a few high schools in central and north Jersey for about five years.

For a short while, *The Insurgent Sociologist* was published at Douglass College, Rutgers, in newspaper format. (It became a journal after it moved to the University of Oregon, under the leadership of Al Szymanski.) The Douglass group (none of whom remain at Rutgers) was instrumental in organizing the first really large East Coast Socialist Sociology conference, which took place during a heavy snow in February 1974. I wrote for the *Insurgent* and was active with ECCSS and with the local New University Conference (NUC) chapter. After NUC dissolved, we kept up a radical caucus among the faculty for some years. The remnant of that caucus still exists.

There is a line in a 1930s play called *The Petrified Forest* by Robert E. Sherwood (Humphrey Bogart starred in the movie version) that goes something like "born too soon for the war, too late for the revolution." Similarly, a character in a Canadian novel, *St. Urbain's Horseman*, by Mordecai Richler, says, roughly, "Young too late, old too soon, was the story of his American generation. Born in the depression, sailing through the Spanish Civil War, World War II, the Holocaust, Hiroshima, the Israeli War of Independence, McCarthyism, Korea, and even Vietnam, with impunity. Always the wrong age, ever observers, never participants."

Is that the way it was? As my cohort of the middle left turned forty in the early 1970s it seemed to some of us, at least, that while life had been exciting, the present state of affairs had become neither kind nor gentle. We had participated in the movements of the 1960s, and they had, to borrow a phrase, given meaning to our lives, as movements do. We had not been mere observers. Yet, at least as far as the student New Left was concerned, we were too old for their revolution, and few of us were much more than marginal figures.

By 1975 the national organizations of the New Left were in shambles. SDS had imploded in 1969. The older New Left, in the form of the New American Movement, was hesitantly groping for unity with Democratic Socialists of America, a splinter group of the old Socialist party. NUC had dissolved itself. The Black Panthers had been effectively repressed. The war was over, black radicals had been killed, exiled, or coopted, and a creeping purge of the left in academia was underway. The Reagan years, actually begun under Nixon and carried on under both Gerald Ford and Jimmy Carter, were in full swing. What remained of the movements of the sixties seemed to have dispersed into scarcely visible local grassroots activity. Our political work in the university increasingly consisted of rearguard actions defending the paltry gains we had made early in the decade. Retreat was the order of the day.

At the personal level, socialist social relations, the term some of us used, were far from satisfactory. The feminist movement had a profound effect on every one of us. Many of us men (not only middle left but also older New Left people) were in conventional marriages, with kids, mortgages, and the rest of the bourgeois paraphernalia. Feminism challenged our domination of family agendas. It was one thing to support the rhetoric of sharing child care, another to have to leave in the middle of a meeting to pick up the kid from day care. It was even more frustrating to have to abandon friends during an ROTC building takeover because your mate had a (different) meeting or demonstration to attend, and household tasks had to be done. The friction of competing agendas was inevitable.

My marriage went through the phases not uncommon in our crowd: stress, therapy, open marriage, affairs, more therapy, separation, more affairs, divorce. Feminism was not responsible for this, but the movement posed questions that served to bring out into the open all the poisonous aspects of even the best relationships. It is futile to think that perhaps we would have led happier lives if we had left the dirt less disturbed. The history of our time did not permit it.

I seemed to spend great energies just staying afloat emotionally in those years, between the depressing and exhausting political situation and my rocky family life. How typical was this? Was our generation more depressed, alcoholic, suicidal, were our sexual adventures and disastrous divorce rates any different from those of our nonpolitical peers in academia or elsewhere in American society? Probably not. We were, or so we would like to think, just more conscious of what was happening to us and around us, and for that reason better able to articulate our problems.

Yet as time went on most of us survived, found new partners, raised our kids, sometimes changed careers, kept roofs over our heads, and, in the university, continued for the most part to do the job of professors: to profess.

Somehow most of us managed to remain cautiously optimistic about the long haul, and therefore survived politically as well. Our journals are still alive. Marxism has become a legitimate, if not exactly respectable (fortunately!), part of academic discourse. The professoriat, the ultimate aristocracy of labor, is becoming unionized. Some of us have developed solid bridges to progressive communities outside the university, and to causes of many kinds. Our networks of comradeship are more or less intact. Although there have been a handful of renegades, and some others have retreated into privatized lives and esoteric scholarship, most of us have stayed the course.

Our reward is to be here at the birth of a new New Left. As before, we will be marginal to it, for the movements of the next decade will have to make their own way. But we will be alongside.

Chapter 8

Critical Sociologists: Born or Made?
Norma Stoltz Chinchilla

A FEW YEARS ago, in a discussion with former classmates at my twenty-year college reunion, I was trying to explain why some of us had come to see ourselves as lifelong radicals while the majority seemed never to have transcended the ambiguities of middle-class liberalism and cynicism about fundamental social change. We all shared similar class and ethnic backgrounds and had all been students during the active political years of the early sixties.

I said I thought the experiences I had had in Guatemala the year after I was graduated (in 1965) and at the University of Wisconsin where I was a graduate student for four years at the height of the antiwar movement (1966–1970) sealed my fate: Those experiences led me to believe in the necessity and possibility of progressive social change, and of making whatever else I did in life compatible with the project of building a broad-based movement for progressive change.

One of my former classmates, clearly anxious to steer the discussion away from politics to lighter subjects like gourmet cooking and physical fitness, dismissed this thesis with the comment, "Oh, come on, you were always a radical!"

The discussion stopped there but the comment surprised me and left me wondering. I had always thought of myself as having been converted to radical politics from the mainstream of middle-class America. Was it possible that I had really been a semi-closeted radical long before I was conscious of it? Were there indications, even in my earlier life, that I would eventually see the world and my role in it different from most of my relatives and early childhood friends? Are activists somehow "born," or are they "made" by the times they live in and the experiences they have?

THE FORMATIVE YEARS

In mulling over the question, I realized that someone who tried hard enough might be able to make a case for "early warning signals" out of evidence such as the following:

I liked church meetings where missionaries came to show their slides and talk about building schools and clinics for people in Africa and Latin America. I even named my favorite doll after a missionary I had read about. (I could be excused for not knowing at that young age that religion and colonialism and charity and poverty are often connected.)

I also loved to go to Democratic party picnics and to the state capitol building with my maternal grandfather, an entirely self-educated small businessman who served in the legislature of the state of Washington for twenty-six years. My grandfather, never forgetting the extreme rural poverty of his German Catholic immigrant parents in North Dakota (from which he had escaped by going to work for the railroad), was a Depression-era Rooseveltian Democrat who believed government should help "working people" and "the deserving poor" through the protection of Social Security and unions. My visits with him to the modest homes of pensioners, who told me that his efforts in getting them their justly deserved pensions had "kept them out of the poorhouse," made an impact on me as a child. I also remember having nightmares about being jailed by the South African government for opposing apartheid after seeing *Cry, the Beloved Country* (a play based on Alan Paton's novel performed at our church by a traveling troupe of actors). I seemed to be the only one in my family (and probably one of few in my church) who looked forward to articles in *Presbyterian Life* magazine about how segregation was being challenged in the South.

As a young adult, I was leader of my church youth group but also had an atheist boyfriend with whom I occasionally escaped to North Beach City Lights Bookstore to hear poetry readings by Allen Ginsberg. I talked my parents into letting me spend a summer at the University of Veracruz in southern Mexico, where I not only learned some Spanish but discovered that some people considered the United States an imperialist power for having "stolen" Texas from Mexico.

It was here I first encountered the writings of C. Wright Mills. *Listen Yankee*, Mills's impassioned critique of the U.S. government's opposition to the Cuban revolution, was the first of several of his books that were to influence the way I saw the world and my role in it.

A high school history teacher, probably the only radical (imported from New York) that our northern California suburban school had ever known, told us about the Wobblies, William Jennings Bryan, the Spanish-American War of 1848, civil liberties, and the House Un-American Activities Committee, then holding its last hearings in San Francisco; he had apparently once been summoned before it. I began to listen to the Berkeley-based alternative radio station, KPFA.

I remember arguing with that history teacher during the first week of class about whether the U.S. war of independence from Britain was fought primarily for ideological or economic reasons (he argued the latter) and later about whether the government had a right to wiretap for the purpose of national security (I argued that it did). He confronted us with the fact that our school, which we thought of as very racially mixed, was de facto segregated by the tracking system: the college-bound A track was almost all Anglo with a sprinkling of Asians while the B and C tracks were almost all Mexican, Chicano, Portuguese, and Filipino (there was only one black student in our high school at the time). We were only vaguely aware of the tracking system, and we simply assumed that it reflected differential ability. Our history teacher shocked our A-track class one day by yelling at us that there were lots of kids in the B track who understood history better than we did, that our only advantage was that we knew how to express ourselves in writing. I think that the majority of the class dismissed this outburst as one more example of his craziness, but I remember thinking that, given what I had learned the previous summer in Mexico, he might be right. There was also the successful ten-minute walkout that we organized, subtly encouraged by our history professor, to support a popular teacher who was about to be fired.

In social science seminar at my small, experimental, liberal arts "cluster" college (Raymond College, a part of the loosely Methodist-related University of the Pacific in Stockton, California), I remember complaining about the functionalism of Parsons and Bellah and the "working-class authoritarianism" thesis of Seymour Martin Lipset, but it was difficult to articulate an alternative explanation since most of what we were assigned to read was one or another version of liberalism or conservativism.

I think I received my most important education as an undergraduate in the stacks of the University of Pacific library, where I found other books by Mills and read everything I could get my hands on about Latin America and the Third World. I began the training to participate in the civil rights movement's Freedom Summer in 1964 but had to drop out when I discovered that parental permission (and agreement to pay bail if arrested) was a precondition. (I never asked my father; I was sure he would explode at the very suggestion and wonder whether or not I should be attending any college that allowed such recruitment on campus.)

I got my SDS card from Bob Ross at the National Student Association (NSA) convention in 1963, the year after the Port Huron statement was written. I went to several NSA conventions as a representative of our student government and listened to SNCC workers tell of the violence that met their efforts to desegregate the South. But I was still relatively uninformed and naive about politics outside the two-party system. My naiveté was dramatically illustrated when I couldn't figure out why the Chicago police would want to attack a nice mainstream group like "the Boys' Club" (which was how I heard "DuBois Club," youth group of the Communist Party–U.S.A.).

All hints of early infections of radicalism such as those recounted above, however, were counterindicated by a generally homogenous middle-class social environment and the social, cultural, and to some extent political values that surrounded my growing up.

My family had a much stronger set of Calvinist German immigrant values than any other family I knew (my parents were both first-generation born in the United States). While the maternal side of the family was Midwest farmers (one set poor and Catholic and the other somewhat more prosperous and Protestant), my paternal grandfather was a skilled worker in the coal mines (a machinist trained in the Krupp factories in Germany). While he came to this country before the rise of fascism in Germany, I always had the impression that the area and social strata from which he came were, if not outright supporters, at least sympathetic to Hitler and his movement to "recapture Germany's place in the world."

Both sides of the family were true believers in the values and world view so aptly described by Max Weber: hard work, self-discipline, asceticism, saving, individual responsibility, religious virtue. They had a visible contempt for people who thought they were better than everyone else, balanced by an assumption that people who worked hard and were without vices did not usually end up poor. There was, in addition, a strong emphasis on respect for authority and keeping your nose clean. The assumption seemed to be that people in authority would eventually right whatever wrongs needed to be righted and that no one who risked his or her credibility by rabble rousing could be effective in changing society for the better. Thus, although it was becoming clear to me that there were important inequities in U.S. society that needed addressing and that U.S. policy abroad was more often on the side of wealthy elites who claimed to be anti-Communist than on the side of reforms that would

benefit the majority of people, I had a hard time thinking of myself as an
activist or potential organizer.

IN THE FIELD

Living in Guatemala for a year (1965–1966) clarified many things for me.
I was one of ten Fulbright fellowship grantees from the United States
who had recently received their B.A. degree from U.S. universities and
colleges. Guatemala was a relatively small country where the differences
between rich and poor were very large and obvious, where class differences among all classes were marked and consciousness about them
widespread, where the manifestations of class conflict were open and
visible, and where the many teachers, professionals, university students,
workers, and peasants believed in the necessity and desirability of *open
political struggle* as a mechanism of social change in spite of attempts by
the government, the army, and the wealthy to deter them through terror
and repression.

I learned in Guatemala, long before Watergate, that governments lie
to protect themselves. There the current government in power was
widely believed to be provoking instability so as to justify more repressive measures and that the U.S. government had deliberately provoked
instability so as to pave the way for a right-wing coup a number of years
before. I learned that with great regularity elections can take place with
the majority of people having no real say over who is allowed to run as a
candidate, not being truly free to vote as they wish, with fraudulent han-
dling of marked ballots, and with the winning candidate having no real
power as president.

I learned that high school and university students, when organized
and informed, can have an important role in shaping the political balance
of forces, especially in a country where illiteracy is high and access to
education is low and where going to a public university means having
access to information and analysis about the social reality of one's country. Most important of all, I met people who were willing to make very
large personal sacrifices to be part of a movement for change, even
though they believed that the changes they were fighting for would probably not materialize in their lifetime.

The year I spent in Guatemala was not an easy one. The use of repression and terror in fighting what the government, the elite, and their U.S.
military advisers considered "Communist insurgency"—the guerrilla
movement, which had its origins in an uprising among nationalist young
army officers—was quite intense. There were shootouts and kidnappings

in broad daylight in Guatemala City as the army and death squads began a campaign that was eventually to defeat this particular guerilla insurgency.

Anti-American feelings among many students at the national university were likewise intense, since the Guatemalan army was receiving its training mainly from U.S. officers and the government was advised, equipped, and influenced principally by the U.S. government. Educational "experts" from the U.S. were attempting to "reform" the national university (to depoliticize it and make it less accessible to the working class, as the students put it). Everybody knew that the CIA was involved in covert operations in Third World countries and other students often viewed people like us with suspicion.

In spite of the initial mistrust, I learned a lot about politics and social change from discussions with Guatemalan university students. Most of our group had enrolled in the school of humanities, as recommended by the Fulbright program. I wanted to go to the law school, however, where I had contact with a female law student. "You can't go there," the cultural attaché had told me. "It's too political. All of the students are Communists. There are very few women students and it's not safe for women." None of those arguments convinced me. I insisted that the law school would be a good place for someone who thought she wanted to study sociology. (I still didn't know what a sociologist really did, but I knew that C. Wright Mills was one and I was interested in the issues he raised.)

Among the student political groups at the law school were the Christian Democrats, whose leader at the time is now the Christian Democratic president of Guatemala. U.S. involvement in Vietnam escalated and the Watts rebellion took place, both of which I had difficulty explaining to my fellow students. When I had left the United States, the President had assured us that we were still only involved minimally in Vietnam as "advisers" and in my undergraduate social science classes we had learned that we were in a postindustrial society where ideological, class, and race conflict had pretty much ended. The students in Guatemala talked about a ruling class or bourgeoisie in the United States. All I really knew about this was what I had learned from Mills, who rejected the concept of "ruling class" in favor of "power elite."

I began to realize that if my goal was to understand politics and societies, I was not very well prepared, in either life experiences or academic training. The experiences I had that year in Guatemala were a beginning, but they raised more questions than answers. I hoped that going directly to graduate school in sociology upon my return to the United States would reduce my confusion and give me the tools I needed. Someone I met in Guatemala suggested the University of Wisconsin in Madison, and in late spring 1966 I activated my application to Wisconsin, knowing very little about its reputation or history.

MADISON DAYS

The first year in graduate school was lonely, frustrating, and difficult. Not only was there culture shock in coming back to the United States, which I shared with my roommate, who had just been in the Peace Corps in Venezuela, but the spirit of C. Wright Mills was nowhere to be found in the sociology department (except maybe in the speeches and activities of some of the more advanced students). Instead, there were largely empirically oriented, ambitious young faculty (mostly male), anxious to publish and not perish and make a name for themselves and the school. Liberal minded, yes, but certainly not the radical critics of U.S. society and its role in the world that I expected. Our class was very large (more than one hundred students) and books and housing were in short supply, a reflection of the rapid growth at the university as a whole and our department in particular.

Our required graduate-level theory class had more than one hundred students. The most radical text we were assigned to read in that class was *The Communist Manifesto*. We were asked to reduce it to one diagram, with variables and arrows showing the connections between them. We were also asked to make a list of propositions (or hypotheses) representing the theory and to find empirical indicators for each variable so that the propositions could be empirically tested. Somehow this approach didn't seem to capture the concept of dialectics on which I had learned Marxist theory was based, but this did not seem problematic to our instructors.

A student once asked, in a political sociology course, why, if we were reading Gabriel Kolko on imperialism, we weren't also reading Lenin. Because, he was told, Lenin's ideas were no longer relevant to analyzing U.S. imperialism. It might be true, I thought, but I sure would like to come to that conclusion myself, since the students I met at the university in Guatemala assumed that all educated people were conversant with his ideas.

In that same political sociology class, we spent a major part of our time reading and critically evaluating the works of Seymour Martin Lipset. The justification was that if we were to be critical of the mainstream of U.S. sociology, our critique needed to be serious and informed. I did not disagree with that reasoning, but so much of our time was spent critiquing "mainstream" work that we never had time to explore alternative forms of sociological analysis (political economy and class analysis, for example). We had no historical sociology, labor history, or social movements courses, to the best of my knowledge. Classmates more clear about the need for such material crossed over into the history department to take courses from a couple of their legendary instructors (Harvey Goldberg, William Appleman Williams). There was a short section in our methodology course about indirect "nonobtrusive" methods of data gathering, but there was little discussion of anything other than large-scale survey and demographic research methods. Large amounts of money came into the department to support this kind of research. Funded research was the god that young faculty were required to worship. Teaching was relatively unimportant in getting tenure or promotion.

The only exceptions to all this were in my Sociology of Development classes in the Department of Rural Sociology (whose graduate studies program was jointly administered with sociology). After endlessly criticizing Western and linear biases in modernization theories of development during our first few semesters, the Latin American students in our Sociology of Economic Change program finally staged a mini-revolt, asking that we spend part of our time studying alternative interpretations. They suggested we read *Capital.* Our much-beloved instructor, Gene Havens, pointed out that it would be difficult for him to teach us this subject since he had never read the book himself. The Latin American students offered to guide us all through this section of the course, and to Havens's credit he allowed them to do it. The little political economy that I learned in graduate school I learned from students from Third World countries, particularly the Latin Americans, of whom there were a substantial number in the Rural Sociology and Agricultural Economics classes. I also learned valuable lessons about political economy and international politics by taking Adam Schesh's course on Vietnam at the Free University, an alternative (noncredit) university in the community where anybody could teach and anyone could sign up for classes.

Discontent with our graduate school experience was apparently widely shared, as I discovered when the more advanced students led a sit-in in our department office, demanding reforms (particularly a reduction in requirements and student representation on departmental committees). I'll never forget one meeting, held to discuss the sit-in: The only faculty member with a leftish reputation in the department, whom I had idolized up to that point, said that if we really knew anything about power in U.S. society, we would be sitting in at the banks rather than at the sociology department. In an abstract sense, of course, he was right, but in a concrete sense it was the character and quality of our graduate department that felt most immediately oppressive to us and over which we might have the most immediate effect. He, on the other hand, was recluctant to participate in any criticism of his colleagues or take any personal responsibility for remedying problems. It dawned on me that reform or revolution is much easier to support somewhere else than in one's own house and that there is such a substantial difference in privilege and power between faculty and students that it can lead to a different perception of where and how political struggle should take place.

A major turning point in the political climate that surrounded our graduate school experience at Wisconsin was the SDS-led demonstration against Dow Chemical recruiters on our campus the fall of my second year (1967). The demonstration occurred in front of the commerce building, which was just across the sidewalk from the sociology building. As the fumes from tear gas thown by the police penetrated the building, all its inhabitants—faculty, students, and staff—were forced to evacuate and confront the reality of police brutality against the demonstrators, a number of whom were sociology students. The ultimate irony of the police violence, for some of us, was that the new president of the university, who had apparently caved in to pressure to call in the police and sheriffs from surrounding towns to counter what would otherwise probably have been a modest-sized demonstration, was a liberal humanitarian-minded sociologist from our department. I was told that this was the first time, in a long history of activism and demonstrations at the University of Wisconsin dating back to the early part of the century, that outside police had been brought to the campus. I remember thinking that this was a good example either of the ambiguity of liberalism about grassroots protest or of Weber's idea that it is the nature of the position rather than the individual occupying it that counts.

I learned most of what I know about political economy, class analysis, and social movements by myself or in study groups after I finished graduate school. The most important part of the Wisconsin graduate school experience, in my opinion, was the political climate on the campus, especially other students. It was particularly the international students and the out-of-state students from families with progressive histories who taught me about a progressive tradition in U.S. history and about international socialist movements.

I learned nothing about feminism or the history or sociology of women until I left graduate school. We were unaware at the time that we were the first class with a relatively large number of women students, most of whom had received some kind of financial aid. I was later told that the decision to fund female students was actually quite controversial since many on the faculty believed that women were likely to get married and not finish (the self-fulfilling nature of that prophecy apparently escaped them).

I do remember asking a faculty member to be my master's thesis advisor and having him say that I should come back in a few years when I had proved that I wasn't just there to get married. There were many aspects of the interaction between female students and male faculty and between male and female graduate students that I later came to understand as sexism—male faculty flirting with female students when they attempted to challenge them intellectually, sexual harassment and sexual exploitation of female students by male faculty (often with tragic consequences for the student), male students' domination of class discussions—but if you had asked me then if I had experienced discrimination or come up against sexism, I probably would have said no. We had no language for describing what we were feeling and no forms of female solidarity through which to share our experiences. Our abilities were, I think, consistently underestimated, but we also underestimated ourselves and were in a constant state of anxiety and insecurity about our situation, each of us thinking we were the only one who felt this way. Anxiety and insecurity seem to be an inevitable part of the graduate school experience for most students, but they were particularly intense for women students in this stage, when the second wave of feminism had not hit the campuses. It didn't occur to us, at least it never occurred to men, that there might be strength in banding together for intellectual and moral support. Although the women in my class were generally very bright and well prepared for graduate work, I later realized that I seldom sought intellectual assistance or advice from them. I always went to the men. No one, to my knoweldge, studied women or what is now known as gender as an academic subject.

DEEPENING AND KEEPING THE FAITH

My first exposure to feminism and scholarship about women was during my first teaching job at Pitzer College beginning in 1970. The students at this small liberal arts college in southern California approached the female faculty to teach a course on women. None of us felt prepared to teach such a course, but the students finally convinced us that we could all learn the material together. As a result of our experience in this course, a small group of women faculty formed a consciousness-raising group, each of us agreeing to participate because she thought one of the *other* potential members "needed" it. Our own feminist consciousness as well as our academic knowledge about women or gender was limited at this point. I later became a founding member of a women's studies program at University of California at Irvine, much to the displeasure of my conservative department chair and the supposedly leftist men who helped me get hired, who believed that Marxism and feminism were inherently antagonistic. Feminism and scholarship about women are now an important part of the academic work I do (along with political economy and social movements), but this interest and expertise were developed completely outside of my graduate school experience.

I remain committed to analyzing, supporting, and educating about social change in the Third World, but I now have an equally strong committment to fundamental progressive change in the United States and believe that the two are very much interrelated. In an attempt to transcend some of the weaknesses of the New Left, I participated in one of the party-building efforts of the 1970s. We attempted to develop a critique of what we considered dogmatism and ultra-leftism in left movements of the 1960s and 1970s and to build a multiracial movement by and for the U.S. working class, broadly defined. That movement, like many of its kind, unfortunately self-destructed because of our political immaturity, separation from the tempering lessons of previous U.S. left experience, the subjectivity of our campaign against white chauvinism, the weakness of our organization's position on feminism, and our lack of understanding of internal and popular democracy. Although I disagreed with Al Szymanski on a number of political positions, I always eagerly anticipated his presence at the American Sociological Association meetings so that we could discuss and debate where the movement for progressive social change in the United States had been and where it should be going.

My current understanding of Marxist theory and practical Marxist political organizing continues to be fertilized by the experiences of Latin American progressive political movements. In Central America, in particular, I have learned valuable lessons about popular democracy, pluralism, the importance of cultural and ideological struggle, and the interrelationship between feminism and socialist transformation. Although the challenge of translating these lessons into the U.S. context remains, and our knowledge of how to organize successfully is still limited, I believe that the experience that is currently being accumulated by grassroots activists across the United States will eventually lead to a stronger, more stable foundation for the national political organization that we still very much need. Although the current employment, tenure, and promotion requirements of major U.S. universities very much militate against sociologists' becoming the activists and organic intellectuals that our students and our society very much need, I hope that scholars and teachers in our field will continue to find ways to make their teaching, their research, and their lives part of the progressive movements that are ongoing, in the making, and not yet conceived.

Chapter 9

Coming Home: A Sociological Journey
Lynda Ann Ewen

SMALL-TOWN GIRL

TELEVISION'S black-and-white "Leave It to Beaver" 1950s were real to me. I came of age in small-town America. Stately elms still lined Elm Street. We all believed Eisenhower sat next to God.

Penn Yan, in rural upstate New York, is an abbreviation of Pennsylvania Yankees. When I grew up there, it was a town of about six thousand people, serving the commercial needs of the area's farmers. All the stores were closed Wednesday afternoon but stayed open Friday nights, when the farmers came to town. It was an unlikely place to breed radicals.

During the height of the Vietnam antiwar movement, psychologists tried to blame the "deviant" behavior of WASP protestors such as myself on our misguided toilet training or some other nonsensical early childhood problem. I had figured out that the war was wrong; why was moral outrage not a sufficient explanation for behavior? Looking back I can see part of the source of that moral outrage in strait-laced and righteous Penn Yan.

My dad, Lyndon Potter, was a veterinarian. He had been raised in a Catskill Mountain family in the the northern part of the Appalachians. He didn't talk about it much, but all his life he struggled against the effects of being raised with alcoholism, divorce, abuse, and poverty. He was the only one of his many brothers and sisters to finish high school, which he did by leaving home and working on a farm for room and board. He then worked his way through college and Cornell University Veterinary School. He never said it directly but I concluded that his passion for science—knowing and understanding—was what made him different from the rest. He had no desire to be rich and undercharged most of the poorer farmers. He often brought home bushels of cucumbers or quarts of wonderful buckwheat honey in lieu of money.

There were no boys in our family, only four daughters. I have often suspected I was a hoped-for son and got "Lynda" because they couldn't

140

use "Lyndon." My gender-role socialization was a mixed bag because Dad willingly shared with me his love of science, logic, and discovery. He had a telescope and showed me the moons of Jupiter. He let me help with operations and explained the biology and procedures. We owned three sets of encyclopedias and subscribed to eight or nine different magazines. Every Sunday we got the *New York Times*. We loved to argue. Dad relentlessly demanded evidence and the debates went on for years. My favorite was whether Roosevelt had given away Eastern Europe at Yalta. I wrote a long thesis on the question my senior year in high school to prove Dad wrong.

Mom and Dad had met in college. Anna Salecker was the daughter of Swedish and German immigrants. Outgoing and athletic, she was a perfect match for the shy, studious, good-looking poor kid. Mom's father died young and my grandmother had to work as a seamstress and then designer to support her two children. My grandmother lost several of her richest clients when the *Titanic* went down. Our sociology textbooks often use the allocation of lifeboats on the *Titanic* as evidence of social class discrimination in its most dramatic form. But the image of my grandmother laboring for twelve to fourteen hours a day in New York City while farming her children out to the care of others so rich ladies could have fancy clothes is what I learned about social class. My grandmother never seemed sorry her clients drowned, only sad to lose the business.

Throughout her life, Mom's love was Girl Scouting. In early twentieth-century America a strong-willed woman had very few areas to express herself legitimately. Girl Scouting was one. In her relationship to my father, Mom always played the expected role—raising his children, staying at home, and doing the books for his business. But in Scouting Mom was a leader. From her teenage years on, she organized, innovated, and taught, holding various positions in the Scouting movement, always as a volunteer. When I got older I often wondered at the irony. As long as she was not paid, her countless hours in Scouting were no threat to the given order of gender roles.

Yet somehow, my sisters and I learned. We lived on the outskirts of town, between two cemeteries (the barking dogs in the animal hospital never woke the neighbors), so we had mostly each other for playmates. Our favorite game was "Wild Girls"; we rode imaginary horses and shot cap pistols. We also had husbands, all of them conveniently stranded on a desert island where they were safe but could not interfere with our lives.

Starting at the age of seven, I was active in Girl Scouting. I also took music lessons—voice, piano, violin, and organ. I learned to paint, em-

broider, and sew. I was an honor student and editor of the school newspaper, sang the lead in "Amahl and the Night Visitors," was elected to
student council, and, in general, achieved. In my high school yearbook
the caption under my picture was "You name it, she can do it." But appearances were deceiving. I was too "smart" to be "popular." I had to act
dumb to get a date, and I hated it.

My sophomore year I took geometry from Mrs. Stewart. She was the
most beautiful teacher I ever had. She was also my Girl Scout leader. And
she was *so* smart! I ended the year with an average of 100 in geometry.
But in New York state that geometry class was all the math required for
the Board of Regents degree. My girl friends stopped, but Dad wanted
me to take more math so I signed up for trigonometry. I was one of two
girls in the class. Mr. S. was balding, fat, and ugly. I hated the class. We
knew he had seven or eight kids and believed that's what women were
meant for. I had never heard the phrase "barefoot and pregnant," and I
didn't think of my failing grades in terms of my sex. I thought it was my
fault for not having the ability. Mr. S. taunted me. I got mad and *mem-
orized* all the old Regents tests in trigonometry. I passed the state exam
with an 87 and he *had* to give me a B. Yet he succeeded in convincing
me I could not do math. For the rest of high school and my entire college career I never took another math course. When I sat down in front
of the math component of the graduate record exam my senior year of
college, I had no advanced math training to fall back on, only my ability
to deduce and analyze. I scored in the ninety-ninth percentile in math.
Perhaps I would have made a great physicist—we'll never know. We understand now, don't we, the incredible damage done by school systems
that stifle, track, and remold children to preserve the class privileges of
the few.

No one ever told me that gender-role socialization or sex discrimination existed. I was very middle class and very white. In small, sleepy Penn
Yan being female was the paramount contradiction to me. I had no other
way to cope, so I created my own world and lived in it. I buried myself in
history, specifically English historical novels. I decided I would ride be-
side John of Gaunt, who would love me and desire me not only for my
beauty but for my moral courage and brilliant advice. I watched movies
(we didn't own a television) about exotic places and fantasized about the
day I would step on the stage of world history and make my mark. Of
course, the content of my dreams was shaped by 1950s Penn Yan. *The
Reader's Digest* (which I read cover to cover because it was always left in
the bathroom) interpreted the Cold War. The Mau Mau uprising was
brought to me by Robert Ruark, Rock Hudson, and *Life*.

I decided I would become a missionary, so charismatic and insightful that I could bring peace and love to atheistic and rebellious lands. I had one specific fantasy of going to Russia and reversing the revolution. After all, we all knew the Russians were coming. In elementary school we were taught how to curl up under our desks, protecting our "vital parts" from the blinding blast that would follow the sirens. Those drills occurred as often as the fire drills. In my Girl Scout first aid class, *half* of our training was devoted to learning "civil defense" and treatment of radiation. We zipped up our yellow radiation suits, picked up our geiger counters, and went out to bring mercy to doomed victims whom the Russians had slaughtered for no reason at all. I wrote an essay about how the Russians invaded Penn Yan and built a bonfire of Bibles in front of my Methodist church, and won an award from the Daughters of the American Revolution. Night after night I had The Nightmare. The fireball rose in the sky and all the people I loved were falling. Their hair was coming out. Their tongues were swelling. The sirens were blasting. I was running. Trying to run away. The light in the sky grew.

Is it any wonder that an entire generation of us became *very* angry when we learned it was all a lie? Our terror had been created in order to give our own ruling class an excuse to build a profitable and dominating military machine. I came to see later that the war-devastated Soviets had no intention of carrying out an aggressive war.

Even then there were contradictions in what I was being taught. In high school I got Mr. Waye for history. He encouraged us to think and argue. I did a paper on General Pershing's expedition into Mexico and discovered it had a lot to do with oil. In my senior year our class had to read the *New York Times* every day. The Belgian Congo was in turmoil and Lumumba was mysteriously killed. The explanations I read in the *Times* did not make sense.

My mother used to say, "The world would be a wonderful place if everybody could have it as nice as we do." The idea, of course, was to replicate Penn Yan, New York, around the world. In my junior year the U.S. State Department validated that notion by picking Penn Yan as the typical American village. The Cold War was thawing and the first group of Typical Russians (artists, scientists, and party functionaries) would come to stay in the homes of Typical Americans (doctors, lawyers, and businessmen) in the Typical Village (99 percent white, 99 percent Republican, 99 percent Protestant). Our family was chosen as a host. Our two visitors were women, a movie star (who was truly beautiful) and the head of the Young Communist League in Armenia. The movie star was not a party member, could speak no English, and only wanted to go shopping.

The Armenian woman spoke English and wore her hair back tight in a bun. When she and my mother discovered that they actually both performed the same social function, they were delighted. They traded songs, campfire games, and Scouting/Komsomol experiences. Listening to them totally freaked me out. Weren't the "Communist youth" supposed to be miniature butchers?

It was fall when the Russians came. On October 17, the anniversary of their revolution, the Penn Yan post of the American Legion held a party in their honor. The visitors had brought their own supply of excellent vodka and their group included the piano player who had won second place after Van Cliburn in the Moscow piano festival. I shall never forget the scene—drunken Legionnaires and Soviets hugging each other, lustily singing as the pianist played revolutionary songs.

SMALL COLLEGE

John F. Kennedy was a Catholic, and Protestant Penn Yan believed there was a papal conspiracy to take over the world. He won anyway and the next year (1961) I went off to a small Christian college for small Christians to study sociology and become a social worker or missionary. Hartwick College, in upstate New York, was very private, very middle class, and very white. It believed in a strong liberal arts education tempered by twelve required hours in religion classes and an annual Religious Emphasis Week (which the students dubbed the "Nod to God Week"). My first two sociology professors—Leon Pastalan and Bob Sheak—challenged and excited me, but they were not warmly received at this college and eventually left. After that my sociology instructors were mediocre to terrible, but I still loved the subject matter. I also enthusiastically absorbed all the psychology, philosophy, literature, and logic I could.

This small college could not escape the wind of youthful rebellion sweeping the land. We had a religion professor who introduced us to the critical religious philosophies of Paul Tillich and the "God Is Dead" debate. A psychology professor, who lasted only one year, taught about dialectics. We organized a massive student demonstration against the campus police, who were harassing students for necking in cars. (Those were the days you shook hands with your boyfriend when he dropped you off at the front door of the dorm.) Other issues were fought out as well, mainly student rights. The social-class composition of the school, its isolation, and its religious orientation prevented our discontent from taking an overtly political dimension.

Wisconsin was one of the schools I applied to for graduate work, and

I was accepted with a fellowship. (I had only an *honorary* Woodrow Wilson, however, because my interview for that fellowship started with the man saying, "My, you're nice-looking. You're probably going to get married and have lots of children.") I had read in the newspapers that small antiwar demonstrations were taking place in Madison but decided to go anyway. I was in favor of U.S. involvement in Vietnam, for I had carefully followed events as reported in *Time*. How could the poor people of the world be helped if the Communists kept taking their freedoms away?

BIG UNIVERSITY

I landed in Madison in the summer of 1965, alone and very out of place. I was drawn to a public antiwar meeting where an emotional speaker talked about dead babies. All the men in the room had long hair and the smell of marijuana hung heavily. I had on white bobby socks, saddle shoes, a white blouse, and a cotton skirt. No one spoke to me and it was clear I did not belong. It was two years before I went to another antiwar meeting.

At the end of that first summer I got married. I had dated Bruce for three years in college. It was implicitly assumed we would get married; it never occurred to me that I could enter grown-up life without a man. It was a shaky premise for a marriage, but Bruce and I tried hard to make it work. We were married for seven years. He is the father of my daughter and remains a friend and colleague.

My beginning cohort at Madison was large and the faculty made it very clear they would weed us out. I made few close friends in the beginning and studied very hard. There were no women on the faculty and very few of my teachers were kind. The "star syndrome" lay heavily on the department, and most of the faculty were very busy being important. They did weed us out; my classes got smaller. I chose Social Organization and Methods and Statistics as my preliminary examination areas. Wisconsin's department was noted for statistical research. The school offered so few on-site research opportunities (you can't interview cows) that secondary data analysis was the only avenue to fame. Methods and Statistics seemed to be the road to science, and I had realized that above all I wanted to be a social scientist. I took the full complement of courses—including a Factor Analysis class where we spent the entire semester doing one problem (by hand, of course). Today a computer could run that problem in seconds. To master the work I had to teach myself the fundamentals of calculus, having no math background.

After completing the course work in Methods and Statistics I realized I could not write my preliminary exam in that area. I now understood that the assumptions of the fancy mathematical models were violated when applied to almost all the variables of sociology. The literature was ahistorical, atheoretical, deductive, and static. The rewards lay in creating more complex and abstract models, not in explaining a real world. I figured out that "pure" empiricism is not science. My alienation from the field was also personal. My grades were as good as my fellow male students but no faculty member ever sought me out, ever talked to me.

I never analyzed it. There was no "women's movement" for me. After I graduated I was told I was only the second woman to get a Ph.D. in sociology from Wisconsin (Cora Bagley Merritt was the first).

My husband was in economics and was taking courses in economic development. Meeting his friends from Africa helped me to decide to switch to Societal Development as my second preliminary exam area, with a minor in political science and an emphasis in African studies. I studied the history of Portugal in southern Africa and Tanzania's experiments in African socialism. The international students patiently explained imperialism to me. My intellectual world began to be reshaped. The great country that I called home was, in reality, a dominating world power exploiting the labor and resources of other countries. I learned the wealth of our rich and the decent standard of living of our middle class were not the result of some inherent greatness we possessed as a people. Bruce and I worked with an interdenominational church group in Madison and wrote a paper that detailed U.S. investments in South Africa. And I painfully learned that the reasons for the Vietnam War had more to do with offshore oil concessions and the securing of Asian labor and markets than democracy.

In the fall of 1967 I had a teaching assistantship. I had to grade on the curve—so many A's, so many F's. I hated that, and I hated the way my supervising professor taught. He was entertaining, clever, and cute but the students were not real to him—and neither were the teaching assistants. I was certainly learning about poor teaching.

I was dressed like a teaching assistant the afternoon of the demonstration. I remember it clearly: I was wearing a dress I had made from a Vogue pattern and a remnant of green wool, and black patent-leather heels. We all knew that students were going to protest Dow Chemical's napalm production for the war by blocking Dow job recruiters in the commerce building, directly across the street from the social science building. I was not part of the antiwar movement and I watched the police lineup from the windows of the sociology department on the third floor. They had on helmets and carried billy clubs. The protesting students were lying down, waiting to be arrested in civil-disobedience style. A question began to circulate: Where are the paddy wagons to take them away? There was none in sight. The chancellor at Madison at that time was William Sewell, a sociologist—one of our own. I went out into the street to observe. The police moved in. They had no intention of arresting anyone. They dragged the students out and beat them. Classes changed and thousands of students passed by the scene of dozens of police beating and kicking prone students. The crowd grew. Soon chants of "Heil Hitler" filled the air. Across the hill, several students climbed up on the roof of Bascom Hall and took down the American flag, to the cheers of the thousands of students now gathered. I remember a cop beating a woman who looked a lot like me. I yelled at one of the TV news reporters, "Take a picture of this!" The reporter yelled back at me, "We're only taking pictures of the hippies!"

A small maintenance tractor pulling a cart filled with bricks for a nearby construction site made its way through the crowd. As it passed students picked up bricks, and soon bricks were flying. (The newspaper reports claimed the students had come to the demonstration with bricks in their book bags.) The police hurled tear gas and the crowd ran, regrouped, and was gassed again. We later heard that the decision not to arrest but merely beat the demonstrators had been made with the acquiesence of our chancellor.

Later that day a mass meeting was called. The auditorium of the social science building was filled to overflowing with outraged students. A leftist "star" from Chicago (I was told it was Rennie Davis) was on stage writing slogans on the backboard quoting Latin American revolutionary Che Guevara and spouting rhetoric. The youth of Wisconsin, from its small towns and farms, were mystified. I had heard talk of a student strike, and that made sense. Now here was this guy talking about having a revolution, and that didn't make sense. I marched up to the stage (still in my green dress and high heels) and grabbed the microphone yelling, "We need a strike!" The leftie grabbed the mike from me and screamed, "Don't you listen to this Mary Worth!" But the strike won out. I had had my first confrontation with the sectarian left.

The Dow demonstration changed a lot of lives, and it changed mine. I learned that due process was not for those who challenged the fundamental policies of imperialism.

That fall a coalition of faculty, students, and progressive people in the community decided to put an antiwar referendum on the ballot. We succeeded in getting 47 percent of the electorate to endorse the most militant position: immediate withdrawal. This was in 1967. The war would drag on for five more years, while those in power chose to ignore the growing evidence that many citizens did not want this war.

I had accepted a research assistantship with Maurice Zeitlin that fall. The work involved analysis of data he had brought back from Chile. It was not in the area of African studies, but it was an opportunity to access data for a dissertation in Societal Development. Zeitlin was a star of the New Left, ambitious and bright. I believe that he wanted a quiet, hard-working research assistant, and my involvement in the antiwar referendum (of which he was the cochair) seemed to anger him. It became difficult to work with him. The sexism and elitism that pervaded the department made it impossible for a productive mentor relationship to develop. When Bruce was reclassified by the draft board, we changed our plans and I became pregnant immediately. I was excited—I wanted a baby. I shall never forget Zeitlin storming into my little alcove and shouting, "You're pregnant and now you'll *never* get the dissertation done!" But my Chilean research led to new friends among the Latin Americans and a close friendship with Norma Chinchilla.

It was a turbulent period. The graduate students went to classes (when they weren't on strike about something) and regurgitated what they were told. But real learning happened in the teach-ins and the study groups we ourselves established. We talked to each other across disciplines. I especially remember Rob McBride in economics and Paul Richards in history. It was not easy to relearn and replace years of accumulated ideological garbage. I learned there was a history of the left in this country. I met a real Communist (and went home and dreamt that the FBI was after me). I watched government agents chase an exiled South African student down the hall, and I met a white South African whose father, an Episcopal priest, had been driven from the country. I met Dr. Jordan, the exiled South African writer, and his wife. I met Puerto Ricans who introduced me to the reality of a Puerto Rican colony. On my own I read black history and black sociologists one summer. (In my entire formal training at Wisconsin I was never required to read a single black sociologist.) I took another summer and read labor history. We all read Malcolm X and Franz Fanon.

I passed both preliminary examinations "with distinction." Someone told me I was the first student to have done that. I had studied hard and knew I had mastered what they wanted me to know. I may be one of the few living sociologists who has read *every* book Talcott Parsons wrote! I was taught what academia defined as sociology. In the protest marches, the teach-ins, and the study groups, I learned what was useful. They were not the same. Others have observed this phenomenon: "science" becomes that which the institution of science claims it to be. It was several years before I realized the only real use for much of my training in sociology was to carry out my criticisms of the discipline; it certainly did little to help me explain social reality.

In my last year I was offered an instructorship. I taught two sections of Principles and discovered I loved teaching. I dedicated my courses to Eduardo Mondlane, leader of Mozambique's National Liberation Front (FRELIMO), who had recently been assassinated by the Portuguese. Mondlane had married a woman from Madison, and his death made a significant imprint on the community. My students wanted to know many things and they were not getting answers from the on-campus sectarian groups. We formed the Committee to End Rhetoric, an attempt to reach the "real" people on campus who had average people's questions. The students and I took a trip to Chicago, where we helped the Young Lords paint a church with colorful Latin murals. I began to understand that much of politics was about teaching and education.

The small percentage of American black students on campus (there were more Africans at Wisconsin than American blacks) began to raise demands for open admission and a black studies program. The administration stubbornly resisted, saying the school could not afford it. A student strike was called, and ten thousand (one-third of the student body, mostly white, mostly farm kids) struck for the right to have a black studies department. The administration called the National Guard, at $80,000 a day, to crush the strike. The students held. I remember vividly the tanks on campus, the campus that held "academic freedom" as its motto. The strike was won; the administration promised an Afro-American Culture course for the fall. However, it claimed there were no qualified blacks to teach the course. After much negotiation, the black leaders of the movement agreed to my appointment as the instructor. (I was acceptable by virtue of my involvement in the anti-apartheid struggle and my "minority" status as female!) I had difficulty with the decision, although I was firmly committed to the idea that the course had to be taught. I sought a compromise with my "whiteness" by asking that a black faculty member coteach the course with me (although I would do most of the work). An African in the history department (whose father-in-law was head of his country's navy) was appointed. I had not yet learned the hard lessons of the primacy of class interests over race. He was unimaginative, conservative, and openly hostile to any aspect of the civil rights struggle that involved the working class.

The first semester my coteacher and I negotiated and compromised our way through speakers and texts. I agreed to an extremely conservative black politician if he would agree to invite Fred Hampton, leader of the Chicago chapter of the Black Panthers. Hampton was assassinated by the Chicago police the week before he was scheduled to speak. My coinstructor seized on the assassination as proof that it was dangerous to have these types of speakers and refused to allow any other Black Panther to speak. When I challenged him, he went to the black students. The student leaders were won by his argument that a white woman was trying to tell him what to do. The international student organization offered me their support. They and their Marxist leadership saw the ultimate issues as class, not race. It was clear to me that I had committed an error when I insisted on taking on this particular fellow as my coteacher. I could not in good conscience set into motion events that would pit international students against American blacks, so I resigned. Some lessons are learned only bitterly.

I was close to finishing my dissertation by the spring of 1970 and began interviewing for jobs. I knew I wanted to teach where my teaching would make a difference—in a working-class school. The department expected me to try for an elite school and Zeitlin encouraged me to apply for a job at Princeton. He also arranged an interview for me at Columbia. I flew to New York for that interview, knowing full well I would not take the job if I were offered positions at either Wayne State or California State at Los Angeles, where I had already applied. The Columbia people took me to lunch at a very fancy restaurant and in the middle of dinner someone asked, "What is your husband going to do if you take this job?" You don't have to be a raving feminist to know that a man would never be asked that kind of question about his wife, and I told them so. There was a stunned silence. They offered me the job anyway, but by the time I got their call I had accepted an offer from Wayne State in Detroit. Five years later I made a very similar conscious decision to go to West Virginia Institute of Technology. At the American Sociological Association meeting in Boston, I ran into one of my former Wisconsin professors, who had gone on to chair a prestigious department somewhere else. He greeted me enthusiastically, then he noticed my West Virginia Tech identification tag and his face fell. "Oh Lynda," he said, "I'm *so* sorry!"

BIG CITY

In Detroit, for the first time in my life I encountered a left that was based in the working class. There were auto workers who were studying Marx and Polish women organizing food cooperatives. I had students who were the sons and daughters of industrial workers, going to school while holding down jobs and raising kids. I met American blacks who talked about the necessity of class unity. I taught at the Detroit Labor School and learned about the relationships between organized crime and unions, about sellout contracts and industrial accidents and death. My marriage broke up in 1972, and I met a man from a West Virginia coal-mining family whose father had been displaced by mechanization and had ended up in the auto plant. I found an inner-city Methodist church where the religion of my childhood could find expression in setting up a day care center and recreation programs for neighborhood youth. I met women who said God might be a female. I learned from the leaders of the Revolutionary Union Movement and the People's Peace Treaty.

In the spring of 1972 I went to Chile. Allende had been in office two years and his government had expressed some interest in the research findings of my dissertation. When I got there Jack Anderson had just released the ITT papers detailing collusion between the U.S. State Department and the corporation to destabilize the Allende administration, and the government went into crisis. I marched with eighty-thousand workers in support of Allende (a march never reported by the *New York Times*, although it reported every small march of several hundred *against* Allende). I saw a working class struggling for an alternative and I saw the storm clouds gathering. Back at home, I worked intensively with Non-Intervention in Chile (NICH) attempting to mobilize public opinion in support of the Unidad Popular and against the seemingly inevitable fascist coup. I also realized that the power structures I saw in Chile—the ruling class and kinship interests I had identified in my dissertation research—also existed in Detroit. I applied a similar methodology and found similar results, which I put into my first book, *Urban Crisis and Corporate Power in Detroit*. At that time I was being exposed to the literature of classical Marxism and applied it, rather mechanically, to my study. As a result, the book has never received much recognition within the discipline. Princeton University Press published it but was so embarrassed by it that a reviewer from the *Detroit Free Press* was told he would probably not want to review it and so would not be sent a complimentary copy.

The department at Wayne was large and deeply divided by rank, jealousy, and "turf" conflicts. I loved my classes and the graduate students, and minimized contact with most of my faculty colleagues. I stayed away from department politics except on what I considered issues of principle, particularly student rights and affirmative action. The all-white faculty were nervous about hiring Bob Newby, who was black, smart, articulate, and militant. His qualifications could not be denied, and the threat of discrimination charges forced the issue. After Bob was hired, the hiring of any other minorities was stubbornly resisted. A competent white women was even turned down because she was married to a black man! Wayne was viewed as a B-level school in the prestige hierarchy of the discipline. Instead of seeing the potential of a diverse and energetic faculty in an exciting urban environment, many wanted to pursue highly individualistic careers and move up and out.

The intense atmosphere of Detroit in the early 1970s was my incubator into the left. As much as I had disliked sectarianism I now came to understand the necessity of political organization. All around me were "vanguards" and "lines." Somehow, out of the checkered history of the working class in the United States a political party had to be built to genuinely represent the interests of the working class. I began to realize the contradictions posed by the roles of political activist and professional sociologist.

SMALL STATE

I married John Taylor in the spring of 1974. A year later he was offered the job as attorney for District 17 of the United Mine Workers, and this son of a coal minor decided to go home. West Virginians seem to remain West Virginians no matter where they are. Even though he had lived in Detroit since he was eleven, John wanted to go back. I had been at Wayne for five years, and a change made sense for me too. I followed John to Charleston and got a job at West Virginia Institute of Technology, located in the Kanawha coalfields east of Charleston. It is a small state school specializing primarily in engineering and technology; I was one of three sociologists in a department of social sciences. We bought a house in a small working-class community in the shadow of a giant DuPont chemical plant and settled in. Our family grew. There were two daughters from John and one daughter from me. We added a son, two cats, and a dog. I was absorbed into John's large working-class family in both Detroit and West Virginia.

Rand, West Virginia, is an integrated community where the children of slaves who once worked the area's salt and coal mines have lived side by side with the children of early Appalachian miners. The surrounding communities, tucked up the hollows, were almost all white and some were notorious for Ku Klux Klan activity.

The infamous right-wing textbook protest of the mid 1970s was active in Rand. District 17 was the hotbed of the coal miners' reform movements for Black Lung benefits and safety in the mines. In our first two years there we were swept into the activities of protesting parents and protesting miners. The antiinjunction strikes of 1975 and 1976 were the largest wildcats of this century and probably the decade's most significant example of sustained collective behavior. (By 1976 one-hundred-thousand miners were idled and the country's coal production largely at a standstill.) The discipline of sociology, of course, ignored them. I wrote an article for an anthology edited by Zeitlin analyzing the wildcats but had to use a pseudonym to protect my sources. I also wrote an article on the role of the Ku Klux Klan in the textbook strike, based on my intimate relationships with key community leaders in the controversy. I presented it at the first Marxist panel ever organized for the Southern Sociological Society. I was not surprised when the articles was rejected by the major journals. To my knowledge, the subject of the Ku Klux Klan has appeared only once in any sociology journal since the 1940s (in *The American Journal of Sociology* in 1960).

The documentary film *Harlan County, USA*, won an Academy Award in 1977, and I was asked to write the story of that strike. The book was initiated by the Independent Publishing Fund of the Americas in conjunction with Vanguard Books, a small leftist press. Writing a book for popular consumption was a new experience, and deeply rewarding. *Which Side Are You On? The Brookside Mine Strike in Harlan County, Kentucky, 1973–1974* was a Vanguard bestseller. I learned that lack of a major critical press and distribution apparatus in this country is one of our most serious problems.

THE SOCIOLOGIST

I had started attending professional meetings while at Wayne. I found them beneficial, for I was always able to meet and talk with sociologists who shared my concerns and interests. But I soon realized that the meetings (and their respective associations) were highly structured elitist organizations. Those of us who were critical had not clearly answered an important question: Did we want to beat them at their own game, playing by the rules of the sociological power elite and trying to reform from within, or did we want to break off from the existing structures and create our own?

The Southern Sociological Association has historically been among the most conservative of the regional associations. Those in control viewed our formation of a radical caucus in the mid 1970s with some consternation. In the beginning the caucus included Jerry Dockery, Carlton (Wally) Smith, Peggy Dobbins, Walda Katz-Fishman, Don Clelland,

Tony Ladd, Jim Friedrich, Tom Hood, John Leggett, and myself. It was not possible for truly hard-core leftists to survive in the South and so the definition of "radical" was different than on the national scene. One young professor came to an early meeting and confessed that he was "a Weberian" and had been ostracized by his department for his political views!

Cracking the American Sociological Association (ASA) appeared next to impossible. During one ASA business meeting in the mid 1970s I stood up to voice some frustration and after the meeting was approached by an older gentleman who introduced himself as Al Lee. He explained that he and Betty Lee had been organizing an alternative, the Association for Humanist Sociology (AHS), and asked if I would be interested. I quickly understood that Al and Betty had been waging a historical struggle on many of the issues that I, a relatively young sociologist, saw as important. I became active in the AHS and became editor of its journal, *Humanity and Society*. The AHS meetings were qualitatively different from the other professional meetings and its membership was intensely loyal. The question remained, however: Could we have an impact on the control and content of the discipline?

There were deeper questions underlying our discussions. As the movements of the sixties and early seventies seemed to die down, radical conflict theories began to be questioned. Many of the Marxists retreated further and further into esoteric philosophical debates. Others, trying to maintain an activist posture, either denounced the working class as backward and gave up, or abandoned a revolutionary posture to pursue limited and reformist goals in trade union or social welfare politics.

COMMUNITY ACTIVIST

Meanwhile, my involvement in the local struggles grew. I did research and wrote for the West Virginia Education Association. I received their support, and the support of the National Education Association, when I ran for the Kanawha County school board on a platform directly opposing the right-wing book protestors. I nearly won. I served as chairperson of a subcommittee on the Board of Church and Society of the West Virginia United Methodist Conference and fought hard to have the conference respond to KKK threats against a minister who refused to let the Klan meet in his church. (The minister was eventually driven out of the state.) Even as the leader of a Brownie Scout troup I ran into the Klan. My girls could not go to day camp because it was held on the field where the KKK held their rallies. I represented my community on the board of the local federal antipoverty program (MULTI-CAPP). After an expensive and poorly built sewer system was shoved down our community's throat, we carried out a boycott that was partially successful—one-third of the customers refused to pay for a year. In all these experiences I learned that working-class politics far transcends many of the clichés of the left.

Local demands on me grew and I developed health problems. I could not continue to be active both locally and professionally, so I made the decision to pull back from the discipline. I resigned the AHS editorship with deep regrets and stopped going to professional meetings for almost eight years.

I spent more time in activities on my local campus, losing the election for chairmanship of the faculty assembly by only one vote and serving two terms as my college's representative on the faculty executive committee. I worked hard on committees to improve advising and helped set up an honors program. I worked closely with black students trying to rediscover their heritage; with women fighting issues of rape, dorm security, and sexual harassment in the classroom; and with international students facing the narrowness of an ethnocentric Appalachian culture. I supported students in two mass demonstrations at the state capitol and numerous lobbying attempts. My health problems also drove me to the medical literature and into the abyss of the American health system. My personal experiences sensitized me and deepened my awareness of the horrors many must endure.

COMING HOME

Conditions change. In the 1970s well-organized groups had the chance to fight and win on issues such as parks, housing, black-lung benefits, clinics, remedial education. In the 1980s it has been different. The effects of worldwide economic contraction are coming home. The electronic/ robotronic revolution threatens to create an unresolvable unemployment problem. Reaganomics is the symptom of a system turning inward and the effects in Appalachia have been devastating. Now, for the first time since the 1930s, large sections of the working class are being pushed into the struggle, not for a better life but for survival. I am seeing the effects on our West Virginia coal-mining community. What is happening here is the precursor to what may be expected in the rest of the country.

Education in West Virginia has been one of the main areas under attack. Most of us who are sociologists are also teachers and academicians. No longer are we somehow apart from the struggles of workers; our academic freedoms, our tenure tracks, our medical benefits, our class sizes—all are in jeopardy. As sociologists we have a great deal to offer faculties fighting for their own interests as workers. Today it is becoming possible to unite engineers, medical school professors, art teachers, and technology instructors around common issues. And as intellectuals we have a great deal to offer by defending and supporting the struggles of those whose immediate survival is in question.

In the spring of 1988 I read William J. Wilson's book *The Truly Disadvantaged*. This book signaled to me that establishment sociology had joined the propaganda blitz being carried out by the bourgeois media to cover up the system's massive attack on civil rights, education, and the standard of living. Wilson's work attempts to recast the old "blame the victim" approach, giving it a new veneer backed by different data. But it is little more than warmed-over structural functionalism. Wilson's version of the "underclass" theory denies the role of class struggle, is ahistorical, and attempts to evade the fundamental contradictions of the system by proposing liberal reform "solutions." Anyone who understands the character of this approach, and has legitimating credentials, cannot help but respond. I went back to the ASA in August 1989.

In the past several years, a number of prominent leftists have written their autobiographies or issued statements in which they denounce their activities of the 1960s. In effect they have become apologists for the bourgoisie. In the coalfields Bernie Aronson had been well known as an articulate spokesperson for the miners and the union in the 1960s and early 1970s. Today he serves as a speechwriter for the White House on Latin American affairs, justifying the use of the Contras in Nicaragua. Fred Carter, a disabled black coal miner, was active in the black-lung movement at the same time as Aronson. Fred kept on fighting. The Department of Labor framed him with criminal charges in an attempt to destroy his legitimacy and that of the movement. Carter had to fight a difficult court battle, which seriously undermined his health, but he won. Out of that fight a revitalized West Virginia Black Lung and Disabled Association was born. Fred Carter remains active.

In almost all cases, the "famous" leftists were not the genuine leaders of the movement. The media needed leaders it could glorify and manipulate. Most of these so-called leaders were created by the press, not by genuine constituencies. Fred Carter was never interviewed by *Time*. The decent and good leaders of the sixties that I knew and respected are largely still around, still learning, and still trying to respond to an unfolding history.

More than ever I see how the failure to learn history accurately is a fetter on our thoughts and actions. An accurate grasp of history allows us to see changes and shifts in conditions and keep our bearings. The next period will be an intense and dramatic chapter in our history. The contradiction between a starving world and a dying planet, on one hand, and the spiraling wealth of a tiny few on the other, will lead to explosions as it confronts the productive capacity of new technologies. Those explosions can be wonderful bursts of creative energy that open up possiblities to feed, clothe, and shelter every human being on this earth. Or that confrontation can lead to fascism, as right-wing political movements succeed in defining the crisis their way and blaming the victims. What I understand now, more clearly than ever before, is that I, as well as everyone else, have no choice but to fight for not only our survival but the alternative future.

Chapter 10

The Making of a Class-Conscious "Race Man": Reflections on Thirty Years of Struggle

Robert G. Newby

WRITING THIS autobiographical sketch gave me an opportunity for introspection that helps me to understand where I and my work fit in the profession. It shows the distinctiveness of my experience as a sociologist, a black sociologist. It also helps me to understand an experience that white sociologists, even of the left, take for granted and, to a large extent, assume to have been basically the same as that of their black counterparts. In that same regard, I think I understand why white sociologists, particularly those who should know that "labor cannot emancipate itself in the white skin where in the black skin it is branded" (Marx [1887] 1967, 301) tend not to fully comprehend the importance of the race question. In fact, I think that not comprehending the depths and centrality of the color question is what Sidney Willhelm's impassioned attacks on them are all about in his *Black in a White America* (1983).

More important, I think I now have a better understanding of the profound impact of race in shaping the social construction of reality for blacks, particularly black sociologists. Though I claim issues of race and class as my specialties, retrospection tells me that a recognition by African-Americans, generally, of the primacy of class requires a considerable intellectual leap of faith, particularly when juxtaposed with their experience. Even more, the intersection of gender with these issues, now being explored by the Center for Research on Women at Memphis State, must also be understood. The work of sociologists, particularly black male sociologists, including myself, must reflect this "triple jeopardy" dimension.[1]

LEARNING THE STRUGGLE OF RACE
Early Development: Context of Orientation

I was born on June 27, 1935, in the heart of the Depression. The stories my mother tells of those days are consistent with the dire conditions faced by many, particularly blacks. I will spare you the details. As she says, "Those were hard times." In 1934, following other relatives, my mother moved from a farm in Arkansas to Wichita, Kansas, in search of a better life—away from the isolation of a small farm, toward better prospects for an income and self-sufficiency. She had two years of post-secondary school and hoped to complete a four-year degree at the University of Wichita.

What she got, however, was domestic "day work" at $1.00 a day. She also found companionship and marriage to my father, William Newby, who was unemployed. In fact, none of the men in the rooming house where my mother and an aunt lived was employed. For heat in the winter, the men would climb onto passing locomotives and pitch coal down to women waiting to gather it in. The men would be arrested, booked, and then released, to repeat the event at the next passing train. For this lodging my mother paid $1.50 a week. Following a divorce from my biological father, she married my real father, Jack Belcher. At seventeen, fearing for his life because of a confrontation with the landlord of his family's tenant farm, he had run away from Covington, Georgia. After a short stay with two sisters in Hutchison, Kansas, he moved to Wichita when he got a job as a section hand for the Missouri Pacific Railroad. He later became a section foreman over an African-American and Mexican-American crew. About 1948 he was "bumped" by a white foreman from Little Rock who had more seniority with the railroad but whom my father had to train for this particular job. Rather than continue the training, my father transferred to the railroad warehouse. Because my father worked for the railroad, which provided the family free transportation, as a child I traveled extensively. I experienced, firsthand, the "separate but equal" segregated South. Until I was thirteen I spent every summer in Warren, Arkansas, with my grandparents. I also went to Georgia several times. As soon as the train crossed the Mason-Dixon Line, we moved to separate railroad cars, segregated terminals, and the back of the bus. I also made extensive trips to the North and to both coasts. By the time I was fourteen, I had been through thirty-five of the then forty-eight states.

My mother and father were both fighters on the "race question." Though my grandmother loved my father, she used to hate to see him come to Arkansas because she feared for his "uppityness" toward whites. When I competed in music competitions and took second place, he would usually tell me, "If you had been white you would have come in first." Now in her mid-seventies, my mother continues these battles today on behalf of her foster children and the poor.

The School Years: Racial Separation and "Race Mixing"

Growing up in Kansas provided me with a unique socialization on the issue of race. Though it is technically a northern state, if there is any doubt about the segregation that blacks faced in Kansas, one need only to remember the full name of the historic 1954 Supreme Court desegregation decision—*Brown* v. *Board of Education, Topeka, Kansas.*

I always took pride in the fact that Kansas did not suffer the stigma of segregation, as manifested in the South. I also found a source of pride in John Brown's victories, which contributed to Kansas's entering the Union as a free state (DuBois 1962). Much later, reading *Race and Politics* by James Rawley, a University of Kansas historian (1969) I found that much of that pride may have been misplaced. Rawley examined the politics of the 1850s struggles surrounding the Kansas-Nebraska Act. From his book I learned that the "free soilers" did not want black slaves in Kansas precisely because they did not want black people in Kansas at all!

These contradictions—"free state" versus total racial exclusion—were precursors to later inconsistent segregation policies. Segregation was permissive where there were enough blacks to sustain a version of the dual system. In pre-*Brown* Wichita, as in Topeka, black population was large enough to maintain segregated elementary but not secondary schools. Only Kansas City had enough blacks to have segregated high schools. In smaller cities with small black populations, blacks more than likely attended school on a nonsegregated basis in all grades.

While segregation is an abhorrent policy, there were certain advantages to attending all-black schools. The black faculty and staff had been trained at predominantly black colleges, and their efforts were assumed to be "advancing the race." The environment for the students emphasized achievement and academic excellence, not hostility and antagonism. Our schools were named after black heroes—Paul Laurence Dunbar, Frederick Douglass, and Toussaint L'Ouverture. We were taught about their contribution to our struggles as well as others such as the educator activist Mary McLeod Bethune and Dorey Miller, a Pearl Harbor war hero.

On the other hand, our opportunities were curtailed by not having opportunities to enter educational programs that required continuity. For example, the selection for vocational programs at the high school level was based on participation in the prevocational program at the intermediate school. But there were no prevocational programs at the lower-level black schools, and so blacks were effectively excluded from woodworking, printing, and other vocational programs. Similarly, since instrumental music was not offered in the "colored" schools, we were

also excluded from band and orchestra. Very much by accident of sched-
uling, however, I was able to overcome this barrier, and during my high
school years became deeply involved in the instrumental music program.
By my senior year, I was the head percussionist in both band and orchestra. I was named the first student director of the pep band, which placed
me at the center of each pep rally. I was also in school plays, a member
of the National Thespian Society, and a student-body leader.

That was the public side. All these activities kept me mired in a very
precarious white world. In the evenings after the rehearsals and other
school activities, I had to guide my white classmates to the few drive-in
restaurants I thought would serve me, to save myself and them from
embarrassment. There was no question of my being served in any sit-
down restaurant.

The Pre-Greensboro Sit-ins

This was the context for 1958, the year in which I participated in the
Wichita sit-ins. The more famous sit-ins in Greensboro, North Carolina,
which are usually considered the beginning of the sit-in movement, actually came later. Thanks to the fine research of Aldon Morris in *The Origins of the Civil Rights Movement* (1984) and Martin Oppenheimer in *The
Sit-in Movement of 1960* (1989), the Wichita sit-ins at Dockum Drug
Stores have been documented. The demonstrations were organized by
Ronald Walters, then president of Wichita's NAACP Youth Council and
presently a political scientist at Howard University. My participation in
these demonstrations was more a matter of following the leadership of
my close friend, Ron Walters, than a deep personal commitment to civil
rights. On the other hand, the experience had a profound impact on me
personally. It was in these demonstrations that I was first told by a white
woman that I should return to Africa.

The policy of segregation in public accommodations in Kansas dif-
fered from that of the South where the dual society was clearly manifested. In the South, separate accommodations were to be expected; in
Kansas, African-Americans were more an afterthought, and so provision
for blacks was not systematic. For example, in train and bus stations there
were no separate waiting rooms for blacks; blacks did not have to ride in
the back of the bus or in separate railroad cars. On the other hand,
blacks could not sit on the main floor in movie theaters. White eating
establishments almost universally excluded blacks. Blacks could not stay
overnight in hotels, not even famous visitors like Duke Ellington or Joe
Louis. Once I and a group of black friends were refused admission to a

jazz concert in a hotel ballroom because the manager decided our tickets were "invalid."

These and countless other daily indignities, coupled with the ambiguity with which blacks in Kansas were treated, may explain why the very first sit-ins occurred in northern cities—Wichita, Oklahoma City, and East St. Louis, Illinois.

The Undergraduate Years

After graduating from Wichita East in the spring of 1953, I followed many of my white classmates to the University of Wichita to major in music. It may not have the reputation of Julliard or an Oberlin, but it is an outstanding music school.

My goal was to play in a major symphony orchestra or to become an orchestra conductor. My academic advisor encouraged these goals, but he told me that I would have to follow the path of Dean Dixon, a black symphonic conductor who had succeeded only by going to Europe. Later, I began to examine the extent to which there were blacks in major orchestras and found only one black, a bassist, in the Denver Symphony.

For me, the pattern of exclusion began when I was still in undergraduate school. Like most working-class college students, black and white, I needed to work during my school years. Talented white music students earned money playing in the Wichita Symphony Orchestra. I was never asked to play in that orchestra, even though I was one of the best percussionists in the school, and so I had to seek jobs outside of music.

Blacks were restricted to "Negro jobs" (janitors, porters), so I had to work outside my field as a hospital orderly, a janitor, and, for a brief spell, on a production line at Boeing. The Boeing job was on the second shift. The money was enticing, but the working hours kept me from evening practices in the drum and bugle corps. Finally, after having to take off from work several times to play band and orchestra concerts, I had no choice but to terminate the Boeing job if I was going to remain in school as a music major.

The job search during the summer following my sophomore year was just as discouraging as the summer before. This time I resolved the problem by going to Los Angeles in early July. I stayed with family, found a job at UCLA, and took conducting lessons at UCLA and timpani lessons with Charles White of the Los Angeles Philharmonic. I did not return to Wichita University that fall, although I did go back later to finish my undergraduate degree in music education.

ENTERING THE STRUGGLE

The Move to Pontiac

I was about to graduate in the summer of 1961, but it was June and still I had not found a teaching job. One of my advisors suggested that personal appearances are much more effective in the job-seeking process. So, around the Fourth of July, my wife of one year and I took off by car for the upper Midwest (Illinois, Wisconsin, Michigan, and possibly Ohio) in search of teaching opportunities. We were unsuccessful in various cities in Illinois and Wisconsin, but the public school system in Pontiac, Michigan, expressed an interest in both Joan and me. What is curious, however, is how it all happened.

We presented ourselves to the apparently white receptionist, who informed us that the district had no teaching openings.[2] When Joan insisted that we be given an interview, the receptionist relented and called the assistant personnel director. After talking to us for a few minutes at the receptionist's desk, he invited us to his office. After further discussion about our professional plans, including Joan's two years of successful teaching experience, he disappeared. In a few minutes he returned, asking if we could come back in the late afternoon to meet with the assistant superintendent for personnel. That afternoon, following another interview, which also included one of the district's black principals, we were told that we would be hired for that fall. The intimation of the assistant superintendent was clear. The primary reason we were hired was that we spoke standard English.

In the fall of 1961, I began teaching in Pontiac, then a city of about 85,000. It was the home of both Pontiac Motors, accompanied by a Fisher Body assembly plant, and General Motors Truck and Coach. This industrial city was in stark contrast to the primarily rural Kansas I had grown up in. While Wichita (approximately 250,000 people in 1960) was in competition with Kansas City, Kansas, for recognition as the largest city in the state, and while the local Chamber of Commerce promoted Wichita as the "Air Capital of the World" because it was the home of Cessna, Beechcraft, and the largest Boeing installation outside of Seattle, it was more noted for its grain elevators than the smoke stacks of auto and steel cities. Also, Kansas was a growth area. For example, by the time I was in college, the three elementary schools I attended had been replaced by new facilities. By comparison, the city of Pontiac and its schools looked very old and bedraggled. The Board of Education's main office was housed in an old factory. I appreciated the job, but I found the city depressing.

Primarily because of its manufacturing capability for producing war materials, Pontiac was profoundly affected by World War II. Before the war the city's employment record was like a roller coaster—30,000 people employed in 1929, down to 7,000 four years later, in the heart of the Depression. Employment continued to ebb and flow until it reached 27,000 by June 1941, where it remained throughout the war years. The war years also made an impact on the city's racial composition. In 1940, the city's population had about 63,000 whites and about 2,800 blacks. By 1950 the white population had risen to about 67,000, and the black population to about 6,800 (see Table 10.1). It was partially in response to this growth that the city's first public housing project was built during the 1950s, in District One, the city's south-side, overwhelmingly black district.

The three very large General Motors installations entered the decade of the 1960s in high gear with high employment. General Motors was the predominant employer in northern Oakland County, particularly Pontiac, and so its influence—and its tax base—were considerable. Blacks who were either escaping from or being pushed out of the rural South were attracted by the jobs there. Pontiac's labor needs shaped the city's population. For both black and white men, approximately 60 percent of the labor force were in the crafts and operatives category (see Table 10.2). Clearly this represents an industrial proletariat.

While there is not much difference in the percentages of black and white men in the industrial sector, for the women the opportunity structure was quite different by race. More than 40 percent of the white women tended to be employed in the clerical and sales category, while about that same percentage of black women were private household workers. Note also the disproportionate distribution of professionals and managers by race, which was certainly characteristic of that time and the basis of much of our struggle for equal opportunity in employment.

My first job was teaching fourth- and fifth-graders at the Bagley Ele-

TABLE 10.1
Population of the City of Pontiac by Race, 1940–1970

Race	1940	1950	1960	1970
White	63,000	67,000	68,600	62,900
Non-white	2,800	6,800	13,600	22,800

Note: Blacks constitute 95 percent of those listed as "non-white" in the 1940 and 1950 statistics. The 1960 and 1970 figures under "non-white" constitute the figures for "Negroes" or "Blacks."
Source: Pontiac Public Library from respective census years.

TABLE 10.2
Occupational Distribution for Employed Persons for the City
of Pontiac by Race and Gender, 1960

	Men		Women	
	White	Black	White	Black
Professional/Managerial	15.9%	3.9%	16.1%	5.3%
	(2,589)	(105)	(1,288)	(78)
Clerical/Sales	13.3	3.6	42.6	10.1
	(2,355)	(97)	(3,414)	(148)
Crafts/Operatives	59.4	64.1	14.6	15.4
	(9,657)	(1,696)	(1,168)	(225)
Private household	—	.3	6.0	40.2
	(8)	(8)	(478)	(586)
Service	6.1	12.9	20.4	26.3
	(1,005)	(341)	(1,642)	(385)
Laborer	5.2	15.1	.4	2.9
	(842)	(400)	(33)	(42)
Total	100.0	100.0	100.0	100.0
	(16,456)	(2,647)	(8,023)	(1,464)

Source: 1950, 1960 Census of the Population; *Characteristics of the Population, Michigan 1960.*

mentary School. Of about forty schools in the city, Bagley was one of six predominantly black schools on the city's south side. Because Bagley had traditionally served the community's earliest black settlers, it tended to be the most highly regarded of the black schools. However, by 1960 the "upper crust" of the black community had begun to move to residential areas newly accessible to blacks. Also, the school's boundaries had been changed so that its clientele tended to be families of newer arrivals from primarily Alabama and Tennessee, seeking work in the auto industry. Most of my students' parents had some direct connection to one or the other General Motors installation. In addition to the black working-class single-family homes served by the school, about one-third of the school's student body lived in the low-income public housing project.

The school's principal was the district's first black administrator, a highly respected man. He had a very warm and genuine regard for Pontiac's black community leaders, who had struggled to have him hired. He knew that the black ministers, one of whom had been elected to the school board against tremendous odds specifically to represent the interests of the black community, had played a key role in insisting that the district hire some black administrators. He tried to instill that same political savvy in his teachers, most of whom lived in Detroit, twenty-five miles to the south.

The staff of about twenty-four was all black, with one exception—a white male who was probably the least competent of the two or three really poor teachers on that otherwise dedicated and highly competent staff. He was not the exception, however, among other white teachers in predominantly black schools, which served as a dumping ground for incompetent white teachers. The outstanding white teachers were assigned to the higher-status white schools. I was one of four black males on that predominantly female faculty.

My fellow teachers told me that I should join the union "because they will protect your job." As blacks they clearly understood that the job protection offered by the union was more important than the so-called professionalism of the National Education Association. I followed their advice and joined the Pontiac Federation of Teachers, but not without some concern. After all, I was from a "right to work" state where unions were the biggest obstacle to blacks' getting jobs.

During my first year in Pontiac I met another teacher who was new that year, Charles Cheng. Charlie was very active with the union and almost every other cause that dealt with notions of injustice. He was instrumental in changing my perspective on unions. I had been thoroughly socialized to believe that teachers were professionals who had three months' paid vacation every summer. Teachers in Kansas worked for nine months but were paid on a twelve-month basis. I was to learn from Charlie and my fellow union members that summer for teachers was not a paid vacation but actually a "forced layoff" without pay. According to the union, the pay of Kansas' teachers was being withheld even though services had been rendered.

Joining the Movement

It was Charlie who, after participating in the March on Washington in 1963, lit the fire under a number of us to do something in the movement. A group of about ten to fifteen schoolteachers, black and white, male and female, became active in the Oakland County (Pontiac) chapter of the NAACP. We became the Pontiac version of the young Turks. We wanted change. We wanted action. We wanted integration. And we wanted it yesterday.

We began by addressing the civil rights issues of the institution we knew best, the schools. In November 1963, on behalf of the local NAACP, we brought to the attention of the school board the problem of racial segregation in the schools. Of course, the board denied that any such condition existed. In March 1964, before many of us had tenure, we organized a march to the school district offices, culminating in a rally at city hall. The march, which drew nearly two thousand people, called for an end to de facto segregation in the Pontiac schools, discrimination in employment, and segregated housing patterns.

We had hoped to have Dr. Martin Luther King, Jr., as our major speaker, but our cause was not big enough. While he was exciting to listen to, there were some aspects of his presentation that were by this time a bit disillusioning: that we should "love our enemies" and turn the other cheek; the point at which he says, "Let us pray"; and finally, the fourth, fifth, or what seemed like the tenth passing of the collection plate. We still wanted King because of his drawing power, but at that point he seemed to be just another Baptist preacher. He did, however, send us a message of support, along with other notables such as Michigan Senator Philip Hart, Roy Wilkins, executive director of the NAACP, and UAW president Walter Reuther.

Apart from our disillusionment with King, other strains were beginning to surface in our group, having to do with the movement's goals. We had selected as one of our major speakers Milton Henry, an attorney, a life member of the NAACP, a trusted friend of Malcolm X, and a former city commissioner for the city of Pontiac. Then, after inviting him to speak, we learned that rather than demanding integration he would probably espouse the separatist views of his newly adopted Black Muslim philosophy. But the march was being sponsored by the NAACP, which sought "racial integration" as the only legitimate goal. The president of the local NAACP chapter, another attorney, was able to coax a more moderate line from Henry in which he made clear our degraded treatment but did not issue a call for separatism.

By this time there was a considerable sentiment for a separatist politics. The Reverend Albert Cleage of Detroit's Shrine of the Black Madonna, like Malcolm, took the leadership in helping us realize that no matter what blacks did, it was never enough. Making yourself socially acceptable to whites did not stop discrimination. More education did not stop discrimination. Moral appeals were often brutally dosed with firehoses. Also like Malcolm X, Cleage would argue that that a Democrat was simply a Dixiecrat in disguise.

The idea of an independent black political party was being viewed as a viable and necessary course of action. To better make our case politically, the militant black leadership in the Detroit area formed the Freedom Now party. Our march provided a fertile setting for signing petitions to place the new party on the ballot. Reverend Cleage, who was named the party's gubernatorial candidate, said of this effort:

> We have got to do something else. . . . We have got to take independent
> black political action. We have got to mobilize the masses of Negro
> people into an independent black political movement. The masses of
> Negro people have got to understand that this is a power struggle, and
> we have got to bring to bear in this power struggle our mass political
> strength. (Conot 1974, 528)

Later, there was a national effort at independent political action through
the National Black Political Assembly. The Freedom Now party, however,
failed to get enough votes to become a more permanent fixture in Michigan politics.

In addition to having the city's largest civil rights demonstration ever,
1964 was an eventful year in other ways. We "young Turks" registered
voters in that presidential election year. We ran membership drives. We
organized more demonstrations protesting numerous instances of racial
injustice. My major responsibility was to chair the chapter's political action committee. Our door-to-door registration campaign in the black
community was highly successful. Our job was made easier by Barry
Goldwater, who, in his nomination acceptance speech, had endorsed
right-wing extremism and threatened to use "the bomb." Because of the
success of our local campaign, I was appointed political action committee
chairman for the statewide Conference of NAACP Branches. I was following in the footsteps of my close associate, Charles Cheng, who had been
appointed administrative aide to the chairman of the State Conference of
NAACP Branches—in other words, statewide organizer for the NAACP.

Then Milton Henry convinced our group to go to Detroit's King So-
lomon Baptist Church to hear Malcolm X deliver his "The Ballot or the
Bullet" speech. For me it was one of the highlights of the year. I had
heard of Malcolm X when I first moved to Detroit and I found his labeling of whites as devils to be extreme, if not absurd. Many of my associates, particularly my fellow musicians, were certainly not devils.

By 1964, however, Malcolm had been released from the strict bonds
of Elijah Muhammad's very narrow, almost reactionary cult. Also, by 1964
his broader, less sectarian, and more secular perspective of black nationalism had a broader appeal to more progressive black masses. Hearing
him in person was a profound experience. His message was revolutionary—he exposed so many truths about how and why a system of white
racism kept blacks in their subordinated position.

That afternoon he clearly spelled out what it meant to be black in
America. He informed us that we were not Americans but victims of
Americanism, otherwise why were we catching so much hell? For us, the
American Dream was really an American nightmare. Malcolm's message

was based on hard facts. He was not diplomatic, he was not polite. The truth he spoke was bold and revolutionary. At one point in the speech he directly placed the oppression of blacks with the government:

> You and I in America are faced not with a segregationist conspiracy but with a government conspiracy. . . . The same government that you go abroad to fight for and die for is the government that is in a conspiracy to deprive you of your voting rights, deprive you of your economic opportunities, deprive you of decent housing, deprive you of a decent education. . . . It is the government itself, the government of America, that is responsible for the oppression and exploitation and degradation of black people in this country. . . . This government has failed the Negro. This so-called democracy has failed the Negro. And all these white liberals have definitely failed the Negro.

At another point he provided an insight that history had obscured:

> We're justified in seeking civil rights . . . because all we're doing there is trying to collect on our investment. Our mothers and fathers invested sweat and blood. Three hundred and ten years we worked in this country without a dime in return—I mean without a *dime* in return. You let the white man walk around here talking about how rich this country is, but you never stop to think how it got rich so quick. It got rich because you made it rich.

The major theme of the speech was its revelations of how blacks were being deceived by white organizations of political power—the Republicans, the Democratic party, and its southern wing, the Dixiecrats.

The flip side of the Malcolm X experience in 1964 found its expression in the internal politics of the local NAACP chapter. Even though we "young Turks" had been the major force in carrying out the NAACP's program locally, from demonstrations to registering voters to successful membership drives, the "old guard" defeated us overwhelmingly in the elections for chapter offices at the end of that year. They did it by charging that we were not "respectable" enough to meet with members of "the white power structure." To discredit our standing within the chapter, they constantly reminded everyone that the white members of our group still slept "on the other side of Telegraph Road" outside the city and outside the black community.

In the fall of 1964, the school district offered me a different position, instrumental music teacher. I accepted the job, which took me to the all-white north end of town, but by this time music was no longer central to my career. My main interest had become the movement, and the new assignment did not slow my activities. Furthermore, my students at

Bagley had served as an inspiration and cause for my commitment out-side the classroom. We had continued to challenge the quality of school-ing for black students.

The PACE Days

Shortly after the NAACP chapter defeat, Pontiac's "young Turks" formed our own grassroots organization, the Progressive Action Commit-tee for Equality (PACE). Like many other grassroots groups around the country, we felt limited by guidelines and restrictions of national organi-zations. One example was the threatened nationwide demonstrations against General Motors for its discriminatory hiring practices of blacks. After considering direct action based upon national agenda, the old guard of the Pontiac NAACP chapter voted against demonstrations at any of the General Motors facilities. They had a fundraising dance instead.

It was in this context that we formed PACE. We modeled ourselves after the Congress of Racial Equality (CORE), but did not formally join them for fear of another national office dictating our limits. These were the days of James Farmer and Floyd McKissick, not the later Roy Innes opportunist period. Farmer and McKissick carried out principled strug-gles to improve the conditions of African Americans, Farmer advocating integration and McKissick advocating black power; both were respected by movement activists. Roy Innes, on the other hand, has been the activ-ists' version of black reactionaries like Thomas Sowell and Walter Will-iams. Our association with CORE coincided with its transition from the goal of integration to community organization. While we were still funda-mentally opposed to segregation, we began to see the necessity for black self-determination.

By this time we had also become the leadership of the teachers union, which meant we had access to the mimeograph machine for our newsletter, "The Pacemaker." In it we challenged the charter revision of the city commission, which, in effect, disenfranchised blacks. We wrote about Selma, the "police riot" in Watts, and the city's racist housing pol-icy. We changed the course of the city, which was only interested in allowing mall magnate Alfred Taubman to build his mall downtown, to the exclusion of much-needed housing. We blocked the building of the mall. A number of housing complexes were built, but downtown Pontiac remains a sore spot for the city, partly because Pontiac is considered by fellow developers to be Taubman's city.

The union provided more than just a mimeograph machine. With Cheng and me on the executive committee, the Pontiac Federation of Teachers took up the civil rights agenda, supposedly consistent with the national union's strong stance in favor of civil rights, as exemplified in its expulsion of its segregated locals in the South and its funding of the Freedom Schools in Mississippi. While 90 percent of the district's black teachers belonged to the union and supported our actions, the civil rights emphasis cost the local many of its white members. In fact, when the collective bargaining election took place that next year, what had been a strong local went down to an overwhelming defeat at the hands of the Pontiac Education Association.

As the chairman of PACE, I was soon identified as a spokesperson for the black community and was offered jobs by both the federal poverty program and the Michigan Civil Rights Commission. All the other leaders of PACE were also offered good job opportunities.

IN THE MOVEMENT'S TRANSITION

The Michigan Civil Rights Commission

In November 1966, I became the first regional director of the Battle Creek office of the Michigan Civil Rights Commission. Twelve such offices were opened around the state. The new directors were a group of young, relatively bright activists who all had the attribute of being "articulate," as we were often told. Our job was to seek changes in race relations affirmatively, by convincing community leadership of the need for change. This meant being "in tune" with the "power structure" and the civil rights community.

Shortly after beginning the job, I discovered firsthand a very deep class cleavage within the black community. The issue was the site for a proposed private-sector rent-supplement housing project. Then (and probably now too) housing for many blacks in Battle Creek was atrocious. The acquired site for the rent-supplement housing was not far from a public housing project. The local Urban League and NAACP opposed the site—and therefore the housing—because it would increase segregation. The poor people who would have benefited from the housing did not care where it was located. Ultimately, the Civil Rights Commission, against my recommendation, sided with the Urban League and NAACP.

With the exception of integration issues, Battle Creek was a much more conservative community than Pontiac, and considerably smaller, about 45,000. It was affectionately known as "Kellogg's Plantation." The influence of the Kellogg family completely dominated the city and everyone was subservient to that legacy. The black community was quite different from the industrial working class of Pontiac. Forty percent of Pontiac's blacks but only about 15 percent of Battle Creek's blacks were employed in manufacturing. Nearly 40 percent of Battle Creek's blacks were employed in professional services and public administration. The high percentage of blacks in these higher status categories can be attributed to the three federal government installations located there. The city was the site of a major Veterans Administration hospital, Custer Air Force Base, and a more general civil service facility, as well as a federally funded Job Corps training center.

Pontiac had the tradition of United Auto Workers union militancy; Battle Creek was a much more genteel community. Many of the city's blacks were federal civil servants who tended to be apolitical, even complacent on issues of race. This, plus their more middle-class lifestyle, militated against the more militant black power ideology that was sweeping the nation by the late 1960s.

Another factor that probably inhibited militancy in Battle Creek was the history of the white community. Battle Creek is the headquarters for the Seventh Day Adventists. For that religious denomination, confrontation is totally inappropriate. An example of the community's low tolerance for confrontation was the negative reaction I received, from both blacks and whites, for writing a letter to the editor criticizing the director of the high school's interracial choir for selecting "Dixie" for their performance at an Urban League dinner.

Apart from my official duties in the movement through the Civil Rights Commission, I was somewhat active in the antiwar campaigns. Charles Cheng and I participated in the 1967 spring mobilization demonstration in New York. This was a mind-boggling experience for me. Standing in the Central Park staging area, I was within fifty feet of that burning of the American flag which was documented by *Life* magazine. Growing up in Kansas during the McCarthy era, I had been taught such acts were treasonous. Stokely Carmichael, then chair of SNCC, called Secretary of State Dean Rusk a buffoon, Secretary of Defense Robert McNamara a fool, and President Lyndon Johnson something equally derisive. He said the contradictory details surrounding the war were worse than "a 'credibility gap'—hell, they're lying!" I had not heard such disrespect for people in high office. But the most startling experience was witnessing the last contingent of the march: a huge throng proudly marching in cadence to a very hip drum beat and carrying a big red banner: COMMUNIST PARTY USA. For someone who had had to sign loyalty oaths to work in the library as an undergraduate, this was truly an unbelievable sight.

The National Conference on Black Power

I insisted on attending the Black Power Conference in Newark, New Jersey, July 20–23, 1967. On June 10 Newark was racked by what was called a civil disturbance. The state police and National Guard troops were not withdrawn until July 17, just a few days before the conference was to start. Since to most officials "black power" meant violence, emotions surrounding the conference were, to say the least, tense. The police patrolled the area, shotguns in clear sight.

In spite of the shotguns and implied threats, conference participants in suits, dashikis, and paramilitary uniforms filled the hallways of Trinity Cathedral House and the Military Park Hotel. A Who's Who of the progressive black movement was there: H. Rap Brown of SNCC; Ron Karenga of US; Imamu Amiri Baraka of the Newark Spirit House; Jesse Jackson of SCLC—the list is quite long. It is also interesting to note that Roy Wilkins, Whitney Young, and Dr. King were not there. Their absence was based on two basic issues: first, black power was an assertion for black self-determination and a rejection of integration and white liberal leadership; second, black power did not reject violence but, following Malcolm X, advocated freedom "by any means necessary." Roy Wilkins of the NAACP and Whitney Young of the National Urban League were spokespersons for organizations dominated by white liberals. King's SCLC program was based on the rejection of violence in favor of nonviolence. All three organizations were heavily dependent upon funding from predominantly white mainstream sources.

That Sunday morning when the plenary session was considering the resolutions, the master of ceremonies requested that all the Michigan delegates step into the hall for a brief meeting. There, we got the news: "It's going down in Detroit." The immediate responses were, "Right on! We're tired of this shit!" The news was sketchy, and soon we were back to the business at hand, conference resolutions. There were calls for various aspects of black control of black institutions and for black self-determination in general. The delegates enthusiastically and unanimously adopted a resolution "to consider a proposal to explore the possibility of negotiating for a five-star homeland for black Americans."

When we landed at Detroit Metropolitan Airport that night, however, reality set in: the pilot announced that entrance into Detroit was prohibited because of the curfew. Watching television that night, we saw the enormity of the problem. Because of the many complaints of police brutality during the "riot," I and other members of the commission staff became observers in the precinct houses. Since the rest of the state, from Pontiac to Benton Harbor, was having its own conflagration, we found ourselves also trying to negotiate humane treatment in other parts of the state.

Over the course of my tenure as director of the Battle Creek office, much of my work centered on the schools. Since there were many sincere white educators who did not understand blacks' complaints about discrimination in the schools, I organized a panel of students to talk to teachers about their school experiences. The five or six students ranged from a kid who had been diagnosed by the schools as a paranoid schizophrenic, to the black president of an overwhelmingly white senior class at the high school. There was some defensiveness on the part of the teachers but, on the whole, the panels fulfilled their goals. I was quite startled the next year, however, when the student who most matched white middle-class expectations—the senior class president—made the cover of both *Newsweek* and *Time* as he, among other black student protestors, exited Cornell's Straight Hall armed to the teeth.

My association with the Civil Rights Commission had been tenuous almost from the beginning. The housing issue had been just the first of several differences. The more serious parting of the ways took root shortly after King's assassination. In response to the assassination, a group of black junior high school students wore black armbands to school. The white principal accused them of inciting to riot and suspended them all. Parents and many others in the black community protested.

Several poverty program staffers and I helped them to direct their grievances toward the real decision makers, the school board. This was the era of the demand for participatory democracy. And participatory democracy in this case meant that parents should have a voice in the disciplining of their children. Someone, possibly me, suggested that they should read page 60 of the *Report of the National Advisory Commission on Civil Disorders*, which described a meeting of the Newark school board that lasted until 5:30 A.M., when the board rendered a favorable decision on a demand raised by the black community.

The Battle Creek parents' group went to the school board meeting and demanded the principal's ouster. When the meeting adjourned at its normal time around 9:30 or 10:00 P.M., the principal had not been fired. The group staged a lock-in, and no one, including the school board, was allowed to leave the room. The board later requested that the commission investigate my involvement in "holding the school board hostage for over two and one-half hours." Though the investigation, months later, exonerated me, my effectiveness as a director had been lost.

POST-MOVEMENT DEVELOPMENT
On the Graduate School

After my experience on the Pontiac Schools and the Civil Rights Commission, I no longer wanted a job in which someone else was going to tell me what to think. Academia seemed the best alternative. I began work on a master's degree in sociology at Wayne State. There I was introduced to Marx and Marxism by Carleton "Wally" Smith. The text for our theory course was Irving Zeitlin's *Ideology and the Development of Sociology Theory* (1968). I also took Smith's special topics course on reform and revolution. But the fact that Marx was white strongly suggested, at that time, that he could be only partially right. Among fellow black-power activists, it was often argued that Marx condoned colonialism and slavery as advances for a backward Africa.

In the fall of 1970 I entered Stanford in a program modeled after Harvard's Kennedy-King Memorial Scholarship. This was post–Kent State but still in the midst of the student movements. This was the era when Bruce Franklin, a tenured English professor, became a martyr of the left after he was fired in 1972 for supposedly inciting students to riot. I became a leader of the black graduate student caucus. Several of us risked degrees by challenging the school in various ways. There were some casualties. But by this time, I was a long way from both Detroit and Kansas and I had two children. My goal was clear: I was not leaving there without a Ph.D.

My development toward Marxist sociology took a rather circuitous route. For my dissertation I investigated the impact of racial (that is, black) consciousness on black-white interaction in small groups. Since racial consciousness, as a concept, had no scientific standing, I likened it to class consciousness, which took me back to Marx and works such as John Leggett's *Class, Race, and Labor* (1968).

I had long since come to believe that integration was not a viable strategy for improving the lives of blacks. Though I was still clinging to a nationalist ideology, the prospect of black control of black institutions seemed remote. In fact, the movement was turning away from U.S. conditions and toward Africa and Pan-Africanism, following this logic track: We must aid in Africa's liberation so that a strong Africa can make the United States treat African-Americans justly. I knew that strategy would have no popular base. The schism between the nationalists and the Marxists in the African Liberation Support Committee triggered a major debate among progressive black scholars. I was heavily influenced by a fellow Stanford graduate student, Ron Bailey, and his collaborator, sociologist Gerald Mc-Worter (Abdul Alkalimat). They endorsed the Marxist side of the debate—class rather than race.

Return to the Community: Wayne State

I returned to Detroit in the fall of 1974, to join the sociology department at Wayne State. The city had changed dramatically. Four years earlier I had left a very race-conscious city where black associations with whites were suspect, at the very least. I returned to a town where jazz concerts at a downtown hotel drew mixed audiences—mainly white, to be sure, but with a clear and heavy black presence. I left a city of politically conscious citizens. I returned to a city where people asked, after being introduced to someone, "What's your sign?"

Much of my development as a Marxist sociologist grew out of a Marxist study group in which I was involved during my first year on the Wayne State faculty. I found that some of my activist friends in the community had changed to a class view of the world, as I was doing. Over in black studies, where I had an overload appointment, we began to seriously debate issues of race and class. Ron Bailey and Gerald McWorter came in to conduct workshops. The more I studied the primacy of the political economy, the less relevant my dissertation on racial attitudes seemed.

Tenure became a struggle for me, as for many others, particularly black scholars. After I had been in the department for four years, the chair suggested that I apply for promotion early; he was sure I would get it. The department supported my application by recommending promotion. The College of Liberal Arts said no. In the sixth year, with more publications to my credit, I applied again. This time the department committee—the same group that supported me two years earlier—would not recommend me for tenure and promotion. Because of the chair's strong support, the committee relented and recommended me for tenure but not promotion. This denial of promotion continued and was later coupled with the denial of tenure to Shirley Nuss. It became obvious that these denials were based on what we studied, race and gender, and the perspective we employed to study these phenomena. A key member of the tenure and promotion committee argued that no Marxist should ever have tenure.

The Arena of Electoral Politics

When I returned from a postdoctoral fellowship at Johns Hopkins during the 1980–1981 academic year, my wife was in the midst of running for a seat on the Pontiac City Council. Her opponent was a white female who had minimal qualifications but, astonishingly, the support of five black incumbents. In spite of this, my wife received about 80 percent of the black vote (she needed 90 percent to win). That campaign experience whetted my appetite for a return to Democratic party politics; I had not participated actively since the 1960s. That led me in 1984 to Jesse Jackson's Rainbow Coalition.

Many local elected officials "shared the stage" with Jackson when he made his campaign swings through Pontiac, but only one of them endorsed him. Because I was one of the few *active* Democrats who supported Jackson and had taken a leadership role in the Rainbow Coalition, I was elected delegate to the Democratic national convention. That experience has provided me several papers on what Jesse's candidacy means for blacks and working-class America.

IN SEARCH OF A RACE AND CLASS SYNTHESIS

On Issues of Race and Class: Where We Stand

In the spring of 1978 I was invited to review William J. Wilson's book *The Declining Significance of Race* for the journal *School Review*. I knew that the general thesis of the book, and especially its title, would be controversial, but my review was generally favorable. I noted that, regardless of its flaws and occasional overstatements (such as his claim that 25 percent of blacks were at that time "middle class"), Wilson made an important contribution by placing the "race question" squarely in the context of the political economy, and away from heavy reliance on the psyche in understanding issues of race. The black leadership of the profession lined up to condemn him through the Association of Black Sociologists (Willie 1979). I found myself the lone dissenter. In fact, the bashing of Bill Wilson has become central to the work of many black sociologists.

What they fail to understand is that there are no "race-only" solutions to the situation of black people. If we want decent health care for all black Americans, we must understand that it is not going to happen in the absence of decent health care for *all* Americans. If we want to see all black Americans employed, that will happen only when we have employment for *all* Americans. Condemnations of racism, no matter how loud or how eloquent, will not provide fundamental change in the lives of black folk. Our criticism of Wilson should be not that he went too far but that he did not go far enough.

While black sociologists need to understand that slavery is really a class question, the (white) Marxist sociologists need to understand the role of race as an obstacle to working-class solidarity and working-class struggle *in both theory and practice*. If, however, we take the concrete actions of the Marxist Section of the American Sociological Association as an example, we find no real interest in untangling questions of race. For the 1981 Toronto meetings, James Geschwender asked me to organize a session entitled "Race, Class, and National Oppression" as a part of the program for the Marxist Section. The session was scheduled to immediately follow a section business meeting. When the time arrived at which the business meeting was scheduled to be over, there was still some business not completed. Consequently, rather than attend the session dealing with the question of "race" or national oppression, the section members found another room and continued their business meeting. A year earlier, *The Insurgent Sociologist* devoted an issue (Fall 1980) to the memory of Walter Rodney on the race question without a single black contributor!

Summary and Conclusions

My choice of title for this essay was deliberate: "The Making of a Class-Conscious 'Race Man.'" I see no basic possibility for justice for black people in a society where inequality is a virtue and the society simply looks for ways to legitimize that inequality. Society says, "They are black," or "They are female," or "They did not stay in school long enough," or offers a myriad other rationalizations that "explain" why some have many homes while others have none. As long as we have capitalism we will have racism, and as long as we have capitalism we will have sexism, and it goes without saying that as long as we have capitalism we will have class oppression. If on the other hand, everyone had essentially the same privileges, the material basis for these ideologies would be eliminated.

That is the "class" side of my commitment as an activist scholar. But I am also a "race man," struggling to change concretely the condition in which black people find themselves, as "race men" have historically done. It must be recognized, however, that in the absence of socialism, or a society organized around the principles of equality, no struggle for "racial equality" can succeed. By the same token, a divided working class that sees no basis for commonality beyond the color question is doomed to continued subordination.

NOTES

1. Frances Beal, in her article "Slave of a Slave No More: Black Women in Struggle," argues that black women face the "double jeopardy" of race and gender oppression as well as that of working-class oppression (*The Black Scholar* 1, no. 6 [March 1975]).

2. When the color barriers began to fall, African-Americans who were hired in what had been traditionally white jobs were usually very light-skinned or nearly white, overqualified, or both. My wife and I later became friends with this secretary who originally provided us the opportunity.

REFERENCES

Conot, Robert. 1974. *An American Odyssey.* New York: William Morrow.

DuBois, W. E. B. 1962. *John Brown.* New York: International Publishers.

Leggett, John. 1968. *Class, Race, and Labor.* New York: Oxford University Press.

Marx, Karl. (1887) 1967. *Capital.* New York: International Publishers.

Morris, Aldon. 1984. *The Origins of the Civil Rights Movement.* New York: Free Press.

Oppenheimer, Martin. (1963) 1989. *The Sit-in Movement of 1960.* New York: Carlson.

Rawley, James A. 1969. *Race and Politics: "Bleeding Kansas" and the Coming Civil War.* Philadelphia: J. B. Lippincott.

Willhelm, Sidney. 1983. *Black in a White America.* Cambridge, Mass.: Schenkman Publishing Company.

Willie, Charles Vert. 1979. *Caste and Class Controversy.* Bayside N.Y.: General Hall.

Wilson, William Julius. 1978. *The Declining Significance of Race.* Chicago: University of Chicago Press.

Zeitlin, Irving. 1968. *Ideology and the Development of Sociology Theory.* Englewood Cliffs, N.J.: Prentice-Hall.

Chapter 11

Living and Learning Sociology: The Unorthodox Way

Hardy T. Frye

WHEN I QUIT high school at age seventeen and left home during the summer of 1956 to join the U.S. Army, I had no idea what lay ahead. I thought maybe I would make a career as a professional soldier. I never imagined I would become a professor of sociology; in fact, I didn't know what sociology was. My path to becoming a Berkeley Ph.D. and a tenured professor of sociology at the University of California was a route very different from that of most Americans trained to become sociologists.

My intellectual growth and political development have gone through many stages—growing up in Tuskegee, Alabama, serving in the army, moving to California and becoming a political activist, joining the civil rights movement and being a participant in the 1964 Mississippi Summer project for voter registration, and receiving a Ph.D. in sociology from the University of California at Berkeley. From the time I left Tuskegee, a small, rural, mostly black town, my experiences have been, more often than not, unlike those of the black world in which I grew up. My life has been a continuing adventure through the prisms of changing American race relations. My study of sociology has provided me with various perspectives through which I could make sense out of my life. Sociology also provided me with analytic tools to engage in critical thinking about American society in general and the black experience in particular.

EARLY YEARS

Growing up in Tuskegee, Alabama

Growing up in Alabama in the years between the beginning of World War II and the growth of the modern civil rights movement meant experiencing the last vestiges of the Deep South's traditional racial segregation. Interestingly enough, although racism existed all around the Tuskegee area, it had little direct impact on me and my peers. In fact, we were somewhat hidden from the raw racism that most black youth in the

South experienced. What we did have was the experience of class difference: In Tuskegee there was definite class segregation within the black community based on educational level and job status.

For all practical purposes, I grew up in an all-black world. Neither of my parents were educated beyond elementary school. My father worked at the Veterans Administration hospital, at the time the only all-black VA hospital in the country. Most of Tuskegee's blacks worked either at the hospital or at the town's other black institution: Tuskegee Institute. This allowed them to be independent of the small local white community for employment but not to escape the class differences that existed within the black community.

Those class differences determined, among other things, where I went to school. The black primary and secondary schools were informally, unofficially segregated by class. It "just happened" that all the black kids whose parents were lower and working class went to a different elementary school from the black kids whose parents held various college degrees. Chambliss Children's House was located on the Tuskegee Institute campus, and most of the children of the professional staff of the college and the VA hospital went there. The children of the other employees of these two institutions attended the other two black public schools. I don't recall any formal rules assigning us to a certain school, but if you were from my side of town you knew what school you were likely to attend and it wasn't Chambliss Children's House. As a sociologist with the advantage of hindsight, I would now speculate that Chambliss was unofficially designated the public school of the black middle class and its enrollment policy was influenced and supported by informal class sanctions that were never explicitly spelled out in public documents.

This segregation by class existed in other areas as well. For example, it was rare for someone from my neighborhood to date a young lady from the community of the educated elite. Many social functions held in the homes of the elites were segregated by class. The forthcoming civil rights movement would provide some challenge to this class segregation.

I do not mean to suggest that racism was magically absent from Tuskegee. The local white community was only 5 to 10 percent of the total population, yet it controlled the municipal government, the agricultural economy, and all the small local businesses. And they viewed all blacks equally. Some studies (Dollard 1949) suggest that even where there is racial oppression, the small elite group is treated differently from the masses of the oppressed group, but this was not the case in Tuskegee. Possibly because most of Tuskegee's blacks (both elite and working class) had secure employment and were not dependent on whites for their livelihood, the white power structure did not make overt distinctions in favor of the elite: *All* segments of the black community were subject to racism.

So, even though class differences were very real in my community, manifesting themselves in terms of the neighborhood you lived in, the school your children attended, the church you attended, where you worked and the type of job you held, and whom you socialized with—our common oppression overrode class differences in many cases. We shared among ourselves the few public facilities open to blacks. All black youth, regardless of class, were allowed to use the recreational facilities of the college and the VA hospital.

Thus racism forced me into a relationship with members of another class. I identified with a major black institution; I interacted with black college students. I was able to experience and observe many of the positive features of a black elite: a strong emphasis on education and becoming a professional, strong emphasis on the family, a unique but interesting brand of black pride, a nice home in a nice neighborhood, membership and participation in black organizations, and fierce belief in the right to become registered voters. Perhaps most important to my community socialization was having black professionals as role models: teachers, doctors, nurses, and many others whom I saw performing a variety of jobs at Tuskegee. It was not possible to find their counterpart in such concentrated numbers in other urban or rural areas of Alabama. Overall, I believe growing up in such an atmosphere skewed the way I reflected upon Tuskegee's local race relations, and this in turn has influenced my view of race relations as a professional sociologist. In my young world, most of the doers and thinkers were black people.

The U.S. Army

Dropping out of high school was very common in my peer group—in fact it was almost a rite of passage for the males—and so I did it too. In 1956, I voluntarily joined the army. I was an electrician in a field hospital.

Enlisting in the military represented for working-class and lower-class southern black youth a sure way to see the world. It helped you "become a man." But, more important, we thought the military would open the door to the job market, particularly in the public sector. It would allow us to go to school on the GI Bill and purchase a home. There was no doubt in our minds that the military was the way to go.

I joined up at the very time the army was working out its newly adopted desegregation policy. For example, on the southern post where

I was stationed for a short time, when we used public transportation we could integrate the bus on the post. But when that same bus left the post, we had to seat ourselves by the local segregation seating standard.

Going from a mostly all-black world to a recently desegregrated U.S. Army took some adjustment. I had to confront white people on a daily basis, and for the first time experienced racial hostility far beyond what I had known as a child. Race relations in Tuskegee had not prepared me for the ethnic and religious bigotry that I would observe occurring daily in the U.S. Army. For the first time, I heard anti-Semitic and anti-Hispanic remarks. Sometimes those statements were made directly to Jewish and Mexican soldiers in my outfit, but most of the time private remarks were made to me by white soldiers. On several occasions I saw a Jewish soldier (who as a child had been in one of Hitler's camps) pushed around and sometimes physically abused by an Irish sergeant who constantly harassed him.

Three years in the U.S. Army brought me into direct confrontation with white soldiers, often forcing me to choose sides, particularly for socializing after duty hours. Actual fights with white soldiers were infrequent because the army had low tolerance for such behavior and took quick and decisive action to prevent it, passing out demerits and various other forms of punishments. However, verbal confrontation was a constant problem. These experiences further broadened my understanding of American race relations, as it became clear to me that racial hostility was not restricted to black–white relations.

Los Angeles—The Big City

After the army, I moved to Los Angeles, where I lived for the next four years. This was my first significant relationship with urban blacks. My contacts with whites were always in a work relationship, supervisor to subordinate. I always held low-paying jobs: a laborer at a sheet-metal factory in south Los Angeles, ward orderly at the VA hospital in Long Beach, and mail carrier and truck driver at the local Compton post office. All three of these experiences allowed me to watch how white employees and bosses dealt with race relations on the job during a period of growing civil rights unrest. The civil rights movement was hardly ever discussed between whites and blacks on the job. The black workers tended to gripe among themselves, never really challenging their supervisors.

Blacks always held the lowest-paying jobs with the least status, and white in nonsupervisory positions rarely worked alongside black employees. The one exception was the white students who held part-time jobs in the post office during their college careers.

Through my contact with these white students, I became interested in furthering my own education. I asked how I could do this without losing my job, and the local postmaster told me that if I wanted to go back to school I would have to quit. I went to see a (white) career counselor and was told I should go to a trade school. So I enrolled in Los Angeles Trade Technical College, where I studied for a year to become a baker.

These early years in Los Angeles brought me into closer contact with the urban black world, of which I had little understanding: ways of acting on the street, crime, densely living in black neighborhoods, and various lifestyles. Living and working in Compton and south Los Angeles brought me into daily contact with street life, confrontations between the police and local black residents, and vices of all sorts. I was beginning to witness a growing black hostility toward whites who came into the area, including social workers, police, merchants, and even white people just looking for a "good time."

GROWING POLITICAL ACTIVISM

The civil rights movement was growing around the country. During the 1960 Presidential election season, I received my major baptism in political activism on a picket line. The Democratic party had its national convention at the Los Angeles Sports Arena, and the local chapter of the Congress of Racial Equality (CORE) established a picket line in front of the building to pressure the party into taking a strong stand in support of the civil rights movement. Being an active CORE member brought me into a growing comradeship with mostly white middle-class people and a few members of the black middle class, all of them well educated.

My new involvement in political activism felt very strange to me for two reasons. First, at this point in my intellectual and political growth, I didn't really understand either the political world or the civil rights movement. Most of what I knew about the movement came from black publications such as *Ebony* and *Jet*. Second, the civil rights activities in which I became more and more gradually involved took me away from the black urban world where I had begun to find some comfort, because most of the political activists in Los Angeles were middle-class whites.

With these new political comrades, I engaged in long debates about strategies and tactics one should use in pushing for civil rights. There was a lot of discussion on the philosophical bases for the political tactics of nonviolence and the morality of this growing movement. Perhaps the most important thing for me at the time was that I had begun to move in circles where these issues were not only debated but in many cases *acted upon.*

In 1963, I participated in a sit-in at the state capitol in support of a fair-housing bill then before the state legislature. This experience kept me in a continuing dialogue with fellow participants, state workers, and observers. For the first time, I found myself having to defend my participation in a demonstration, as we debated the legitimacy of the tactic we were using. The intellectual discussions caused me to seek out more information about past struggles by black Americans, and I began to do the background reading that would later become a pathway for my training in sociology (Franklin 1948; Frazier 1951; Mills 1959a, 1959b).

The fair-housing bill passed, the first in the nation (it was later overturned at the ballot box). We in the Los Angeles CORE chapter knew we had played an important role in this legislation. This encounter started me on the road to both becoming a committed political activist and pursuing my intellectual interests. In my private life, meanwhile, I was dealing with a separation from my wife and an inability to find work.

I had done well in baking school (top 5 percent of my class), but when I tried to find a job in the industry, from which blacks had been excluded, I was given the runaround. Potential employers said I had to be in the union to get a job, the union said I couldn't become a member until I had a job lined up.

I decided to migrate to northern California, where I heard that a major baking firm in a place called Berkeley was willing to hire blacks. However, my sojourn took me first to Sacramento.

Sharpening My Critical Thinking Skills

Sacramento proved to be of utmost importance in my political and intellectual development. There I got the chance to observe firsthand the workings of California politics (Sacramento is the state capital). And it was in Sacramento that I completed work for a B.A. degree in sociology, and became a leader in the local chapters of CORE and Friends of the Student Nonviolent Coordinating Committee (SNCC).

I never planned to go to Sacramento. I was on my way to Berkeley in early summer of 1963 when my car broke down. I didn't have enough money to get it fixed, so I started looking for work. I applied unsuccessfully for baking positions in the local baking industry and finally found a job working at the Greyhound bus station as a shipping clerk. I quickly immersed myself in civil rights activities, and that fall I enrolled in the local junior college, Sacramento City College.

My academic training and political radicalization began at Sacramento City College. Two professors from Sacramento State College, a sociologist and a historian, had much to do with my becoming engrossed in critical thinking and intellectual debates on subjects that ranged from the contemporary civil rights movement to the 1917 Russian Revolution. The history professor became one of my closest friends during the summer of 1963. He gave me a job as his driver because he had been stripped of his California driving license. As we traveled from Sacramento to Berkeley and other cities in the San Francisco Bay area, we had long Socratic conversations on a variety of topics. Encounters with graduate students and state workers similarly broadened my intellectual understanding of the larger context in which the growing civil rights movement could be understood. I emerged as a leader in the local civil rights movement, which gave me entry rights into the local political activist camps, which included members of the state legislature. I was now in constant dialogue with middle-class scholars and politicians, and I spent a lot of time rethinking my own positions.

You Can Go Home Again

During the summer of 1964, I journeyed to Mississippi to take part in the project known as Mississippi Summer. The project was sponsored by the Council of Federated Organizations, an umbrella organization of national civil rights groups including CORE, SNCC, the National Association for the Advancement of Colored People (NAACP), and the National Urban League. I was going home, but it was clear that I was returning to a southern reality about which I knew little.

Even before my cadre of volunteers could enter the state, we were confronted with racist violence. One of the summer volunteers and two civil rights veterans had just been released from jail in Philadelphia, Mississippi, and were now missing. They would be found dead about a month later, buried in a gravel pit.

My experiences in the South strengthened my commitment to political activism. I became a member of SNCC and did political work in northern Mississippi; western Tennessee; Jackson, Mississippi; and Selma, Alabama. I was involved in the debates about the direction of the movement and the strategies and tactics that should be used. My experience with Mississippi, the hardest of all southern states to crack, with its tremendous resistance to civil rights and the high level of violence toward black citizens and all civil rights workers, pushed me further in the direction of radicalism.

I had little faith in our ability to challenge Mississippi's racism through negotiation. I began to believe that only radical activities could change Mississippi. I became involved in direct action and participated in nonviolent picket lines and sit-ins. In addition, I began to organize in the black communities. We helped organize blacks into the Mississippi Freedom Democratic party to show that black Mississippians should be allowed to participate in the local, statewide, and national political arenas. Local party officials, by refusing to let them register to vote, had denied blacks access. We began to encourage blacks to build political organizations to challenge institutions where the black community was getting shortchanged—school boards, county agricultural boards, and so forth. Many of us in SNCC began to branch out in our civil rights activities. I attempted to organize people into farm cooperatives in Marshall County and unions in Tupelo, Mississippi. We tried to get black workers to talk about starting unions in the plants or mills where they worked.

I continued to do this type of civil rights work in northern Mississippi and western Tennessee over the next two or three years, periodically returning to Sacramento to school for a time, and then traveling back to the South. Whenever I was in Sacramento, I worked with the local Friends of SNCC chapter to help raise funds to carry on the struggle in the South. Primarily my job was giving talks about southern racism and political oppression, and usually I commented that the federal government appeared to be as much on the side of the oppressors as the oppressed. Many people in the audiences had no understanding of the South or Mississippi culturally, socially, or politically, and to them it seemed that I was talking about another country. They also knew little about the relationship among the federal government (specifically the FBI), state and local governments, and the various civil rights organizations. The audiences usually believed—or wanted to believe—that the federal government was strongly committed to helping black southerners secure their rights, and they seemed shocked when I presented counterevidence.

Later I found that, in order to represent SNCC successfully, I often had to defend its radical positions on issues such as the war in Vietnam. At that time, SNCC discouraged blacks from fighting in Vietnam. Our position was that black Americans had no obligation to fight in Vietnam since the Vietnamese were fighting for their liberation from colonial oppression and many black Americans were denied their basic civil rights here at home, that blacks had a greater obligation to fight for our rights here in the United States. All these activities strengthened my commitment to radical politics and the movement. On reflection, I view this as enhancing my ability to analyze regional and national racism.

The civil rights movement next took a direction that would call into question many aspects of the internal relationships of civil rights organizations themselves: the call for black power. What did it mean? Was it reverse racism? What did it mean for whites who had gained their experience in the civil rights movement? These questions helped raise an issue that the movement had not addressed: the need to organize against white racism within the white community. To that point, most of the energy of the movement had been concentrated within the black community. Would white civil rights workers organize against white racism in the white community? That question was at the heart of the break between black and white civil rights workers, at least in SNCC.

ACADEMIC YEARS

Studying Sociology and Being Political

My political consciousness greatly influenced my academic studies at both the undergraduate and graduate levels. While I worked on completing my undergraduate studies at Sacramento State College, I found my interest sparked in two fields of study, political science and sociology, but it was sociology that would excite me. For one thing, the sociologist's approach felt relevant to black experiences in this country and addressed my own concerns in this area. For another, a significant number of the sociology professors were sympathetic to the civil rights movement, and their critical analyses legitimated my continuing analysis of American society. While attending Sacramento State, I continued to do community organizing. This work allowed me to better understand the issues under sociological scrutiny in class, and that in turn gave me deeper insight into the problems we faced in our attempts to organize the community. This was particularly evident with the community alert patrol we organized in black neighborhoods to monitor police behavior toward black youth. As a cooperative effort, we and some community people established the Oak Park Service and Action Committee (OPSAC). Its major goal was to address the community's grievances, mainly with the school board and the police department. During my work with this group, the Black Panther party was born and made its bold foray into the state capitol carrying guns. It was OPSAC that organized efforts through a local bail bondsman to get them out of jail.

Discussions and debates with my professors were commonplace and provided an important counterpoint and backdrop to my activism. This all contributed to my intellectual growth, and also to my increasing self-confidence. I was asked to lecture on the nature of the contemporary civil rights movement, poverty, and racism in American society. This led to my first essay, "Negroes in Early California History, 1849–1870" (published in 1967 in *The Movement*, a national civil rights movement newspaper), a sociological analysis of racism in early California history.

I graduated from Sacramento State College with a B.A. in sociology in January 1968. My experience on and off campus strengthened my belief in my analytic ability. I read a great deal in sociological and political theory and philosophy. I had closely observed major players in state politics, understood the black community of Sacramento from a sociological perspective, and participated in continuing debates on the need for black liberation. Political allies, both black and white, gave me the confidence to challenge many of the assumptions and positions of established white scholars. For example, Seymour Martin Lipset claims that for many students, political activism was a passing phase. But this was not the case for me and many of my civil rights colleagues, both black and white.

Before I left Sacramento State, one of my professors told me I should call a professor at U.C. Berkeley; the sociology graduate department, he said, was interested in me. To my knowledge, no one had ever gone from sociology at Sacramento State to graduate work at Berkeley. Even though I had received the department's "Student of the Year" award in 1968, I knew I was being asked to apply partly because of my race.

Arriving in Berkeley

In January 1968 I went for my graduate interview at Berkeley. (I remember walking down the hall noting the names of many familiar authors on the office doors.) Although I had been invited, my introduction to the department was cold but typical in a big department—very few personal greetings are passed on to undergraduates. The receptionist probably saw me as just another student wanting to see an important professor. This is typical. When I asked the receptionist where the professor was, she told me to come back during his office hours. I then informed her that I had an appointment and was told to go to his office and wait—he should be there soon. No smiles or friendly greetings—welcome to Berkeley!

When he arrived and we sat down to talk, I told him I realized they were recruiting blacks but I wanted it understood that "I am not interested in being the department nigger." He quickly assured me that I would not be. His phone rang; as he talked on the phone, I scanned his bookshelves, noting a few titles that I had read. After his phone conversation, I told him I had written an essay critiquing one of his books. We discussed what I had written, and he was polite enough (I know now) not to point out the weakness of my analysis. After the interview, I felt the department was interested in me and my self-confidence increased. My classes were not due to start until September, and so I took a position as a researcher on a departmental project studying racism, manhood, and culture.

That year the sociology department had enrolled eight blacks and one Latino in its graduate program. This was a major increase in minority enrollment; only four American blacks had been in the Ph.D. program over the last five years and no Latinos, out of more than 250 graduate students at Berkeley. One day a white sociology professor, a specialist in ethnic relations, asked me if I was aware that the department was admitting a large group of black students; what did I think would happen, he asked. I was insulted by this question; all the incoming blacks (he didn't realize I was one of them) were qualified holders of B.A. degrees. I told him I didn't know, but perhaps we would decide to burn the damn place down. The next morning, as I was leaving the department to return to the research center where I worked, we met at the elevator. He asked what department I was coming to in September. Sociology, I replied. Over the next four years he never engaged me in conversation again.

Other things clearly showed me that many people were uncomfortable interacting with black graduate students. When I first reported to work at the research center, the administrative assistant of the research center stopped me and asked what was I doing in the building. It took the head of the project to give her a satisfactory answer. So much for Berkeley liberalism in early 1968!

I was a bit unsettled when I met the graduate students who were to be in my cohort. Many of them were bright elite students who talked radical, but most had little experience in the trenches actually working in radical politics. Although I had firsthand experience, my academic training was perhaps less rigorous than theirs, forcing me to work hard to compete with them.

Berkeley was the right place for me to continue my intellectual and political growth. Many of the graduate students and some faculty were engaged in serious intellectual pursuit of an understanding of the civil rights movement, radical intellectual thought, the Black Panther party emerging next door in Oakland, and challenges to mainstream sociological and social science thought all at the same time. The professors were excellent and the program provided me with the flexibility I needed to not only excel but to do it in my own style—engaging in intellectual debates on historical and contemporary issues, especially the assumptions surrounding the nature of American society and its western heritage, while remaining committed to political activism. I participated in a "Third World strike" for an ethnic studies program on campus and campus demonstrations surrounding People's Park, advocated the inclusion of more minority students in the department, particularly Latinos, and demonstrated for the need for curriculum change in the department to provide courses more relevant to minority students.

For my dissertation I decided to study the rise of the National Democratic party of Alabama (NDPA). I read an article in a popular magazine on this mostly black independent third political party in Alabama, which had run a black for governor against George Wallace in the 1970 general election. NDPA was largely concentrated in the Alabama Black Belt, an area where SNCC had worked during the mid and late 1960s. I became interested in the possible connection between SNCC's work in this area and the rise of this third party.

My research uncovered the fact that indeed many of the original members of the NDPA had participated in the local and national civil rights movement. SNCC organizers argued that Black Belt blacks should establish a separate political party because white Alabamians would not open up the local and statewide democratic parties to meaningful black political participation. At that time, many of these Black Belt Alabamians rejected the idea of a black-only party and continued to push to open up Alabama's Democratic party. Several years later, however, they were involved in NDPA, which was 90 percent black. An important point that arises out of this research is that a growth in political consciousness for oppressed group members is likely to occur through strategic planning only after they have tried traditional methods and failed.

My research, published as *Black Parties and Political Power: A Case Study* (1980), confronted me with the limitations and successes of a black political party. I found that in rural counties where the politics was still based on "us" versus "them," blacks on a third-party ticket could win local political offices only where 70 or 80 percent of the population was black, where a large number of blacks were registered to vote, and where 60 percent of the registered voters turned out on election day—and mostly all voted for the black candidates. When blacks attempted to run for office beyond their county's base, they lost in areas where the ratio of whites to blacks was larger. They lost simply because they were outnumbered by white Alabamians who voted along racial lines, particularly in statewide and congressional races.

Perhaps the most important finding of my research, which I rethought some years later, concerned the effect on local black constituents when black politicians were elected. In several visits back to these counties, I noticed no significant change in the economic power structure. Capital still remained in the hands of the landed aristocracy. Did it make any difference that blacks were now in control of City Hall, the local sheriff's office, the local school boards, and the county commission?

I concluded that it did, that indeed the quality of life had changed under these black leaders, and changed for the better. Blacks were no longer afraid to go to City Hall or the courthouse, black parents did not worry on Friday night that their teenagers had been arrested and physically abused by the local sheriff or police or that they would be subject to racial abuse when they went to check on their teenagers. The outward migration to go north in search of jobs and "freedom" did not occur as much as it had when whites were the political leadership of the county or town. There appeared to be a sense that the political control of the black community's future was in the hands of the black community, at least at the local level.

This doesn't address the macro-problems affecting the community from the shifts in outside structural forces, but it does suggest that activity at the micro level must not be overlooked as we attempt to find solutions to address our community's social problems. Some changes can be made by the people themselves. This research heightened my interest in grounded theory. I began to feel strongly that sociologists should look more closely at what people do, not just "structure," the "state," "values," and so forth.

Graduation was the end of a long haul. I was tired of graduate school, but I was satisfied, perhaps even triumphant. I remembered back to my undergraduate days, walking a picket line with a friend who was planning to transfer to Berkeley and wondering if I should do that too. I remembered mentioning it to my (white) counselor. I remembered his reaction: "People like you don't go to Berkeley."

Going to Yale

A couple of weeks after I turned in my doctoral thesis, I headed east for a new job at Yale, where I had a joint appointment in sociology and Afro-American studies. Yale was the epitome of an elite American university. There I could observe how the children of the elite are trained.

When I arrived in New Haven, I was surprised to note that the university was located in the middle of the city. Black people lived next door to the university, but the two worlds were miles apart. Community blacks were low income and did not send their kids to the university. Yale blacks—students or faculty—did not relate to the black community.

One Afro-American faculty member talked to me about the social graces that Yale faculty members were expected to display. He liked me;

he seemed to admire my Berkeley "radical" spirit. He only wanted to smooth off my "rough edges."

My interactions with him and my other colleagues in the Afro-American studies department were mutually respectful. Unfortunately, my colleagues in Yale's sociology department were different. My junior colleagues were interesting, smart, and not afraid to engage black scholars. The senior faculty was a different story. Many of them acted as if we didn't exist, and even when they did recognize our existence, it was in a derogatory manner. Perhaps that's why so many of the black faculty members hired in the sociology department quit after the first year.

One instance comes to mind. The department was asked to write up a short plan describing how it intended to diversify its faculty. During faculty meetings, the discussion was always put off to the end, and so it took several meetings to agree on a fairly short plan. After several sessions, during which I kept quiet on the subject, a senior faculty member stopped me in the hall and asked why I was not participating. I replied that I had chosen not to participate because I questioned my colleagues' sincerity. "Well!" he said, "if you think we are going to hire in this department like they do in the telephone company or the post office, you are sadly mistaken." To which I replied, "That cool, boss," and walked away. It was clear to me from that short confrontation and a few others that I would not be sticking around.

In the spring of 1976, I received an invitation to return to Berkeley to help develop a research institute. I quickly accepted and asked Yale for a year's leave. At the end of the year, I did not return to Yale; I resigned.

Back to Berkeley and on to Santa Cruz

I returned to Berkeley on a postdoctoral fellowship and worked with three professors to rebuild the old Race Relations Institute into the Institute for the Study of Social Change, funded by the National Institute of Mental Health. We set up a postdoctoral program for new racial-minority Ph.D.'s, and we began a doctoral training program for Third World minority students in anthropology and sociology. We were very successful at this task, producing more than thirty racial-minority students with Ph.D.'s, most of whom we placed in major universities. We also worked with Berkeley's local government and with various community groups, such as the Center for Third World Organizing, an organization that trains racial-minority members in community organizing; with racial-minority members of the San Francisco Bar Association; and a local group in Richmond, California, working against the targeting of black communities by the cigarette industry.

In 1977, I became a visiting professor at the University of California at

Santa Cruz, and in 1978 I joined the faculty as an assistant professor. Since that time, I have carried out the functions of a professor located at a research university. I have been particularly hard at work attempting to diversify our faculty, recruiting racial-minority graduate students, and working closely with several black and white graduate students.

In 1982 I received tenure and promotion to associate professor and in 1987–1988 served as the associate dean of the social sciences division. When the dean resigned over a principled disagreement with the higher administration concerning teaching load, sabbaticals, and other faculty issues, I resigned along with him to make clear it was principles, not personalities, that were at stake. It seemed at the time, and still does, that the long and complex path from Tuskegee to an associate deanship was the culmination of an incredible journey, but it was not an end point because it led me to even a stronger commitment to the liberation of the African-American community, politically and intellectually.

INTELLECTUAL REFLECTIONS FROM THE 1980s

During the 1980s, I continued my studies of black politics in several pragmatic ways. I worked for the black socialist-oriented mayor of Berkeley, Eugene "Gus" Newport, as his executive assistant from 1980 to 1981; I carefully analyzed the 1984 Jesse Jackson campaign; and I observed and researched self-help movements in the black community.

I'm still in the process of completing a manuscript on my experiences working in Berkeley's progressive government. Several insights have affected my thinking on the working of urban governments: (1) the complexity of the problems faced by such governments; (2) tensions in race relations between white liberals and progressives and the black community, usually arising from mistrust; and (3) the many progressive programs such as rent control that threaten the economic security of many of the city's senior citizens (specifically black seniors).

This work also led me to develop my own ideas on some of the issues facing the black community. Whereas many social scientists call for the removal of external restraints and an infusion of national resources into our urban black communities, I believe they overemphasize the external restraints at the expense of understanding the internal strengths and resources of these communities. Even if external resources are ultimately necessary, what are the communities to do in the meantime until a national administration responds to the community needs?

My research on black inner-city community mobilization against the current crack crisis has shown the communities' willingness to organize toward a new standard of acceptable normative behavior. In short, we might be seeing from this activity the beginning of what Herbert Blumer called an amorphous general social movement, which has the potential to establish across the country a more structured social movement against drugs and street violence.

It is in this context that we should understand the significance of the Jesse Jackson phenomenon, for he has shown that inner-city blacks can be mobilized for political action and he has unified the black community to bring pressure on the national leadership of the Democratic party. Such mobilization of these internal strengths of the black community might lead to change in the external restraints that so imprison the community. Lest we forget, spontaneous mobilization efforts by members of the black community in the civil rights movements of the mid-1950s and 1960s and the urban riots of the mid-1960s and early 1970s loosened the external restraints on the black community and brought in national resources.

Of course, to be effective over a long period, such efforts need to be institutionalized through the development of sophisticated organizations. Unfortunately, Jesse Jackson's major weakness appears to be in this area of organization building. Nonetheless, I am convinced that within the urban black community there exist levels of organization that can be built on, and a strong belief in and active practice of the conception of self-help.

The needs of the urban black community have to be addressed through these internal strengths and resources. I hope in the 1990s we will learn more about the dynamics of the various black communities. For I believe no macro-change can significantly rebuild these communities without using these inner strengths.

NOTE

Acknowledgment: I wish to thank G. William Domhoff for his strong support and critical commentary.

REFERENCES

Dollard, John. 1949. *Caste and Class in a Southern Town.* Garden City, N.Y.: Doubleday Anchor Books.
Franklin, John Hope. 1948. *From Slavery to Freedom.* New York: Alfred A. Knopf.

Frazier, E. Franklin. 1951. *The Negro in the United States*. New York: Macmillan.
Frye, Hardy T. 1980. *Black Parties and Political Power: A Case Study*. Boston: G. K. Hall.
Mills, C. Wright. 1959a. *The Power Elite*. New York: Oxford University Press.
————. 1959b. *The Sociological Imagination*. New York: Oxford University Press.

Chapter 12

At the Center and the Edge: Notes on a Life in and out of Sociology and the New Left

Robert J. S. Ross

> *We have come far, we are going farther yet.*
> Carl Sandburg, *The People, Yes*

THE SIXTIES did not end in 1969. The movements that began then influenced a cohort of young adults who, imprinted by the experience of those movements, moved on through their life cycles and work lives. This is an essay about one person riding that "long wave."

BECOMING A SOCIOLOGIST

I read C. Wright Mills's *The Power Elite* early in 1962, starting late in the evening on a winter night. I was seized by the power of Mills's language, by his craft, his anger, by the power of the powerful he depicted. I was nineteen-year-old junior at the University of Michigan, vice president of Students for a Democratic Society (SDS). The Port Huron Convention was a few months away.

Ann Arbor dawned cold and gray, and I wandered the streets weeping. How could we *ever* call them to account? No matter, I had also read Camus: We would try, even though hope might be obscure. On to Port Huron, to Chicago, to becoming a sociologist, a Marxist, a socialist, a department chair, a MUDPIE (middle-aged, upwardly mobile, disaffected professional).

The ethos of the early New Left, of SDS in particular, was rather different from its later images. The "old" New Left as a political movement embraced Mills's call, in *The Sociological Imagination* (1959), for a social science suffused simultaneously with the values of reason and freedom. That Mills was not preoccupied with issues of racial or economic justice did not make his indictment of American democracy any less compelling. I was a younger activist with perhaps precocious responsibilities, and the messages I received from my political environment, from slightly older comrades and age peers, were consistent with what Mills called the "classic tradition" in social science (1960). In the year after Port Huron I wrote a senior honors thesis on Mills and the most important influences on him: Marx, Weber, Mannheim. Those are still the figures in whom I am most interested when I teach theory.

It was only later, during 1964–1968, when I was a graduate student at the University of Chicago, that antiestablishment politics became confounded with the counterculture's antiscientific animus. These years were fateful. Our cohort of young intellectuals was burdened with a frightful handicap in its mission to remake the social sciences and to communicate to a wider public. For me, the cross-cutting messages of this era of the movement and the profession produced a prolonged period of intellectual stalemate. It was not until the late seventies that I was to shed these confusions fully and embark on serious work in political economy.

The emphasis on reason in human affairs was a great asset in the early New Left, and my exposure to Mills was the chief reason I switched from an undergraduate major in political science to a decision to seek graduate training in sociology. It seemed to me that in sociology one had the opportunity to study the basis for power in society, rather than merely its formal codification. But it took a year in Great Britain to alert me to the blind spots in the Port Huron consensus.

A careful reading of SDS documents of the early sixties—the "Port Huron Statement" (SDS [1962] 1987) and the equally cogent "America and the New Era" (SDS [1963] 1969)—reveals an analytical emphasis on the mechanisms of bureaucratic elitism, and concern for racial equality; poverty is seen as an outrage, and the arms race as a threat to humanity. The source of renewal is seen as movements of "local insurgency," a conception at least as Jacobin as socialist. The social order is not analyzed as a class system. The documents are arguably "anticapitalist," certainly "anticorporate," but without a view of fundamental dynamics.[1]

This emphasis in early SDS on "local insurgency" was a response to Mills's *Power Elite*. Where Mills contrasts, somewhat despairingly, real "publics" with mass society manipulated by elites, SDS called for building challenges to the powerful from the bottom up.

In the spring of 1963 Dick Flacks was drafting *America in the New Era* and he and I were discussing with Paul Booth the notion of "corporate liberalism," contrasting it to popular liberalism and progressive versions of populism. We were trying to find an *American* political tradition that would support our radical, democratic, socialist politics. But we were not depending on Mills's model of the intellectuals, as such, as the base of a movement.

In my honors thesis on Mills, which I was writing at that time, I wrote: "Mills did neglect the potential of organizing power from below the heights of the elite, . . . the potential of ferment and force being exercised from the middle and bottom levels of society. Social movements can (and do) generate power; some elections do (and more can) have importance."

A year later, as community-organizing projects were just beginning, Tom Hayden's response to Mills included this: "What Mills overlooked was the underdevelopment within the US as well as the Third World. The contradictions between underdevelopment and potential abundance, between growing social protest and degenerate institutions, are bringing political ferment back to the US" (1964, 184).

After I was graduated from Michigan, I won a fellowship to London, where I took courses with Ralph Miliband. I knew Miliband's name from the acknowledgments in a number of Mills's books and from his memoir of Mills published after Mills's death (Miliband 1962). In Miliband's courses, and in London, I encountered a vigorous, nonsectarian Marxism and a popular socialist tradition in a social order where the lines of class and culture were clear.

Reflecting on my own background as a son of a schoolteacher and a class-conscious garment worker from the Bronx, I concluded that Mills's critique of the "labor metaphysic" was best understood as a rejection of the politics of the right wing of labor and of American social democracy in the midst of the Cold War. His view seemed less appropriate as a guide to the use of class analysis in social theory.

Returning to the United States in the summer of 1964 I joined SDS's community-organization project in Chicago, an experience that would stamp my subsequent intellectual and political life. From London I had been following the initiation of the Economic Research and Action Project (ERAP). Carl Wittman and Tom Hayden (1966) had written a paper in the winter of 1963–1964 in which they argue that poor people could better their condition through organization; that is, that poverty of power underlies the absence of income. If poor people were to effectively organize for jobs or income, the pressure on the national budget would make a full-scale arms race impossible. One could strike a blow for peace and justice through community organization and, in the meantime, unite the black and white poor.

The SDS approach was different from its immediate ancestor, Saul Alinsky's community-organization strategies, in its long-term strategic focus on the national level and its explicit objective of broad political coalition. The implicit strategy was not so very different from that later articulated by Bowles, Gordon, and Weisskopf (1983) as wage-led growth.

The economic analysis upon which community organizing of the poor was based was perhaps "premature." Embodied in a working paper by economist Ray Brown called "Our Crisis Economy and the End of the Boom," it essentially depended on a view that automation would cause unemployment to reach crisis proportions. It predicted that monopoly capitalism would stagnate. Of course, by 1964–1965, a major path of economic stimulus was emerging: war. Even as we walked the streets of Chicago's North Side, leafleting the unemployment compensation office, war production for Vietnam was soaking up excess labor, and soon the army would absorb excess young men.

I spent the months of June through September 1964 at Jobs or Income Now (JOIN), attempting to organize unemployed white immigrants from Appalachia on Chicago's North Side (Gitlin and Hollander 1970). Late in August I faced a decision. I had been admitted to Brandeis for graduate work. If I went, I would have to leave JOIN and Marion, the woman I still love (and am still married to after twenty-four years). Or I could stay in Chicago and maintain involvement in JOIN and with Marion. My friend Dick Flacks was beginning an assistant professorship at the University of Chicago, and he proposed that I reactivate my application there. Late in August I was admitted with a fellowship, thus ensuring a fine marriage and a terrible mismatch between myself and my chosen department.

In October 1964, I began graduate work at the University of Chicago. My first few days were a terrific culture shock. From the survival concerns of Uptown, living on peanut butter and with cast-off furniture, I found myself in an elite institution where my passions for justice were, well, unusual. To my fellow graduate students I was somewhat exotic, perhaps a bit admirable but certainly not a good example for a successful career in the Big Time.

In my first semester, I took Peter Blau's Theory course. He was interested in formal theory construction in a positivist model. I wrote a term paper on poverty. The issue had become quite visible and the War on Poverty had been announced. I was still deeply involved with the JOIN project. I steeped myself in the data about who was poor, where they lived, what jobs—if any—they held. At the end of the paper I argued that there was a selective vulnerability of oppressed minority groups. Blau noted that I had not really constructed the assignment around the requirements of a formal theory; less relevantly, he prodded me about the "success" of overseas Chinese. I was given a *C* grade. A revision of the paper was published in *Liberation* magazine, and it eventually appeared in a textbook of radical sociology (Ross 1966). And so it goes: our profession manages to punish us for all of our virtues.

THE IMPACT OF THE WAR

By 1967 relations between the growing body of leftist students and the faculty at Chicago and elsewhere had deteriorated. The Vietnam War changed the tone and the content of the protest movements. Emotionally, a desperate anger now overwhelmed hopeful vision. Politically, as the movement grew and the horrors of the war became deeper, increasing numbers of activists thought of themselves as "revolutionaries" and thought of the historical moment as revolutionary crisis. The resultant atmosphere was not conducive to traditional learning, and the Left bore some responsibility for this.

The culture of the later New Left included an antiempirical, antiquantitative ethos. The counterculture hybrid with left politics denigrated science as an enterprise (Gitlin 1987). The line between madness and reason became fashionably obscure (for example, see Laing 1967). Many of us moved through the program by avoiding technical methodology and, for that matter, much of the substantive knowledge that a student, even a left student, should absorb from conventional but learned faculty.

Some of the senior members of the Chicago faculty, however, were more fractious than the most militant of the students. Some were personally committed to the war in Vietnam, and took antiwar activity to be unpatriotic. Others were offended that graduate students would intrude themselves into departmental affairs.

Once a faculty member called me in my role as chair of the sociology graduate student organization after we had submitted a memo calling for a more open process in research assistant assignments. He asked whether I trusted the faculty. I replied that secrecy was not conducive to trust. He pressed me for a more direct answer, and I repeated my "sociological" observation. He pressed again, adopting an "old buddy" tone of voice: "Come on, tell me, what do you really think?" I demurred once again. Finally, he provoked me by accusing me of being mealy-mouthed. I broke down and said: "I just don't trust any of you fuckers." It was then reported to the faculty that I had, in rage, called the faculty a bunch of fuckers.

I did not do a dissertation with Dick Flacks, on his study of young activists, because I wanted to understand and move the world outside of academe, to address class and power, not just the movement. But the mainstream faculty with whom I shared these urban and social policy concerns cut me off after I had a visible role in a campus sit-in protesting complicity with the draft.

Substantively, sociology was just beginning the long sea change that would produce the generation of structuralists, resource mobilization theories, power structure researchers, and the rethinking of urban sociology. These were in the future; in social psychology leftist social movements were still seen through the eyes of Eric Hoffer's *True Believer* (1951) and Cold War attempts to force western communists into the "authoritarian personality" mold.[2] To the faculty at Chicago, we activists were mad dogs, and I suppose some of us lived up to expectations.

The Vietnam War also influenced our perspective on Mills's theory. Mills had seen the military establishment as an independent leg of a tripartite power elite. Among left intellectuals it was apparent that the war was directed from the White House, and that the military and the CIA served the President. If this vast and terrible undertaking was the product of civilian political leadership, generously interleaved with corporate influence, it was natural that the new interpretations both of Mills and of power would move toward a more nearly classical class analysis. This was precisely the direction of Bill Domhoff's early extensions of Mills's project (1967, 1970).

Further, despite the peculiarities of Vietnam's role in the world political economy, the general search for "the roots" of American foreign policies gave birth to a vigorous debate about contemporary imperialism, and a variety of neo-orthodox and not-so-orthodox theories. This too moved discussion away from Mills's model; he had written of a "military definition of reality" and had said, with Weber, that Marx's economic materialism should be supplemented with an "administrative" and "military" materialism.

As the Vietnam War and opposition to it continued, the personal, intellectual, and political dimensions of conflict between traditional faculty and the protest movements reached greater heights. The result was deep enmity. This was made vivid in the spring of 1969, when Dick Flacks was attacked in his office and nearly killed. We later had reason to believe a Minute Man–type rightist (never apprehended) did it, fracturing Dick's skull, and nearly severing his right hand. Dick was taken out of his campus office on a stretcher, gravely wounded, headed for intensive care. I recall that one sociology faculty member was overheard to say that given Dick's public antiwar stance, he got what he deserved. Other, even uglier speculations were reported to us.

I was on leave from the graduate program during 1968–1969, working as the founding organizer of the New University Conference (NUC), an attempt to build a New Left graduate student and faculty organization. Part of our activity, and my responsibility, included support for the "radical caucus" at the ASA meetings. Among my "executive decisions" that fall was to print Martin Nicolaus's speech "Fat-Cat Sociology" as a working paper for the organization (see Chapter 15). The general conception had been discussed for a few years within SDS under the rubric of "radicals in the professions." Even though I was organizing among academics, Marty's essay added to the reservations about the social role of intellectuals I had expressed in my honors thesis.

At the end of the 1968–1969 academic year I was suspended from Chicago, even though I was on leave. There had been a sit-in, an occupation of the administration building, originally protesting the firing of Marlene Dixon. I had privately opposed the action as a strategic dead end. A strike, I thought, might be more effective (unless, as the future Weather Underground types no doubt feared, there was little mass support), and would put students at less personal jeopardy than a building takeover. But the rage against the war and the guilt-laden consciousness of many movement activists from affluent families would not be denied. Militance in tactics had come to be synonymous with radicalism in strategy. To put oneself in jeopardy was a badge of honor, regardless of careful calculation of objectives and resources.

Working as the NUC organizer, I was not active in the SDS chapter, and I hardly knew of the sit-in plan until some chapter leaders asked me to chair a campus mass meeting where they would seek a mandate for their course of action. I had, in those days, a reputation for some knowledge of parliamentary procedure. The meeting of well over a thousand people (including those who did not support the SDS chapter's goals of reinstatment for Dixon) was a cacophonous scene, over which I presided with some humor.

A vote gave the chapter the mandate it wanted, and the administration building was occupied. Inside the building, I was asked to chair once again, a neutral figure among the contending factions, which included a very small Third Camp socialist group, a group whose leaders later became part of the Weather Underground, and a group led by the Progressive Labor party. When I returned from a week-long organizing trip for NUC, I went to the occupied administration building just in time to be identified by a squad of faculty Madame Defarges, taking down names for future administration action. I left once again for an NUC organizing trip, to return on the day the defeated students left the building.

The University of Chicago had learned from the Columbia University experience a year earlier. No embarrassing head breaking for them: they waited out the occupation. When the students gave up, a series of university trials began in which a substantial number of people were expelled. After passionate pleading I was merely suspended.

The eventual result of this was that I was to submit a dissertation to a thesis committee I had not met. Five years later (in the meantime I had directed a funded study of advocate planners at the Institute for Social Research [ISR] at Michigan), there was no one left at Chicago with whom I was even on speaking terms. The department asked Bill Wilson to chair the thesis, though we had never met. At the time of the oral defense of the completed dissertation, I had met no one else on the committee. Quite strange. To this day I am grateful to Bill Wilson, who presided over the acceptance of my thesis, eleven years after I entered graduate school, under extraordinary circumstances.

WORKING

In the interim, in 1969, I had gone back to Ann Arbor as a research associate. I had decided to stay in academia. It was in part a political decision, because universities seemed a relevant place to be; it was in part personal, for my own inclinations were toward conceptualization, research, analysis.

The early seventies were very hard. SDS had been torn apart by factions, and even from the peripheral vantage point of the New University Conference the level of bitterness in inner movement circles was ferocious. The spirit that produced the Weather Underground had an important impact on all of us. We would refer to those who had become "Weatherized," generally meaning people who were inclined to "pick up the gun," to argue a view of imminent revolution. Often, this meant posturing. Sometimes it meant bizarre desertions: we heard of people who left their children with others in order to join the "Red Army."

I was talking occasionally with a retired former Young Communist League leader and McCarthy-era convict whose son was a fellow sociologist. At one point he exclaimed, "Why can't you intellectuals just accept that there is a role for intellectuals? Why are you so guilty about it?" He was right. The antiintellectual culture of the late New Left was wrong.

NUC experienced all the inner conflicts of other late 1960s organizations, except that in the early 1970s, we were trying to build a new group while others were falling apart. As a white male "leader," during a political moment of guilt and suspicion, I paid some dues, took my share of trashing. I was burdened, from 1969 to 1976, with debilitating skin diseases.

The movement of the sixties was falling apart, and with it marriages, careers, and individuals. But my sanity was (barely) preserved by a bit of perspective, for I realized that a good bit of the madness around me was the predictable result of the breakdown of a social movement.

In the early sixties I had read Doris Lessing's *Golden Notebook* (1981), Clancy Sigal's *Going Away* (1962), and Simone de Beauvoir's *Mandarins* (1979). Each deals with the emotional crises of people who had been in and around the communist movement through the end of World War II. In each, principal characters go bananas as their movements are defeated, repressed, or discredited.

In retrospect, my work in NUC at the end of the sixties and the early seventies has some continuing relevance to strategies of organizing intellectuals and professionals.

The NUC idea was to create a New Left organization of those who worked "in, around, and in spite of" universities. Faculty members and graduate students were our constituency. At the outset, there was a conflict about emphasis: Were we radical teachers, or teachers in the radical movement? Some felt we should emphasize radical pedagogy. I took the latter stance and advocated active participation in "movement" events, such as the Chicago convention demonstrations. (My FBI file has a nice dialogue about this. Washington FBI headquarters wants to indict me along with the Chicago six or seven or eight. Chicago investigates, and gets comments to the effect that Ross opposes the war, but is a patriot who believes in civil liberties everywhere. This is my most definitive character reference on "official" books.)

Another alternative proved more lasting: the Union for Radical Political Economics (URPE). URPE concentrated on developing alternative paradigms of economic analysis—arguably more successfully than we sociologists managed, and clearly with more lasting effect than NUC could sustain across diverse disciplines.

My model was based on a model of a social movement in active combat, whose members conceived of themselves, as we sometimes said, as the higher-education section of an imagined socialist party. The URPE model was more "professional," more segmented. It encouraged the development of an intellectual discourse within a given discipline. As the seventies progressed, no unified socialist movement or party emerged. Though the URPE model did not satisfy our (my?) need for action in those times, it seems to have had more long-term viability.

NUC, or my activist conception of it, had another problem. On a given campus it was often the case that the most prominent left intellectual(s) would not participate in chapter affairs, and would not take the lead in local struggles. These were men and women whose battles were fought in the pages of the *New York Review of Books*. Mundane, local, democratic organizations were not for them.

Perhaps the most problematic aspect of the cultural politics of the early 1970s was the enshrinement of the elusive proposition that "the personal is the political." For early feminists this was a liberating doctrine that gave legitimacy to their anger at male chauvinism. However, when elaborated and overextended, as it was, the doctrine justified a righteous sense of superiority that attacked conventional lifestyles. Monogamy, legal marriage, mortgages, children, eventually red meat: All became suspect. For a time, some women were made to feel defensive about their heterosexual attachments.

A peculiar radical patina was painted on all this, calling itself an attack on "bourgeois" lifestyle. But of course it was the culture of a fraction of the upper middle class that was asserting its moral superiority over the culture of the working class. In the course of the emergence of this doctrine, organizations were turned into arenas for invidious attacks on persons. The large and small irritations of getting along with others were transformed into grand conflicts. Did a person talk too much in a meeting: male chauvinist ego-tripping. Alternatively, experiments in day-to-day living arrangements, communes in particular, were preferred over political organizations trying to change institutions, policies, the world.

The corollary to the "personal is the political" is the idea that one should live, with one's family and comrades, as if the Revolution had occurred, as if we could prefigure in our everyday affairs the ligaments of a new society. We could, this doctrine presumes, live as if the Future were the present (and by the way, along with the misled fads of the times, as if the Future would do away with families, marriages, personal space, private discourse, and sexual fidelity). Funny now, but conflict over these matters turned the fading remnants of the New Left into psychic cannibalism. The tribal image *was* in vogue, and the remaining days of the New Left of the early seventies were nasty, brutish, and short.

By contrast, at the Institute for Social Research (ISR), where I worked in these years, I enjoyed the businesslike atmosphere and fast pace of work. I nevertheless observed that too often the real work of craft, the challenge in the soft-money game, was the production of a successful proposal. The intellectual work of absorbing, interpreting, making meaningful theoretical or strategic conclusions from empirical work was often swamped by the need to churn out another proposal. And the proposal, as a matter of course, was always tailored to a client—the government, a foundation, a corporation. Not likely sites of support for radical work.

The mix of research and teaching in a graduate/undergraduate faculty situation seemed, then, a more attractive course. Now, after seventeen years in a private, collegiate, undergraduate setting, I know there are no heavenly perches in this oh-so-earthly gilded cage.

In 1971 I arranged my salary at ISR to include some teaching at the University of Michigan campus in Flint. I taught political sociology at night, to a class composed primarily of GM workers, with some wives of the managerial cadre and occasional wild cards such as a woman of about fifty who owned a farm north of Flint and who brought hilarious stories of Flint school kids visiting the bell pepper fields.

One night I was discussing bureaucracy, authority, and the power of superordinates' expectations over subordinates. I used the example of inflated body counts in Vietnam. One of the women in the class, the wife of a GM middle manager, a good student not pleased with the political spin she perceived in my views, challenged: "How do you know? Were you there?" No, I had not been there.

I asked the class how many of the men had been in the army. All but one. How many had served in Vietnam? Of the twenty-five or so, all but a handful had been in 'Nam. I asked, "Did I get it right? Is that how it worked?" The assent was unanimous, ranging from out-loud "yeahs" to affirmative nods. Inwardly and visibly I sighed in relief. Yes, sociology really did work; I could teach this class. It was a great moment in teaching, and I decided to look for a hard-money teaching job.

As 1971 ended I had collected all the data for my study of advocate planners, eventually to be my dissertation, and was on the job market. I was offered a position at Boston University and one at Clark University. Boston's John Silber, by 1972, was already notorious as a red-baiter. Given that I had not completed my Ph.D. thesis, my unusual academic path, I chose Clark. At Clark a new sociology chair, Ed Sampson, was a sympathetic Berkeley veteran, and the provost was an Ann Arbor friend, Al Guskin, with whom I had written my first essay on advocate planners. My role as a movement activist and a scholar seemed to be understood and appreciated. I was right and wrong.

An Academic Position

The sociology department at Clark had collapsed the year before I arrived. Sampson was invited by Guskin (now president of Antioch College) to reconstruct the department. Around Sampson was an involved circle of students who shared some of the community concerns of the late sixties movements. For the next eight years I would be in a unified department with a basically progressive consensus. Even after the break-down of the sixties movements themselves we were able to nurture a steady stream of student organizers, many of whom had older siblings who had been movement activists.

In 1973 Sid Peck joined us. We created a department that succeeded in training activist intellectuals and functioned democratically. But our protection at the administrative level was soon removed. A new president had neither John Silber's flair nor talent for provocation, but he was fully as conservative, and just as vindictive. When our department became identified as a base of opposition to many of his policies, the troubles began.

I completed my dissertation on advocate planners in the unusual fashion already described, and then became an untenured chair in 1975.

I was fired on May Day 1978. I was thirty-five, married, with two kids, two cars, one mortgage, a dog, no savings to mention, still with some political skills, and, in terms of university politics and stereotypes, I carried heavy baggage from the sixties.

My supporters and I thought that the president had communicated his negative views to the chair of the personnel committee, an old Clark hand, a philosopher of "right-Hegelian" views. We thought that the committee found it difficult to believe that an activist could be a good scholar, especially if he was a public socialist. My record of publication was superior to all but one or two of the approximately twenty people promoted to tenure in the social sciences after 1970, but the initial judgment was that my scholarly work was found wanting.

In the fall of 1978, a massive student campaign was organized by a relatively experienced cadre of former and current students of Sid and myself. An appeal committee found that the original personnel committee had discounted positive letters of reference through a disrespect for sociologists, and ordered a *de novo* consideration of the case.

At one point my student supporters were inflamed. They wanted to stage a sit-in. I explained to Sid Peck that the students "felt" they had to do this. He said, "Well, it may *feel* right, but our objective is to win, to get you promoted. The question is not whether it feels right, but whether it helps that objective." A fitting epitaph for adventurism.

Finally, after new recommendations had been submitted, the committee voted to promote me to tenure in March 1979. At last I could get down to work. During the tenure fight I had begun work on regional political economy and deindustrialization. I knew a gread deal about the symptoms of all this because I had maintained ties with organizers, especially with Massachusetts Fair Share, a neighborhood-based statewide populist organization. But now I began to work with political economy in a more serious way. By 1980 I was beginning to make an intellectual contribution to understanding the new global era of capital.

The progression had been in many steps, but the themes were consistent since my days in JOIN. I had set out as an SDS-oriented graduate student concerned about poor communities and power. As a teacher and scholar I was concerned with the crisis of the older cities. By the mid-1970s, the groups I was interested in, and the neighborhoods in which they were working, were running down and their residents were losing jobs. Plants were closing. The old industrial belts were decimated. Capital mobility and disinvestment became my focus.

My reflection about the political economic basis of superficially local matters led me once again to refine my view of Mills. He had acknowledged that the "middle-levels of power" had a certain pluralistic tumult in local and legislative matters. But the big decisions, those he said were of historic importance and national scope, were made by the power elite: war and peace and boom and bust. But many middle-level decisions, I now realized, aggregate, often at a moderate pace, into just such importance and scope: regional and national deindustrialization; inner-city decay and gentrification; the steady assault on unions and the erosion of industrial workers' economic and political power. I shared with Mills, still, a rejection of the superficiality of celebratory pluralism. But I saw the importance of these so-called middle levels, and also perceived here an opening for fruitful political work.

The tradition that seemed to encompass these contradictions best appeared to be political economy, and that became my mode of expression for the eighties (Gibson and others 1984; Graham and Ross 1989; Ross 1983; Ross and others 1984; Ross, Shakow, and Susman 1980; Ross and Trachte 1981, 1990; Trachte and Ross 1985). Mills had great impatience for Marxian political economy, perhaps because his most productive years were during the postwar boom: The stagnation and crisis of the 1970s and 1980s have reoriented intellectual work in ways Mills simply did not anticipate.

ANOTHER CRISIS

In January 1980 I started my first sabbatical after eleven years of full-time academic work and eight stressful years at Clark. I studied the political economy of New England and I spent two days a week working with a coalition developing plant-closing legislation. In June our Clark Regional Development Unit convened a conference of regionalists at a conference center in Luxembourg.

My intellectual and political work were converging. I was studying classical theory in political economy and learning about New England. Our group's theory of global capitalism was developing (Gibson and others 1984).

Then the sky fell in. After the conference I learned that Sid Peck had been charged with sexual harassment by a visiting professor in our department. She had been encouraged, it appeared, to make her formal charge, with no attempt at informal resolution, by a hatchetman provost who had had a hard time with Sid when Sid had chaired a faculty compensation committee.

My observations and experience led me to doubt the complainant's charges and to trust in Sid's integrity. I defended him. The (liberal) dean of the college called me in and suggested that my signature on a letter describing the attack on Sid as political harassment and an attack on academic freedom was inappropriate. I told him that if the FBI had failed to intimidate me or censor me, he would damn well not succeed either.

The case became notorious and complex, with many complaints and countercharges, and constant fear of penury from legal expenses. Eventually, after suits and countersuits were filed in the courts, all charges were mutually dropped.[3]

By 1982, I was in my fortieth year, embarked on intellectual work that constituted a life's project—the theory of global capitalism. Except for thirteen weeks in 1980, however, Clark had been one exhausting life-and-death struggle after another. The sociology department was no longer unified, and I had been "Zinned": a verb I invented to describe John Silber's vindictive salary freeze on the radical Howard Zinn at Boston University. Relatively immobile geographically, I had also experienced a change in my relationship to the left, that is, that community that had its origins in the movements of the sixties.

My experience of the attempted lynching of Peck was bruising in three ways: Never before, despite twenty years of political engagement, had my reputation as a person of principle and honesty been challenged. And until then, despite all, I had held to a kind of historical faith that the left was in some way a morally distinct community. I had enjoyed a secure identity, feeling that the left community was my home. The events of 1980–1982 wrenched loose all three of these cherished anchors of my adult life.

Sid, I felt, had been a victim of guilt-by-gender reasoning. I found the culture of the left lacking in personal trust: people who had been my comrades for years chose to believe my adversaries, with whom they were unacquainted. The right was ascendant and the left was eating itself alive. As I saw it then, demagogues and opportunists were able to exploit the sympathy of good people who were disoriented by a need to be on the side of underdogs, but who could not perceive the machinations of our common enemies.

People of the left, I realized, were part of the human species, *not* especially saintly. I left the ideal of the "beloved community" behind, because it no longer existed for me.

Along with personal distance, I faced life-cycle issues: inadequate income, and a sense that after twenty-two years of protest I needed to leave my mark somewhere, to put my fingerprints on some real policies.

The page turned. My work had come to the attention of the staff of the state senator who had sponsored the plant-closing bill I had worked on for two years. He needed a policy person/speechwriter/link to intellectuals. An Italian-American progressive, State Senator Gerry D'Amico promised an opportunity to work on the issue about which I cared the most, plant closings. He knew who I was and where I came from. I joined his staff as part-time intellectual and jack-of-many-trades in early 1983, while maintaining my position at Clark.

CLASS LOYALTY VERSUS LEFT FADS

Capital mobility had become a new weapon in class struggle. What working people lost at work, they could not win back in community action. So political action around plant closings, industrial health and safety, job training, child care, and union recognition took priority over so-called consumption issues. D'Amico was an advocate of plant-closing legislation and "right-to-know" (about chemical hazards in the workplace and community), and economic development that would preserve blue-collar manufacturing jobs. He was also among the Massachusetts Senate's more effective human service advocates.

I felt comfortable with his Worcester base of working-class and upwardly mobile middle-class Italian-Americans. They were the mothers and fathers and sons and daughters of the people who had formed, analogically, the Italian segment of my father's garment workers' union in New York.

It wasn't long before I experienced the 1980s split in Democratic party circles. Left "liberals" among political activists were often upper-middle-income persons and organizations concerned sometimes about the poor, and usually about social issues and civil liberties and victims of American foreign policies in poor countries, and procedural reforms in the legislature: the so-called suburban liberals. Populists and urban ethnics were often political activists who cared about working people. The two groups did not have the same agenda.

In 1986, D'Amico ran for lieutenant governor in the Democratic primary. I was the "issues director." His opponent, Evelyn Murphy, was equally (but not more) liberal in her support of abortion rights and other social issues, but she had taken the business community's position on plant closing and "right-to-know" against D'Amico. The circuit of fashionable liberals, weighty in Massachusetts opinion formation, preferred the symbolism of a female candidate and could not trust that an Italian from provincial Worcester with "conservative" labor support was really progressive. We lost the primary. A pro-business candidate got the liberal vote.

I took another step away, emotionally, from the cultural ambience of the fashionable left.

In the meantime, my departmental base at Clark was under new stress. Sid retired in the fall of 1987, as I was beginning sabbatical leave. My closest age-peer comrade, Andrea Walsh, was denied tenure. Our once-progressive department was put in receivership. Although I was the most senior faculty member, the administration decided to recruit an outside chair. After fifteen years of maintaining a bridgehead of progressive education, it appeared that a coalition of conservative faculty and technocratic administrators would be able to exploit the divisive history of gender war and take control of the sociology department. But the long wave of the sixties frustrated this. The supply of qualified academic labor is such that the finalists for the position, as of this writing, all come from outside the bland mainstream.

RETROSPECT

After the New Left disintegrated, the absence of an organized social movement left its intellectuals at the mercy of the conventional professional labor markets. In sustaining a practice, an involvement in public affairs oriented to the historic interests of working people, and a commitment to a progressive department and colleagues, I took some risks. But after all, why should it have been easier? Activists in a social movement that succeeded in frustrating an aggressive war but not in substantially altering power relations would obviously experience some rigors in succeeding years. And why should those who challenge the powerful and their intellectual dependents expect to be coddled? It's all so predictable, so normal.

Emotionally, my experience of these constant struggles has involved both losses and gains. The losses are that I have come to be less spontaneous or open in my professional and work encounters.[4] One learns, Everett Hughes taught, to be "objective," lest one be constantly, dangerously drained. Perhaps I appear to be colder and more calculating than I really experience myself. The gain is something I realized during the Peck case. I needed a way to continue to fight the good fight, necessarily involving some losses, and still remain fundamentally, strategically optimistic—to perceive even in grim situations the possibility of redemption, triumph, transcendence, even, however far-off, justice. My way has been a kind of ruthless objectivity about strategic analysis.

I remain optimistic. This too has roots in my experience of the sixties. Between age sixteen and twenty-six (1959 to 1969), years in which the left grew, I was part of many successes in organization, action, and even in impact on the nation. This was an imprinting experience, even more than the rigors of those and succeeding years.

I am fundamentally encouraged by developments in and around sociology. There has been a renaissance of an empirically oriented, nondogmatic Marxist, neo-Marxist, in-argument-with-Marxist sociology. The cohort of sociologists influenced by the movements of the 1960s has produced some landmark work. The left in our field is no longer a speculative critical philosophy; it approaches science. Despite the continuing cycle of fragmenting fads, despite a great deal of foolish misreading of organizational practice, there is a rich development of urban political economy, social-movement analysis, study of the state and of class formation. Sure, it's sometimes ivory-towerish: some ivory towers give good views.

Finally, the generation-long dialogue with Mills is reaching maturity. When Mills died in March 1962, we were thunderstruck. He would have been the figure against and with whom we would have measured our views, had our debates, addressed our new formulations. Ideas about the new strata of the working class would have seen the author of *White Collar* in action; the analyses of corporate networks and class power would have engaged the author of *The Power Elite*. The new problems confronting the labor movement would have challenged the author of *The New Men of Power*. If Mills had had a typical American male life span he would be with us now, commenting on the criticism of his work, perhaps acknowledging his underestimation of the sources of renewal in Marxism.

This too is the fate of the "youth" of the sixties: their parents pass on, so they must carry on the dialogue, now with their offspring.

As a theoretical heritage the movements of the sixties are a mixed and complicated bag. But great deeds were done, large thoughts were contemplated, new visions were tested. All in all, democracy was served well.

NOTES

1. Only later did the criticism of "corporate liberalism" become socialist, but by then the gap between "revolutionary" leaders and the mass student base had grown gigantic.

2. See the excellent refutation of the authoritarian personality research as applied to the left in Roger Brown's *Social Psychology* (1965).

3. Years later, newspapers reported that the original complainant had resigned a position as director of women's studies at another university after the women's studies committee protested her alleged homophobia, racism, and anti-Semitism.

4. An example: My office door is always open. After Sid's entrapment, I dare not close it. That means no possibility of a charge of inappropriate advances, but also no privacy for a troubled student.

REFERENCES

Bowles, Samuel, David M. Gordon, and Thomas E. Weisskopf. 1983. *Beyond the Waste Land: A Democratic Alternative to Economic Decline*. Garden City, N.Y.: Anchor Press/Doubleday.

Brown, Roger. 1965. *Social Psychology*. New York: Free Press.

De Beauvoir, Simone. 1979. *The Mandarins*. New York: Regnery Gateway.

Domhoff, G. William. 1967. *Who Rules America?* Englewood Cliffs, N.J.: Prentice-Hall.

————. 1970. *The Higher Circles*. New York: Random House.

Gibson, K., and others. 1984. "A Theoretical Approach to Capital and Labor Restructuring." In *Restructuring Regions in Advanced Capitalism*, ed. Phil O'Keefe. London: Croom Helm.

Gitlin, Todd. 1987. *The Sixties: Years of Hope, Days of Rage*. New York: Bantam.

Gitlin, Todd, and Nanci Hollander. 1970. *Uptown: Poor Whites in Chicago*. New York: Harper & Row.

Graham, Julie, and Robert J. S. Ross. 1989. "From Manufacturing-based Industrial Policy to Service-based Employment Policy?: Industrial Interests, Class Politics and the 'Massachusetts Miracle.'" *International Journal of Urban and Regional Research* 13:22–35 (corrected version inserted June 1989).

Hayden, Thomas, 1964. *Radical Nomad: Essays on C. Wright Mills and His Times.* Ann Arbor: University of Michigan, Center for Research on Conflict Resolution.

Hoffer, Eric. 1951. *The True Believer.* New York: Mentor.

Laing, R. D. 1967. *The Politics of Experience.* New York: Ballantine Books.

Lessing, Doris. 1981. *The Golden Notebook.* New York: Bantam Books.

Miliband, Ralph. 1962. "C. Wright Mills." *New Left Review* 15: 15–20.

Mills, C. Wright. 1959. *The Sociological Imagination.* New York: Oxford University Press.

———. 1960. "Introduction." In *Images of Man.* New York: Braziller.

Ross, Robert J. S. 1966. "Notes on the Welfare State." *Liberation*, March, 12–17, 32. Reprinted in *Where It's At*, ed. S. Deutsch and J. Howard. New York: Harper & Row, 1969.

———. 1983. "Facing Leviathan: Public Policy and Global Capitalism." *Economic Geography* 59:144–60.

Ross, Robert J. S., D. Shakow, and P. Susman. 1980. "Local Planners—Global Constraints." *Policy Sciences* 12:1–25.

Ross, Robert J. S., and Kent C. Trachte. 1981. "Global Cities, Global Classes: The Peripheralization of Labor in New York City." *Review* 6, no. 3 (Winter): 393–431.

———. 1990. *Global Capitalism: The New Leviathan.* Albany: State University of New York Press.

Ross, Robert J. S., and others. 1984. "Global Capitalism and Regional Decline: Implications for the Strategy of Classes in the Older Regions." In *Regional Restructuring Under Advanced Capitalism*, ed. Phil O'Keefe. London: Croom Helm.

Sigal, Clancy. 1962. *Going Away: A Report, Memoir.* Boston: Houghton Mifflin.

Students for a Democratic Society. (1962) 1987. "Port Huron Statement." Appendix in James Miller, *Democracy Is in the Streets.* New York: Simon & Schuster.

———. (1963) 1969. "America and the New Era." In *The New Left: A Documentary History*, ed. Massimo Teodori. Indianapolis: Bobbs-Merrill.

Trachte, Kent C., and Robert J. S. Ross. 1985. "The Crisis of Detroit and the Emergence of Global Capitalism." *International Journal of Urban and Regional Research* 9:186–217.

Wittman, Carl, and Tom Hayden. 1966. "An Interracial Movement of the Poor?" In *The New Student Left*, ed. Mitchell Cohen and Dennis Hale. Boston: Beacon.

PART III

Sociology in Action

The two essays in this part investigate radical sociology in practice, both inside and outside the academy. Anthony M. Platt examines the origins of radical criminology. Before the 1960s, the study of criminology was, he says, "little more than a technocratic instrument of state rule." The urban insurrections of the 1960s and the vast array of social movements reflected the crisis of social control in that period. The ensuing policy debates over the restoration of law and order created an intellectual opening in the study of criminology for those who wanted to go beyond the established frameworks. As participants in the movements of the 1960s came to question the neutrality of the law, the repressive and discriminatory practices of the state came under close scrutiny. As Platt points out, "Proponents of radical criminology were primarily activists, involved in and committed to public education about the biases of law; to struggles to make the police accountable through community control and civilian review boards; to prison reform through demystifying corrections, opposing medical experimentation, and supporting prisoners' rights; to the provision of resources for battered and raped women; and to the severance of university complicity in the military-industrial and police-industrial complexes." Although radical criminology suffered repression and co-optation during the 1970s, the spirit of radical criminology persisted and witnessed a resurgence in the late 1980s.

Howard J. Ehrlich discusses the use of radical sociology outside the academy. Ehrlich resigned his position as sociology professor at the University of Iowa in 1972 and began organizing Research Group One and the Great Atlantic Radio Conspiracy. Ehrlich chronicles his disenchantment with university life and discusses his many organizing adventures as an independent radical sociologist. Research Group One was an attempt to build a local resource as a base for doing community research and for radical social scientists outside of academia. The underlying principle of Research Group One was to contribute to build-

217

*ing a good society by designing research that leads to some sort of so-
cial action, and to make radical ideas and radical research accessible
to a wide audience. Research Group One developed a pamphlet series, a
radio show, and a magazine. The Great Atlantic Radio Conspiracy produced radical critiques of important issues within American society that
have been played on almost two-hundred radio stations around the
world. The Great Atlantic Radio Conspiracy is still in existence, and
tapes of its various programs are stocked in libraries in the United
States, Canada, Australia, and New Zealand and have been used in
classrooms, in community-organizing efforts, in union halls, and in
study groups.*

Chapter 13

"If We Know, Then We Must Fight": The Origins of Radical Criminology in the United States

Anthony M. Platt

THE SUBJECT MATTER of criminology—law and the definition of illegality, criminal behavior and deviance, social control and criminal justice—addresses sensitive aspects of a social system's mechanisms and ideology of power. Not surprisingly, in the United States this academic discipline has been kept on a short rein and until the 1960s was little more than a technocratic instrument of state rule.

By the early 1970s, however, I was coteaching (with Paul Takagi and Barry Krisberg) a radical curriculum in an undergraduate course called "Introduction to Criminology" at Berkeley. There were several hundred attentive and politicized students in the class, and the readings included Lenin on the state, Mao on contradiction, and a variety of materials about U.S. imperialism and U.S. war crimes in Vietnam. During this same time, I also cotaught another criminology class with David DuBois, the editor of the Black Panther party's newspaper. By 1974, there was a national journal devoted to radical criminology and all the leading commercial publishers were competing to put out best-selling critiques of the police, courts, and prisons. How did it happen that one of the most conservative and firmly regulated academic disciplines became so radicalized in the late 1960s and early 1970s?

Social Control: Crisis and Reorganization

The ghetto revolts of the mid 1960s, followed by waves of protest movements that shook the fabric of American society, generated considerable debate within ruling-class policy circles—especially government officials, technocratic researchers and academics—about how to prevent, respond to, and control these movements. The crisis of control was reflected in the use of think tanks and commissions to investigate, report, and make policy proposals. These commissions were by no means simply efforts to delay reforms or whitewash official violence (Platt 1971). They played a significant role in formulating and legitimating new strategies of social control that emerged in the 1965–1975 decade.

These far-ranging policy debates, funded by millions of federal and foundation dollars, engaged intellectuals and practitioners, furnished unprecedented grants and other perks to criminologists and those investigating the sociology of deviance, and provided limitless data for publications. Criminology was exposed to scrutiny and debate, thus creating an intellectual opening in the academy for those who wanted to go beyond the boundaries of Cold War liberalism that had ruled American social sciences at least since World War II (Schrecker 1986).

The first major black urban riot of the 1960s took place in Watts in August 1965. After the six-day revolt was brought under control, involving the death of thirty-four civilians, over one thousand injuries and close to four thousand arrests, Governor Edmund Brown appointed John McCone to head a commission to investigate the Los Angeles riots. McCone was a corporate businessman, a political conservative, and a former chief of the CIA (1962–1965). The level of this appointment, a reflection of the concern of corporate and political leaders, set the tone for future government commissions.

Watts was the first of many explosions of social protest that tested the state's mechanisms of control. In 1967, President Johnson appointed the National Advisory Commission on Civil Disorders (known as the Kerner Commission) to investigate the wave of black riots that swept the country after Watts. Its final report, published in 1968, included major recommendations regarding the criminal justice system. In 1968, President Johnson appointed the National Commission on the Causes and Prevention of Violence (headed by Milton Eisenhower). In 1969, this commission issued *To Establish Justice, to Insure Domestic Tranquility*, plus several task force reports on related issues. In 1970, following an escalation in student protest against U.S. policies in Vietnam, President Nixon established the National Commission on Campus Unrest (chaired by William Scranton).[1]

The black riots of the 1960s generated considerable debate within the technocratic stratum of government officials and intellectuals about how to contain and reform the ghettos. This debate, which had significant international and national ramifications, was reproduced in the corporate media.[2] In addition to the "riot commissions," President Johnson in 1965 appointed the President's Commission on Law Enforcement and Administration of Justice, whose final report (*The Challenge of Crime in a Free*

Society) and task force reports were published in 1967. This national crime commission, chaired by Nicholas Katzenbach (Under Secretary of State and former U.S. Attorney General) and composed of high-level state and political functionaries, was the first major assessment of criminal justice since the Wickersham Commission some thirty years earlier.

While the crime commission was publicly justified as a response to the growing crime problem, its main task was to develop proposals for the modernization and reorganization of the criminal justice system, which was poorly coordinated, often anachronistic, ill equipped, and unprepared to deal with protests and riots. Its policy recommendations urged a variety of economic and social reforms, but only its social-control proposals were actually implemented. The legacy of all the crime and riot commissions was an expanded, more sophisticated, more rationalized, and more repressive criminal justice system.[3]

With the expansion of criminal justice came increased involvement by the federal government in the funding and policies of local agencies. This trend was reflected in the growth of a "police-industrial complex," a rapidly growing industry that took technical developments originally created for overseas warfare or for the space program and, backed by government subsidies, applied them to the problems of domestic "order" in the United States; in the growth of educational programs to service the research and development needs of this growth industry; and in the reorganization of criminal justice, especially the police, along the lines of a military-corporate model that emphasized technology, specialization, and managerial techniques of "command and control" (Platt and others 1982).

While the riot and crime commissions of the 1960s ushered in a reorganized and increasingly repressive state apparatus, this era also generated political and ideological challenges to long-standing, liberal conceptions of justice, as well as a radicalization of significant sectors of the academic community, including the seemingly impenetrable field of criminology.

Rebellious Ideas

As participants in the social movements of the 1960s battled the police and troops, joined "common criminals" in the jails and prisons, and politicized the courts and legal system, the esoteric field of criminology literally became the subject of news headlines, television specials, literary critiques, best-selling autobiographies, and journalistic investigations. The lines between journalism, polemic, and scholarship were often blurred, sometimes erased, and often crossed. This movement produced trenchant critiques and muckraking investigations that demystified liberal myths about the neutrality of law and benevolence of the state, communicated the subjective experience of oppression, and exposed the raw, mean-spirited underbelly of the U.S. political economy.

Long before "radical criminology" emerged in academia, the popular imagination was fired by the writings of activists who had personally experienced the racial and political biases of justice in the United States. By the time that the Union of Radical Criminologists (1973) and the journal *Crime and Social Justice* (1974) emerged out of the School of Criminology at Berkeley, a popular and militant critique of criminal justice was well established outside the university.

From the black movements (civil rights, ghetto rebellions, and revolutionary organizations) came a flood of personal accounts, critiques, and exposés of the racist and political functions of criminal justice, often published by leading commercial publishers. Malcolm X's autobiography (1964), which included his years of struggle in prison, was issued as a best-selling paperback soon after his assassination in 1965, the same year that Claude Brown's autobiographical account of his experience in juvenile reformatories was published. Then 1968 saw the publication of Eldridge Cleaver's *Soul on Ice* and Bobby Seale's *Seize the Time*.

George Jackson's letters from prison were first published in *The New York Review of Books* in 1970 in the same month that his *Soledad Brother*, with an introduction by Jean Genet, was released. This revolutionary critique of the prison system became widely read, especially after Jackson was killed in prison. A year later, the collective autobiography of the New York Twenty-one, members of the Black Panther party who had been tried for subversion in 1969, was published as *Look for Me in the Whirlwind*, a savage indictment of racist America. Also in 1971, a collection of writings by Angela Davis and "other political prisoners" was published, with a foreword by Julian Bond. It included James Baldwin's celebrated "open letter to my sister, Angela Davis," in which he expressed solidarity with her, with George Jackson, and "with the numberless prisoners in our concentration camps. . . . We know that we, the Blacks," he continued, "and not only we, the Blacks, have been, and are, the victims of a system whose only fuel is greed, whose only god is profit." Baldwin urged people to act on this knowledge. "If we know, and do nothing, we are worse than the murderers hired in our name. If we know, then we must fight for your life as though it were our own—which it is—and render impassable with our bodies the corridor to the gas chamber. For, if they take you in the morning, they will be coming for us that night" (Davis and others 1971, 16, 17, 18).

As the New Left (the predominantly white student and antiwar movement) increasingly found itself in court and subsequently in prison, it became integrated into the prison movement, which was led primarily by black prisoners. This produced additional critiques and exposés of the criminal justice system. For example, Tom Hayden's *Trial* (1970) was one of many widely read accounts of the trial of the Chicago Eight. Activist Samuel Melville's *Letters from Attica* was published in 1971, a year after he was killed in the massacre at the prison. Philip Berrigan, imprisoned for his antiwar actions in the early 1970s, discussed his experience in *Widen the Prison Gates* (1973). *Seven Long Times*, the memoirs of Piri Thomas, a Puerto Rican writer and activist, about his years in a New York state prison, was published in 1974.

During this period, there was also a proliferation of radical writings from left organizations and periodicals, from left-liberal journalists, from former criminal justice functionaries, and from feminists and movement professionals (especially lawyers). This literature exposed the inner workings of criminal justice, corroborated the first-person accounts of defendants and prisoners, and stripped American justice of its self-justifying rhetorics. Also, for the first time, activists inside and outside the university called for the public recognition of rape as a serious crime rather than simply a private problem between individuals (Griffin 1971).

As political activists confronted secret grand jury hearings, informers and provocateurs, indictments and trials, the legal system itself became the object of investigations and scrutiny. For example, *The New York Review of Books* carried Murray Kempton's (1970) critique of how the New York court system violated the rights of the Panther Twenty-one; Robert Lefcourt's *Law Against the People* (1971) provided activists with a radical anthology of legal essays.

The police, as the front-line functionaries of social control and counterinsurgency, received unprecedented critical scrutiny. *The Nation* called attention to how "the federal government has taken the first dangerous steps toward transforming the United States into a society whose police agencies have a repressive capacity unparalleled in history" (Goulden 1970). The ACLU focused its attention on police brutality and malpractice, especially in black communities (Cray 1972). An ex-FBI agent, William Turner (1970), went public with his inside stories about J. Edgar Hoover; another ex-agent, Robert Wall (1972), explained in *The New York Review of Books* how the FBI operated as a "relentless guardian of orthodoxy" and "is all too effective in harassing legitimate political activity" (17–18). These confessions were more than confirmed in 1972 when antiwar activists publicized an important set of documents that they had stolen from the FBI's office in Media, Pennsylvania. The first serious analysis of its kind, "The Theory and Practice of American Political Intelligence," written by Frank Donner (1971), also appeared in *The New York Review of Books*. This was followed by other thoughtful investigations of political policing, notably by the American Friends Service Committee's National Action/Research on the Military-Industrial Complex (NARMIC 1971), by journalist Jeff Gerth (1972), and by a new magazine, *Counter Spy*, that began in 1973.

As can be seen from this partial survey of the late 1960s and early 1970s, the nonacademic criminology of this period was militant, innovative, and reached an audience that ranged far beyond the small circle of professional leftists. Hundreds of thousands of people, even millions, became educated about the injustices of American justice by reading the paperback autobiographies of best-selling revolutionaries and radical exposés by liberal journalists. The commercial success of Jessica Mitford's *Kind and Usual Punishment* (1973), a muckraking attack on "rehabilitation," prison industries, and medical experimentation, was testimony to the public interest in radical criminology.

CRIMINOLOGY AND SOCIOLOGY OF DEVIANCE

I have suggested that the roots of radical criminology are to be found in the ideas that emerged out of the social protest movements of the 1960s and the policy debates that accompanied the breakdown in "law and order." In addition, it is important to examine the intellectual traditions within academia that also shaped the emergence of this movement.

Before the 1960s, there was not a radical tradition in academic criminology. Applied criminology had always been closely tied to the technocratic demands of the state and professional training (Platt 1974). The liberal wing of criminology was able to assert its interests during the 1960s with the full-blown development of New Deal policies, especially the War on Poverty, with its emphasis on the problems of youth. This tendency, which was grounded in theories of opportunity structure, supported expanded state intervention (including Keynesian reforms and diversified forms of social control) and a reliance on higher education in changing the attitudes of "unenlightened" professionals. There was nothing radical in the theories of the criminologists and sociologists who wanted the *existing* political-economic system to create more openings for meritorious members of the "lower classes" (Wolfgang, Savitz, and Johnston 1962).

While radical criminology broke with these assumptions, it did draw on the civil libertarian and antistate perspectives that characterized an important left-liberal tendency among an influential group of intellectuals. Both labeling theory and conflict theory, which had traditionally been used apolitically or to justify social control, were now used by humanists and radicals to examine the repressive, discriminatory, and arbitrary practices of the state, its managers, and professional surrogates. Howard Becker's *Outsiders*, the most widely read example of this new use of the labeling perspective, was published in 1963; Thomas Szasz's denunciation of psychiatry, *Psychiatric Justice* (1965)—a curious blend of civil libertarian and laissez-faire ideologies—gave further ammunition to critics of social control.

During the mid- and late 1960s, this perspective produced a variety of studies that exposed the malevolent practices behind benevolent state intervention and called for protection of individual rights against child savers and social workers (Allen 1964; Platt 1969), the police (Skolnick 1966), and correctional do-gooders (Nasatir and others 1966; Carey and Platt 1966; American Friends Service Committee 1971; Mitford 1973; Wright 1973). As labeling theorists tried to understand the state and the class forces behind repressive reforms (such as the juvenile court, rehabilitation, parole, indeterminate sentencing, and so on), they later turned to the neo-Marxism of such "revisionist" historians as William Appleman Williams (1966), Gabriel Kolko (1967), James Weinstein (1969), and Howard Zinn (1970).

Another important intellectual influence on radical criminology was the sociologists who as participant observers reported positively and romantically on "subcultures of deviance." We paid close attention to Goffman's (1961) rebels subverting the authority of total institutions and Becker's (1963) bohemians smoking marijuana and playing jazz. Ned Polsky (1967) taught us procedures for hanging out with pool hustlers and beatniks. These cool, cynical, and detached critiques of American life accurately expressed the alienated disenchantment of middle-class students and young intellectuals for whom cultural rebellion and political activism were inextricably linked. This petty bourgeois radicalism, while certainly a break with the positivist tradition in sociology and criminology, generally rejected (or ignored) Marxism and failed to offer any lasting insights about the political economy of American society.[4]

RADICAL CRIMINOLOGY

Radical criminology was not simply a spontaneous *response* to the crisis in the state or to social protest. Activism was not external to the university. By the mid 1960s, a significant number of students and intellectuals were politically active in the civil rights and student (Free Speech) movements, the future cadre of the antiwar movement. At Berkeley, radical criminology was self-consciously organized and built by a small core of faculty and students who had been politically active for many years or who had been radicalized by their experiences in the 1960s. For example, Herman Schwendinger had a long history of political commitment and a long-standing interest in Marxism; Paul Takagi had been radicalized by his personal experience of racism (including imprisonment as a Japanese-American during World War II) and by his firsthand knowledge (as a functionary in corrections) of the bankruptcy of criminal justice; before coming to teach at Berkeley in 1968, I had also been active in the student and antiwar movements, and I inherited a leftist perspective from my family.

Radical criminology in academia was born as an activist movement. From its earliest days in the late 1960s, it emphasized practice over theory, tactics over strategy. This was a result of several interconnected factors. First, criminology had always been more concerned with policy and professional training; second, there was, unlike sociology, no radical or Marxist tradition in criminology; third, the emerging group of radical criminologists generally underestimated the long-term significance of theoretical work. At the same time, however, there was considerable debate within radical criminology, and an intellectual expansion of the field took place through the study of Marxism and critiques of the dominant theories.

Proponents of radical criminology were primarily activists, involved in and committed to public education about the political biases of law; to struggles to make the police accountable through community control and civilian review boards; to prison reform through demystifying corrections, opposing medical experimentation, and supporting prisoners' rights; to the provision of resources for battered and raped women; and to the severance of university complicity in the military-industrial and police-industrial complexes. For example, at Berkeley between 1969 and 1972, we were variously involved in a local electoral campaign for community control of the police, a regional "Prison Action" conference that organized hundreds of activists in prison reform, defense committees for political activists, educational programs in prisons, educational forums on U.S. war crimes, and an antirape hot line.

Theoretically, radical criminology was eclectic, derivative, and undeveloped. It borrowed heavily from political polemics and muckraking journalism, interwoven with civil libertarian critiques of the state, labeling theory, revisionist history, and the sociology of deviance. With the exception of Herman Schwendinger, the pioneers in radical criminology discounted the significance of theoretical work. It was Schwendinger (along with Julia Schwendinger) who stressed the importance of creating the journal *Crime and Social Justice* (which did not come out till 1974) and whose 1970 article, "Defenders of Order or Guardians of Human Rights?" was the intellectual bedrock of radical criminology.[5] Other theoretical contributions were made by Richard Quinney (1972, 1973), whose critique of positivist legal theory was widely read; by Erik Wright (1973), whose sociological analysis of prisons challenged the assumptions of liberal penology; and by contributors to *Issues in Criminology*. But overall, these contributions were quite limited, and radical criminology did not generate significant theoretical work until the late 1970s and 1980s.

The poverty of radical criminological theory in the United States encouraged an intellectual dependency on intellectuals in other countries. Rusche and Kirchheimer's materialist study of punishment and social structure in Europe, originally published in 1939, was reprinted in the United States in 1967 and 1968, though it was not widely read until late in the 1970s. From England, Taylor, Walton, and Young's *The New Criminology* (1973) was closely studied. The abolitionist perspective of Norwegian sociologist Thomas Mathiesen (1974) was influential in the United States, as was Franz Fanon's *The Wretched of the Earth*, first published here in 1965. Similarly, the influential philosophical work of Michel Foucault (1977) was later imported via French Canada.

The theoretical weaknesses of radical criminology in this country were in part the result of an emphasis on short-term activism and idealist expectations about the impact of social protest on the established political structures. They also reflected antiintellectual tendencies within the overall New Left, the lack of a Marxist tradition in American universities, the discrediting of the theoretical legacy of the Old Left, and the institutionalized hostility of Cold War liberals to any kind of radical theory in the social sciences (Schrecker 1986).

Consequently, radical criminology in its earliest days tended toward ultraleftism, romanticism, and a messianic utopianism. The prison movement, which exaggerated the revolutionary potential of most prisoners, adopted "tear down the walls" as one of its slogans. Accounts of socialist experiments in criminal justice, such as the Ricketts' *Prisoners of Liberation* (1973), were often mechanically imported from Third World countries without serious discussion of what was applicable from a China or a Cuba to this country (Horton and Platt 1986).

CONCLUSION

Radical criminology, like all the movements of the New Left, suffered repression and cooptation in the 1970s. With the closing down of Berkeley's School of Criminology and firing of its radical wing in 1976, radical criminology lost an organizational base for a critical mass of activists. Individual activism continued but the capacity for training and recruitment, and for building an esprit de corps, was gone. The traditionally conservative ambience of criminology was reestablished. Thus, by 1979, the American Society of Criminology could even publish a special issue of its journal on the topic of radical criminology without consulting or including any of its leading representatives. By the early 1980s, criminological textbooks included sections on radical criminology as a historical tendency that, like Lombrosianism, was dismissed as a misguided intellectual fad.

But the spirit of radical criminology persisted through the Reagan era and is even witnessing a resurgence. The journal *Social Justice* (formerly *Crime and Social Justice*) continues to be published and is now in its sixteenth year; Marxist and radical writings also appear in *Contemporary Crises* and other publications; the criminological work of the Schwendingers has received several academic awards; William Chambliss, a pioneer in conflict theory, was elected the president of the American Society of Criminology (for 1987–1988); the criminology section of the American Sociological Association elected Paul Takagi as chair (for 1986–1987) and has given special awards to radical criminologists from Latin America (including Vilma Nunez from Nicaragua, Margarita Viera from Cuba, and Rosa del Olmo from Venezuela).

Radical criminology, for all its theoretical immaturity and utopian activism, did make a significant contribution to criminology and the sociology of deviance. It seriously challenged conservative and corporate liberal domination of an important academic discipline. It helped to expose the fiction of ideological freedom in university life and introduced debate and dialogue where none had previously existed. It defended the intellectual legitimacy of revolutionary and Marxist ideas. It raised questions about the supremacy of Western civilization and opened our eyes to the possibility of a pluralistic world.

Most of all, radical criminology offered some of us a way out of the jaded, alienated cynicism that characterizes most intellectual work in this country. Bold, innovative, and optimistic, it enabled us to integrate mind and heart, to imbue intellectual life with personal meaning and social value, to make our knowledge serve the mass of humanity. It gave us a precious opportunity to know that there are alternatives to, in the words of James Baldwin, the "deadly—and, finally, wicked—mediocrity" that poses in the name of "democracy" (Davis and others 1971, 17).

NOTES

Acknowledgment: Thanks to Herman Schwendinger and Paul Takagi for their helpful critiques of a first draft of this chapter.

1. In addition to these nationally prominent commissions, there were also locally appointed commissions that investigated specific events. For example, *Rights in Conflict* (known as the Walker Report) investigated violence at the Democratic national convention of 1968; Archibald Cox led a fact-finding commission to investigate "disturbances" at Columbia University in the spring of 1968 (the report was published as *Crisis at Columbia* [Cox Commission 1968]); and Mayor Richard Daley established a study committee to investigate the riot that followed the assassination of Martin Luther King on April 4, 1968.

2. For example, *Newsweek* did a cover story entitled "The Black Mood" in its issue of August 21, 1967, followed by an in-depth story called "The Negro in America: What Must Be Done" in its issue of November 20, 1967. On March 8, 1968, *Life* published a special section called "The Cycle of Despair: The Negro and the City." In its issue of May 17, 1968, *Time* included "A Nation Within a Nation."

3. Between 1955 and 1971, criminal justice expenditures increased enormously from 0.5 percent to 1 percent of the GNP. From 1971 to 1974, spending on criminal justice increased over 42 percent, from $10.5 billion to about $15 billion. Of this, over $8.5 billion was spent on the police in 1974, eight times the amount spent on the police in 1964. By 1979, well over half (approximately $14 billion) of all public funding of criminal justice was spent on the police (Platt 1987).

4. As Alvin Gouldner pointed out in 1968, labeling theory "is taking up arms against the ineffectuality, callousness, or capriciousness of the caretakers that society has appointed to administer the mess it has created. It is essentially a critique of the critique of the caretaking organizations, and in particular of the *low level* officialdom that manages them. It is not a critique of the social institutions that engender suffering or of the high level officialdom that shapes the character of caretaking establishments" (107).

5. But even the Schwendingers postponed their significant theoretical works on rape and delinquency until the 1980s. (Their 1974 book, *Sociologists of the Chair*, however, did include a critique of the social-control assumptions of the pioneers in American sociology.)

REFERENCES

Allen, Francis. 1964. *The Borderland of Criminal Justice*. Chicago: University of Chicago Press.

American Friends Service Committee. 1971. *Struggle for Justice*. New York: Hill & Wang.

Becker, Howard. 1963. *Outsiders: Studies in the Sociology of Deviance*. New York: Free Press.

Berrigan, Philip, 1973. *Widen the Prison Gates*. New York: Simon & Schuster.

Brown, Claude. 1965. *Manchild in the Promised Land*. New York: Macmillan.

Carey, James, and Tony Platt. 1966. "Nalline Clinic: Game or Chemical Superego." *Issues in Criminology*, Fall.

Chicago Riot Study Committee. 1968. *Report to the Hon. Richard J. Daley* (August 1).

Cleaver, Eldridge. 1968. *Soul on Ice*. New York: McGraw-Hill.

Collective Autobiography of the New York 21. 1971. *Look for Me in the Whirlwind*. New York: Vintage.

Cox Commission. 1968. *Crisis at Columbia: Report of the Fact-Finding Commission Appointed to Investigate the Disturbances at Columbia University in April and May 1968*. New York: Vintage Books.

Cray, Ed. 1972. *The Enemy in the Streets: Police Malpractice in America*. New York: Anchor.

Davis, Angela, and others. 1971. *If They Come in the Morning: Voices of Resistance*. New York: The Third Press.

Donner, Frank. 1971. "The Theory and Practice of American Political Intelligence." *New York Review of Books*, April 22.

Fanon, Franz. 1965. *The Wretched of the Earth*. New York: Grove.

Foucault, Michel. 1977. *Discipline and Punish*. New York: Pantheon.

Gerth, Jeff. 1972. "The Americanization of 1984." *Sundance* 1, no. 1.

Goffman, Erving. 1961. *Asylums*. New York: Anchor.

Goulden, Joseph. 1970. "The Cops Hit the Jackpot." *The Nation*, November 23.

Gouldner, Alvin. 1968. "The Sociologist as Partisan: Sociology and the Welfare State." *American Sociologist* 3 (May).

Governor's Commission on the Los Angeles Riots. 1965. *Violence in the City—An End or a Beginning?* Los Angeles: College Book Store.

Griffin, Susan, 1971. "Rape: The All-American Crime." *Ramparts*, September.

Hayden, Tom. 1970. *Trial*. New York: Holt, Rinehart & Winston.

Horton, John, and Tony Platt. 1986. "Crime and Criminal Justice Under Capitalism and Socialism." *Crime and Social Justice* 25.

Jackson, George. 1970a. "Two Letters from Soledad Prison." *The New York Review of Books*, October 8.

——————. 1970b. *Soledad Brother*. New York: Bantam.

Kempton, Murray, 1970. "The Panthers on Trial." *New York Review of Books*, May 7.

Kolko, Gabriel. 1967. *The Triumph of Conservatism: A Reinterpretation of American History, 1900–1916.* Chicago: Quadrangle.

Lefcourt, Robert, ed. 1971. *Law Against the People: Essays to Demystify Law, Order and the Courts.* New York: Vintage.

Malcolm X. 1964. *The Autobiography of Malcolm X.* New York: Grove.

Mathiesen, Thomas. 1974. *The Politics of Abolition.* London: Martin Robertson.

Melville, Samuel. 1971. *Letters from Attica.* New York: William Morrow.

Mitford, Jessica. 1973. *Kind and Usual Punishment: The Prison Business.* New York: Alfred A. Knopf.

NARMIC. 1971. *Police on the Homefront: They're Bringing It All Back.* Philadelphia: American Friends Service Committee.

Nasatir, Michael, and others. 1966. "Atascadero: Ramifications of a Treatment Maximum Security Institution." *Issues in Criminology,* Spring.

National Advisory Commission on Civil Disorders. 1968. *Report to President Johnson.* New York: Bantam Books.

National Commission on the Causes and Prevention of Violence. 1969. *To Establish Justice, to Insure Domestic Tranquility.* Washington, D.C.: U.S. Government Printing Office.

Platt, Anthony 1969. *The Child Savers: The Invention of Delinquency.* Chicago: University of Chicago Press.

———. 1971. *The Politics of Riot Commissions.* New York: Macmillan.

———. 1974. "Prospects for a Radical Criminology in the United States." *Crime and Social Justice* 1.

———. 1987. "U.S. Criminal Justice in the Reagan Era: An Assessment." *Crime and Social Justice* 29.

Platt, Tony, and others. 1982. *The Iron Fist and the Velvet Glove: An Analysis of the U.S. Police.* San Francisco: Global Options.

Polsky, Ned. 1967. *Hustlers, Beats, and Others.* Chicago: Aldine.

President's Commission on Campus Unrest. 1970. *The Scranton Report.* Washington, D.C.: U.S. Government Printing Office.

President's Commission on Law Enforcement and Administration of Justice. 1967. *The Challenge of Crime in a Free Society.* Washington, D.C.: U.S. Government Printing Office.

Quinney, Richard, 1972. "The Ideology of Law: Notes for a Radical Alternative to Legal Oppression." *Issues in Criminology,* Winter.

———. 1973. *Critique of Legal Order: Crime Control in Capitalist Society.* Boston: Little, Brown.

Rickett, Allyn, and Adele Rickett. 1973. *Prisoners of Liberation: Four Years in a Chinese Communist Prison.* New York: Anchor.

Rusche, Georg, and Otto Kirchheimer. 1939. *Punishment and Social Structure.* New York: Columbia University.

Schrecker, Ellen. 1986. *No Ivory Tower: McCarthyism and the Universities.* New York: Oxford University Press.

Schwendinger, Herman, and Julia Schwendinger. 1970. "Defenders of Order or Guardians of Human Rights?" *Issues in Criminology* 5, no. 2.

————. 1974. *Sociologists of the Chair*. New York: Basic Books.

Seale, Bobby, 1968. *Seize the Time*. New York: Vintage.

Skolnick, Jerome. 1966. *Justice Without Trial*. New York: John Wiley.

Szasz, Thomas. 1965. *Psychiatric Justice*. New York: Macmillan.

Taylor, Ian, Paul Walton, and Jock Young. 1973. *The New Criminology*. London: Routledge & Kegan Paul.

Thomas, Piri. 1974. *Seven Long Times*. New York: Praeger.

Turner, William. 1970. *Hoover's FBI*. New York: Dell.

Wall, Robert. 1972. "Special Agent for the FBI." *New York Review of Books*, January 27.

Walker Report. 1968. *Rights in Conflict: The Violent Confrontation of Demonstrators and Police in the Parks and Streets of Chicago During the Week of the Democratic National Convention of 1968*. New York: Bantam Books.

Weinstein, James. 1969. *The Corporate Ideal in the Liberal State, 1900–1918*. Boston: Beacon.

Williams, William Appleman. 1966. *The Contours of American History*. Chicago: Quadrangle.

Wolfgang, Marvin, Leonard Savitz, and Norman Johnston, eds. 1962. *The Sociology of Crime and Delinquency*. New York: John Wiley.

Wright, Erik. 1973. *The Politics of Punishment*. New York: Harper & Row.

Zinn, Howard. 1970. *The Politics of History*. Boston: Beacon.

Chapter 14

Notes from an Anarchist Sociologist: May 1989

Howard J. Ehrlich

1.

BY THE YEAR 1965 the war in Vietnam had come to American campuses. Teach-ins had begun at the University of Iowa and Students for a Democratic Society (SDS) were organizing on campus. In my mid-thirties, I was already the model young professional. I had by then published two books and placed articles in all the right journals. I had tenure, a light teaching load, a good salary, graduate research fellows and assistants, even a part-time secretary.

But it became increasingly clear to me that the university was in complicity with the war makers, permitting faculty to conduct secret research, supporting military training on campus, reporting student grades to draft boards, and providing information on students and faculty to the FBI. Radical faculty were being fired and radical students were being flunked. Informants and provocateurs made their appearance. ROTC students audited certain courses to document deviant professors. As student activism increased, university managers became active agents of repression. Campus security people took notes on who attended political gatherings. False charges were brought against radical faculty and students; civil rights were trampled. All these were part of my personal experiences in those years. I was certainly too old to be a child of the sixties, but I definitely became of political age then.

I went from being a concerned, antiwar, liberal faculty member who counseled radical students and signed petitions to being a committed radical. I became an insurgent sociologist organizing students and faculty for the coming revolution. I felt that I could no longer comfortably pursue a professional career. I traded in my three-piece tweed suit for drawstring pants. They may have both been uniforms, but certainly my new one was more comfortable. By the time I left the university my hair was down to my shoulder blades and I carried a bag on my shoulder, usually filled with leaflets and posters and paraphernalia to hang them.

Much of my hair has since gone, but I still sport my Zapata-style mustache (grayed, of course) and my shoulder bag is still full of posters and political propaganda.

2.

For me it all started at a campus rally on the steps of the Old Capitol on the Iowa campus where a group of students carrying a black flag made an appearance. I was puzzled, and so I asked one of my radical faculty friends what the flag was all about. That's the black flag of anarchism, he told me. The expression on my face must have been a giveaway. "You mean," he said with that tone of condescension that authoritarian faculty reserve for their graduate students, "you haven't read the Marx-Bakunin correspondence?"

3.

And so I went in search of the Marx-Bakunin correspondence. Looking for it was a great experience; the political encounters of the two men presaged the encounters of marxists and anarchists for this century. I was, however, unable to locate any serious preserved correspondence. I simply chalked up the experience to my being victimized by yet another academic pretension.

I did find one interesting letter, however. It was from Kropotkin to Lenin. In 1920 Kropotkin wrote:

> One thing is indisputable. Even if dictatorship of the party were an appropriate means to bring about a blow to the capitalist system (which I strongly doubt), it is nevertheless harmful for the creation of a new socialist system. What are necessary and needed are local institutions, local forces; but there are none. . . . Without participation of local forces, without organization from below of the peasants and workers themselves, it is impossible to build a new life."

I also set out to look for references to anarchism in the textbooks on the history of social thought. Except for some references in the writings of Sorokin and Nicolas Timasheff, both Russian sociologists who cited some Russian anarchists in passing, not a single other text of the late 1960s recognized the existence of anarchist social thought.

4.

In the process of my search, I realized that I had been an anarchist all my life and that, without being aware of it, I had recapitulated in my own world view what writers like Malatesta, Kropotkin, and Bakunin had been doing, saying, and writing. It was still a while before I would encounter the writings of Murray Bookchin who, more than anyone during the last twenty-five years, articulated the fundamental differences among anarchists, liberals, and marxists.

5.

I want to now make a disclaimer. The combination of time and ego have doubtless smoothed the edges of my narrative, while the constraints of space have led to my overlooking many things. What I am trying to do here is present my odyssey as a radical and a sociologist, to let a new generation of radical academics know that there is a good intellectual life outside the academy. But I am also trying to present the political ideas that guide this odyssey.

As I have struggled to develop that life, I have come to believe that the role of radicals in society today is to create other radicals.

6.

In the late sixties many of us saw ourselves as creating "the revolution" without comprehending that a revolution is a process, not an event. I can vividly recall sitting in a study group and seriously debating two Weatherman documents that had set a timetable for the new American revolution. We knew that we were engaged in revolutionary times, but we hadn't allowed ourselves to confront what that actually meant. What makes the recollection so vivid is that the telephone in our meeting room (which was in my basement) began smoking. A poorly installed or faulty transmitter had overheated. Few events can increase your political zeal more than knowing that agents of the state are listening in.

7.

Well before the activities of the New Left and the new feminist movement came to formulate the equation of the personal and the political, Errico Malatesta was writing: "Revolution is the creation of new living institutions, new groupings, new social relationships; it is the destruction of privileges and monopolies."

Colin Ward, the distinguished British anarchist, wrote in *Anarchy in Action* (1973) not of revolutionary change but of the "prospects for increasing the anarchist content of the real world." Like other social anarchists, he sees anarchy as "an act of social self-determination." It is in that conjuncture of social and self that the revolutionary process comes into being. So like earlier anarchists I came to believe that one must change oneself in the process of changing society. There can be no personal liberation without revolution; there can be no revolution without personal liberation.

8.

In 1971, I was promoted to a full professorship at the University of Iowa after bringing charges of political discrimination against the sociology department. Although I had been the head of the department's largest graduate program and was quite well published professionally, I had been frozen in rank and was being systematically deprived of students and student assistants. Some graduate students were told not to take courses with me since it would endanger their career chances, and some others were just advised that I was a known revolutionary and should be avoided. Graduate students who worked with me were being sanctioned, and several were actually failed by a right-wing professor. The university's investigating committee ruled that while I had indeed been unjustly denied promotion, the denial was not political. I accepted the promotion despite the wormy decision and awarded myself an unpaid leave of absence. I never returned, submitting my resignation the following year when I was threatened with being fired for being AWOL.

Supported by my former wife, who some years later was to be fired (that is, "not renewed") for her political activities by the University of Maryland, Baltimore County, I was able to complete work on my book *The Social Psychology of Prejudice.* As I was finishing the book, I also began to organize Research Group One and the Great Atlantic Radio Conspiracy, my first organizing adventures as an independent radical sociologist. I want to write about these here, but first I want to describe some of the reasons I left the academy.

9.

When I left the university, I knew it was the end of my academic and professional career. I was what the psychologist Milton Rokeach called an "ideological renegade." Few persons are rejected more intensely, as Rokeach's research on open- and closed-mindedness documents, than those who defect from a sacred institution. Even though I had worked closely with Rokeach, I wasn't fully prepared for the level of hostility and rejection that followed. One old friend set up a meeting with my daughter, who was then only thirteen, to determine if I was having severe psychological problems. Many of my marxist comrades in the academy simply wrote me off. Clearly I no longer mattered in the profession, and I had to warn all my former students who had relied on me for a reference that their association with me might no longer be helpful.

The problem for me was how to put into practice my developing conceptions of radical sociology. Several of us had agreed, in Iowa City, to move to Baltimore, where we would establish a "people's research center." Much as the "Science for Vietnam" and the "Science for the People" groups were trying to harness scientific knowledge to "serve the people," I thought we ought to be able to do the same from a social science perspective.

Moving our commune and multiple marriages turned out to be more complex and traumatic than we had anticipated and some stayed behind. The result was that we incorporated Research Group One in Iowa and printed letterhead that read "offices in Iowa City and Baltimore."

Even printing the letterhead was a personal/political act. While some radical academics went out and practiced target shooting and others studied guerrilla revolutions, I had decided to learn how to run a printing press. Once a week for several months I practiced on the press at a local community college north of Iowa City. As tacticians as diverse as Napoleon and Che Guevara have said, one newspaper is more to be feared than an army.

If I ever had any doubts about my preparations for what was to come, they were dispelled one night when I was returning to Iowa City from the print shop. Military searchlights lit the sky. I could see them miles from the city and followed them back to town. Large numbers of sheriffs and police and firefighters had surrounded a high-rise men's dorm. Earlier that night several students had been painting over the windows of parking meters. (At a time when we had been demanding free education, free food, and free love, free parking seemed a modest demand.) When the students were spotted by the police, they ran into the men's dorm. The police, believing, like many of the radical students, that we were already at war, began lobbing tear-gas canisters into this high-rise dorm. At least one area was set on fire, and hundreds of men, many of whom had been awakened from sleep, were evacuated under surveillance. My encounters with the police and National Guard were to become more frequent and more direct over the years.

10.

Research Group One (RG-1) was a serious attempt to build a local resource as a base for doing community research and for radical social scientists. In our flier we described ourselves as "an anti-profit collective

engaged in social science research and the application of research findings for social change." There were far more people involved than I can
possibly recall, but among those who achieved recognition in other contexts were Carol Ehrlich, Fred Pincus, Chris Bose, Natalie Sokoloff,
Glenda Morris, Nancy Henley, and David DeLeon.

First let me tell you some of things we did over the years: an evaluation study of the outcome of a conference on radical teaching and
teacher unionization; a study of recruitment and defection from a national left organization; an evaluation study of an organizing meeting of a
proposed new national coalition of population, ecology, and minority
defense groups; two extensive community surveys dealing with unethical
food-store and loan-company practices, and community perceptions of
alternative services in local neighborhoods (free clinics, food co-ops); a
readership survey of a local socialist triweekly newspaper, and a study of
community response to the first issue of an alternative newspaper.

One of our last studies illustrates what we were trying to do as well as
the problem of supporting ourselves financially. The coordinator of the
major food co-op in the city called us in to consult; he was having difficulty assessing the members' food preferences and also their motivations
to participate. With the coordinator and several other co-op members we
designed a study to make that assessment. Some co-op members were
trained as interviewers, others as coders. The findings were presented
orally at co-op meetings, written up in a pamphlet distributed to all members, and eventually incorporated into two radio programs, one on how
to organize a food co-op and the other on the politics of food co-ops. Of
course the co-op had no money to pay for our services, but they did give
us a worker's discount on our groceries.

11.

Basically we found ourselves doing surveys and evaluation studies. We
did some "self-defense" work. For example, we uncovered the kinship,
friendship, and corporate ties of a federal judge who was presiding over
an important political trial, looking for a clear conflict of interest. Although I believe such defensive work is important, it was hard for us to
convince others to become involved. Since such work often involved the
police and the courts, many people were frightened away.

We had hoped, also, to study ourselves in the process of doing our
work. What we really needed was a skilled observer, a member of the
research collective, who would study us while we were working. Unfortunately, we never ever had an "extra" person. Instead we settled for
reflection and self-evaluation sessions after the fact.

We did formulate a set of principles of radical research; in fact, they became the guide for our work.

First, *we tried not to impose our research on anyone*. Our concern, rather, was to try to involve the "subjects" not only in formulating the goals of the research but also in the research process itself. This is not easily done. For large-scale surveys, you need different means to ensure that the research is neither exploitative nor irrelevant.

Straight sociologists testing hypotheses derived from formal theory are actually rare. But even for such rare occasions, we need to understand that the long-term needs of a sociologist are not necessarily, or likely, to be the needs of the people being studied. And the rewards will go the sociologist, not to the research participants. Most sociology, even where serious though not formal theoretical hypotheses are being tested, is based on the intent of the researcher: either to make a contribution to the field or (mainly) to enhance his or her publication credits. I do not mean that pejoratively, although it's obviously not what I want to do with my skills. Being a sociologist means working in a hierarchical, bureaucratic organization that measures job performance primarily by writing productivity. Successful straight sociologists are required to make some contribution to that body of knowledge called sociology. Radical sociologists may use the same rigorous methodology, but their goal is *to contribute to building a good society*. (I will say more about that later.)

Relevance and social significance are insured by designing what Kurt Lewin called action research, what in today's jargon is called policy research. So in RG-1, in my current work, and indeed any radical social science enterprise, *the important guiding principle of research is how one can act on its findings*. All radical researchers must have in mind a sketch of what can be done with their findings. Excluding serendipitous findings, you ought to be able to say that if the results are X, we do C, and if the results are not X then we do B. And one can then assess whether B or C are good things and whether they are feasible. The radical researcher needs also to assess whether B or C are outcomes that can be more easily manipulated by an elite than by the people for whom the research is intended.

With respect to the research process, *radical research is a collective effort*. At the very least it is not hierarchical. We do not have to deny training, experience, or expert knowledge to function collectively. We do need to deny that such authority gives a person extra privileges. It is one thing, as anarchists throughout history have insisted, to be *an* authority; it is something else to be *in* authority.

Finally, with respect to the communication of research findings, the radical sociolgost knows that most research is written up in a specialized language and published in relatively inaccessible journals or books. The function of that is to further empower those already in power. *The findings of radical research must be accessible.* To that end, RG-1 adopted a multimedia strategy. All research had to be reported through many means, and publication in professional outlets as our lowest priority. In our first two years we began a radio program and a pamphlet series, and many years later we began a magazine. All were seen as alternative means to our end of making radical ideas accessible to a wide audience.

Research Group One Reports started as a set of reports published by the Liberated Xerox Press. They became so popular that in 1973 we issued our first four printed pamphlets. By the time we hung it up, we had published eighteen pamphlets in editions ranging from one thousand to five thousand; several were reprinted around the world. The pamphlet series paid RG-1's overhead for years. Many were adopted by radical teachers for classroom use, and some are still being used in photocopy in study groups and classrooms. We quit publishing pamphlets because it was no longer economically viable. For one thing, when we began we could mail a pamphlet at book rate for ten cents. Today, with a ninety-cent book rate, the postage may cost more than the printing. We sold most of our early pamphlets for under a dollar, figuring that their low price would make them affordable to most people. That same pamphlet today would have to sell for three to four dollars.

12.

I want to make some final comments on the politics of research. Many forms of research are terrific organizing tools. People involved in the research become its advocates. They have a personal involvement in communicating the results and in acting upon them. The research process itself can involve even more than the researchers. Doing research on matters of deep personal concern also shows those who agree to be interviewed or tested or observed that some people do really care about them and about the issues that concern them. And telling someone you are studying that you care is an important personal and political act.

There is another component of radical research that I haven't discussed, and that is *research on critical issues.* Our pamphlet series allowed us to publish our research on strategic social issues—the politics of news media control, alternative forms of education, how to locate nuclear weapons sites in your home community. The series also enabled us to address issues that concerned the left. One of our best sellers and most widely reprinted pieces was Carol Ehrlich's "Socialism, Anarchism, and Feminism," which was the first major comparison of these positions. We also published pamphlets on how to do radical research and on the conditions of feminist research.

13.

"This is the Great Atlantic Radio Conspiracy. We are still at large." Since 1972 myself and other members of the Conspiracy collective have opened our weekly radio program with this announcement, part pretentious and part portentous. We have survived by our wits and through our commitment. For many years the Radio Conspiracy has been the largest circulating left periodical in the United States, though my comrades are always embarrassed when I state it publicly.

14.

In late 1972 we took to the airwaves. The Great Atlantic Radio Conspiracy (billed as a production of Research Group One) began its weekly half-hour series on a National Public Radio affiliate in Baltimore. The founding group included Carol Ehrlich, Chris Bose, Bob Zeffert, Paul Kreiss, and myself. Paul is a biochemist, the rest of us were trained in the social sciences. Later we were joined by historians, theater and radio people, and by listeners who came to volunteer.

We began with great excitement and little understanding of the medium. Not only did we not realize that writing for radio was different than writing for publication, we also didn't realize until we walked into the studio that we were expected to be our own recording engineers. Our first program, "What's New with the New Left?" was boring and technically incompetent. Our second program on alternatives in education was interesting but technically incompetent. At that point the program director called us in and said he was assigning the news director to coach us. The news director called in the operations manager, and they both tutored us for almost a year. And by that year, 1973, we had achieved such a level of competency that we won the first of what were to be nine national awards for radio production. The winning program was "The IQ Fallacy" and with it we had solidified our style—a dense, highly produced mix of scripted research, interviews, music, comedy, and special effects. The competition, sponsored by the American Psychological Association, awarded prizes that year to *The New Yorker* for magazines, to ABC for television, and to the Conspiracy for radio. We decided at that point to go national and we began to syndicate ourselves. In January 1988, we produced our five hundredth program, celebrating the event with a nationally distributed show about currents in media control.

15.

I happen to like radio. In fact I have more radios in my house than the American average, which is four. Radio is an important medium; more people listen to radio every day than watch TV. Average adult listening is about three hours daily, a good deal of that on car radios.

Producing good radio is intellectually challenging and esthetically satisfying. It is also personally gratifying to realize that we have been played on almost two hundred radio stations around the world. Tapes of our shows are stocked in libraries in the United States, Canada, Australia, and New Zealand. In addition our tapes have been used by teachers, in community organizing, in union halls, and in study groups.

Several years ago we collectively produced a "political statement" to describe the Great Atlantic Radio Conspiracy. For me and my companions, the statement summarizes what we are about as we sit in an isolated studio ostensibly talking to only a microphone and ourselves. Here are a few excerpts.

> We are a working collective. Those aren't just words to us. Our perspective is that fundamental social changes are going on right now. Change is a process, not a sudden apocalyptic event after which everything will be perfect. Part of the process of radical change is how we organize ourselves in our work. If a group divides itself into leaders and followers, into skilled and unskilled, into cadre and mass, then that group is recapitulating many of the pathologies of bureaucratic and authoritarian organizations.
>
> We are a political collective. Most of us identify with social anarchism. We reject older forms of organization such as unions and political parties that claim to be working for change. We reject the political economies of both capitalism and socialism. We have no "party line," nor even a "correct line." And we don't expect to find one.
>
> We all believe that if the promises of ongoing changes in society are to be fulfilled, they cannot and will not be "led" by a small group claiming the correct line and imposing it on everyone else.
>
> We are a political radio collective. Producing radio programs is our primary political work. Although members of the Conspiracy do work in other political contexts, we see our primary task as that of countering the cultural/political domination of the American mind by the capitalist media.

We see ourselves as presenting alternative ways of looking at the world and at specific events of the day. In doing so we work to increase the density of radical thought and of revolutionary symbols.

That about sums up our perspectives. We believe that revolutionary social change is essential; that it is going on right now; and that how we implement our ideas has as many implications for building a good society as do our abstract goals.

Do we have a program for revolutionary change? We think that, at best, all we can do is assist others in organizing themselves. We can't do it for them. We can't liberate anyone from above; people have to participate in their own liberation. We can, as a media collective, present an analysis of present conditions and a sketch of alternatives. That's what we see ourselves as doing.

16.

In October 1975, TBS—The Baltimore School issued its first catalog. Glenda Morris and I, along with two others who were soon to drop out, designed what we hoped would become an alternative learning network organized on anarchist principles and built on the model of the "free university." We offered short-term, evening and weekend courses in the homes and workplaces of our teachers. Our collective was joined by Tom Knoche, Vicki Dello Joio, and Chris Stadler, among others. At various times we had more volunteers than we could coordinate.

Our commitment was to offer courses on political philosophy (anarchism, marxism, feminism); survival skills (from nutrition and bread baking through bicycle repair and Aikido); and courses for personal development.

The school persisted for seven intense years. More than two hundred teachers had offered workshops and courses to approximately three thousand students. TBS also developed a series of public forums and cultural events at a neighborhood coffeehouse and began a radio program featuring our teachers and local activists.

Out of our activities the "no nukes" alliance in Baltimore began so did the first citywide housing coalition. The Group for Anarchist Studies organized around the school. Many of these groups as well as the TBS Radio Forum and several self-help "classes" persisted for years after we closed shop in 1982. We didn't realize until late in the game that what we were creating was not just a network of classes, teachers, and students, but that we were building an alternative community institution that required our efforts not just as coordinators but as community organizers.

17.

Lecterns, seminar tables, and classroom buildings are all part of the props that teachers often unconsciously use to distance themselves from students. And behind these props, should they be shaky or should the professorial role performance be flawed, lie the ultimate weapons— grades and course credits. Hold a class in your living room for no credit and with no grades, and you learn what it is to be a teacher.

There were other political lessons that I learned through TBS. One had to do with state control of education. By calling ourselves a school, we became subject to the rules and regulations of the Maryland State Department of Education. It appeared that under state law, Maryland has the exclusive right to use or control the use of such names as "school," "academy," "college," and so on.

We became a target of the regulators early on, and it seemed to me that their zeal in pursuing us was as much a part of their hostility to our political character as to the fact that they feared losing control. We variously ignored their claims and threats, attacked them, met with them as reasonable folk, and even staged a bit of guerrilla theater in their offices. The net result was that we garnered a fair amount of publicity, a good deal of public support, and held them at bay for as long as we were around. We were the first to challenge their authority, but it was clear that had we continued there would have been a showdown. For the state, we learned, education is too dangerous to let people build their own institutions.

18.

Through the 1970s as I became involved in my own study of anarchist thought, I began to germinate the idea of an anarchist anthology. The two earlier anthologies—one strange collection by Irving L. Horowitz (*The Anarchists*, 1964) and the other by Len Krimerman and Lewis Perry— collected mainly older writers. I mentioned to David DeLeon, who was then a member of the Conspiracy collective and was at work on his book *The American as Anarchist*, that there was a need for a contemporary collection. As it turned out David had already developed an outline. So we quickly recruited two other co-Conspirators, Carol Ehrlich and Glenda Morris, and set off to read everything that had been written by anarchists in the past ten years. Out of our reading and discussions came the anthology *Reinventing Anarchy* (1970).

It seemed at the time only a short step from the book to recruiting many of the contributors to participate with us in establishing a serious intellectual journal of anarchism. It turned out to be a very long step, but by the winter of 1980 we produced the first issue of *Social Anarchism: A Journal of Practice and Theory.*

We organized the journal on a professional model with an editorial board and the requirement that articles be refereed. We have fourteen members on our editorial board—men and women who are activists, academics, performers, artists, and writers. Every article we receive is reviewed by at least two editors. We were able to assemble some of the most productive and creative anarchist thinkers in the country as editors and as contributors. The journal has grown steadily, from the first edition of 54 typewriter-type pages to 128 pages typeset on our own computer. The journal was reviewed by the editor of the English *Bulletin of Anarchist Research*, who called it the leading intellectual magazine of anarchism in the English language.

On its masthead, my coeditors Chris Stadler and Mark Bevis and I wrote, "As both political philosophy and personal lifestyle, social anarchism promotes community self-reliance, direct participation in political decision-making, respect for nature, and nonviolent paths to peace and justice."

19.

In 1986 economic necessity and an opportunity I couldn't resist returned me to a regular job. A new, small nonprofit organization in Baltimore advertised for a research director. My friend Jean Grisso out of loving concern read the want ads every Sunday looking to place me in something that would make me happy and relieve her worry for my economic well-being, found the ad. The organization was the National Institute Against Prejudice and Violence.

As the institute's first research director, I was called on to develop policy research in the area of sociology I knew best—prejudice and intergroup relations. I developed a research agenda that was consistent with my principles of radical research and found a positive reception from institute staff. Although the organization tends toward the bureaucratic, it functions paradoxically at a cooperative level that borders on collectivity. There is a higher level of collegiality than on any college faculty I have experienced.

At the institute I have initiated a program of research on ethnoviolence. "Ethnoviolence" is a term I coined to refer to psychological or physical assaults on people that are motivated by group prejudice. The studies cover ethnoviolence at the workplace, on campuses, in residential areas, and the communications media—all conducted from the standpoint of the victim. The objective is to determine the conditions under which ethnoviolent acts occur and the impact on the victims. Again, in keeping with principles of action research, the policy options have already been charted: options in regard to intervention, reporting, consulting, and victim assistance. A multimedia strategy for the communication of our findings is already in place.

A full description of the details of the ethnoviolence project must wait for another day and another forum.

20.

I think that Mao was right in his understanding of the role of intellectuals: that they were an essentially amoral force in society, most likely to shift their allegiance if their own class privileges were threatened. The Cultural Revolution, its failure notwithstanding, attempted to change the role of the intellectual. One need only look at the behavior of the American marxist or socialist or allegedly radical faculty during the period of New Left activism on campus to realize that they were, in fact, trapped in their role. They were authoritarian and hierarchical in their professional as well as their political life. They talked of democracy, but their conception was really of a democracy for the elictes.

Let me tell you a story about that. At one of the national gatherings of the New University Conference, which was the major organizational outlet for nonsectarian left faculty at the time, the Iowa chapter came with an organizational proposal. Concerned with the elitism that seemed to be developing, we made a modest proposal that central organizing committee members not be allowed to succeed themselves and that terms be staggered so that each year half the committee membership would expire. In most contexts you might take that to be nothing more than a liberal democratic proposal. In this context, our chapter became labeled the "anarchist" chapter. A powerful speaker, Al Szymanski, jumped to his feet after our resolution and declared that if Lenin had been on the organizing committee "these people would have kicked him off." He was applauded wildly. Our proposal had generated much tension and his riposte led to its overwhelming defeat.

Mao wrote in his Red Book that "a revolution is not a dinner party," but many of my comrades, I came to realize, really wanted it to be just that. They were not about to seriously endanger their careers or to take to the streets. They were not about to deal with their students as peers. Sure, they may have felt guilty about grading them, but they went on grading them—for the draft board, for their potential employers, for the sake of control, and for the sake of their own jobs. Most were trapped by the golden fetters of a good-paying job, a three-month vacation, sabbaticals, and grants, and no doubt mortgages on car, home, and boat. A marxist professor is not a marxist revolutionary. I have the feeling that they are the people Mao warned us about.

Many of the more experienced analysts of the sixties quickly grasped what even the current wave of writers still have not understood. The major impulse of student radicalism then was essentially anarchist. Paul Goodman wrote, in 1968, "The protesting students are Anarchist because they are in a historical situation to which Anarchism is their only possible response." To this he added that students "are new as a mass and they are confused about their position." (For those interested, Greg Calvert and Carol Neiman's nearly forgotten study, *A Disrupted History* (1971), and Kirkpatrick Sale's *SDS* (1973) are excellent analyses of the ferment and confusion of the period.)

21.

One of the primary slogans of the sixties, and there were certainly many, was that "the personal is the political." I believed it then; I believe it now. There is a major difference between opposing sexism in your study group and opposing the institutionalized sexist practices of your academic department. It is hard to take seriously some male intellectual calling for gender equality when his everyday behavior conforms to the traditional patriarchal role, or when he has done nothing more than profess his remorse over his inability to change his behavior.

Many leftists rationalize the discrepancy between their political ideology and their personal behavior as an understandable smudge (dare we say flaw?) in their otherwise politically correct lives. They see the causes for that discrepancy as external to them, something that will be taken care of after the revolution. They have fallen victim to the "ordinal fallacy"—first I will do this, then I will do that. Personal liberation will come after the revolution. The fact is, we are what we do. And if we do not do today what we believe to be true, it is the nature of life that we will probably not do it tomorrow.

22.

In his 1988 presidential address to the American Sociological Association, Herbert J. Gans wrote, "We ought also to confront once more an old, recently forgotten question: what is a good society and how can sociology bring it about?" Aside from the fact that I thought the question had been long forgotten, underlying its formulation is the elitist idea of the sociologist as the certified agent for constructing models of society and social relations.

For Gans, however, this is neither the primary task of sociologists; nor are they to be involved, as sociologists, in the actual building of that society. In contrast, I view the primary task of social scientists as participating in developing a sketch of the good society. But, unlike Professor Gans, I think that all research and scholarship should be judged by its relevance to that task, that is to the task of advancing us toward that society. Furthermore, we must live as if we were resident in that society—as if, as the poet Marge Piercy put it, we were part of an experiment in the future. It is the strategy of the anarchist sociologist not merely to do sociology but to help build that new society in the vacant lots of the old.

NOTE

The title and format of this essay are modeled on a piece I wrote for the first anthology of radical sociology. The anthology, titled *Radical Sociology*, was edited by J. David Colfax and Jack L. Roach (New York: Basic Books, 1971). To spare you the search, the Kropotkin-Lenin exchange is printed in P. A. Kropotkin, *Selected Writings in Anarchism and Revolution*, ed. Martin A. Miller (Cambridge, Mass.: MIT Press, 1970). Most of the other works cited are readily available. The Great Atlantic Radio Conspiracy is still broadcasting and its catalog is available from them at 2743 Maryland Avenue, Baltimore, MD 21218.

PART IV

Documents

We include two documents that we feel capture the essence of the development of radical sociology in the late 1960s. Martin Nicolaus's "Fat-Cat Sociology" was prepared as a speech given at the annual meetings of the American Sociological Association (ASA) in August 1968 in Boston. Nicolaus was on the platform with Wilbur Cohen, then Secretary of Health, Education, and Welfare and keynote speaker at the convention. Organizers of the Sociology Liberation Movement (SLM) had met with ASA officers to protest Cohen's appearance as a major speaker. For proponents of the SLM, Wilbur Cohen represented an administration that was carrying out an illegal war on the Indochinese people. To them, ASA's willingness to have Cohen as a keynote speaker merely indicated the complicity of the sociology profession with the war effort. SLM organizers requested that Martin Nicolaus be allowed to speak alongside Cohen to represent the views of radical sociologists. In many ways, Nicolaus's speech outlined the major views of the Sociology Liberation Movement.

The "Women's Caucus Statement and Resolutions to the General Business Meeting of the American Sociological Association" on September 3, 1969, was an attempt to draw attention to the forms of discrimination most commonly experienced by women in sociology departments and professional associations. In 1969, 67 percent of women graduate students in the United States had no senior female sociology professor during the course of graduate studies. No women were associate editors of the American Sociological Review *or members of the advisory board of the* American Journal of Sociology. *Although these resolutions were introduced two decades ago, and even though some forms of discrimination have been addressed, many of the statements and resolutions are still applicable today.*

Chapter 15

Fat-Cat Sociology
Martin Nicolaus

THESE REMARKS are not addressed to the Secretary of Health, Education, and Welfare. This man has agreed voluntarily to serve as a member of a government which is presently fighting a war for survival on two fronts. Imperial wars such as the one against Vietnam are usually two-front wars—one against the foreign subject population, one against the domestic subject population. The Secretary of HEW is a military officer in the domestic front of the war against people. Experience in the Vietnam teach-ins has shown that dialogue between the subject population and its rulers is an exercise in repressive tolerance. It is, in Robert S. Lynd's words, dialogue between chickens and elephants. He holds some power over me—therefore, even if he is wrong in his arguments, he is right; even if I'm right, I'm wrong.

I do address myself to the secretary's audience. There is some hope—even though the hour is very late—that among the members and sympathizers of the sociological profession gathered here there will be some whose life is not so sold and compromised as to be out of their own control to change or amend it.

While the officers of this convention and the previous speaker were having a big meal in the hotel, I was across the street in a cafeteria having a hot dog and two cups of coffee. This may be why my perspective is different.

The ruling elite within your profession is in charge of what is called health, education, and welfare. Those of you who listened passively to what he had to say presumably agreed that this definition—this description of what the man did—carried an accurate message. Yet among you are many, including the hard researchers, who do know better or should know better. The department of which the man is head is more accurately described as the agency which watches over the inequitable distribution of preventable disease, over the funding of domestic propaganda and indoctrination, and over the preservation of a cheap and docile reserve labor force to keep everybody else's wages down. He is secretary of disease, propaganda, and scabbing.

This may be put too strongly for you, but it all depends on where you look from, where you stand. If you stand inside the Sheraton Hotel these terms are offensive, but if you gentlemen and ladies would care to step across the street into Roxbury you might get a different perspective and a different vocabulary. If you will look at the social world through the eyes of those who are at the bottom of it, through the eyes of your subject population (and if you will endow those eyes with the same degree of clear-sightedness you profess to encourage among yourselves), then you will get a different conception of the social science to which you are devoted. That is to say that this assembly here tonight is a kind of lie. It is not a coming together of those who study and know, or promote study and knowledge of, social reality. It is a conclave of high and low priests, scribes, intellectual valets, and their innocent victims, engaged in the mutual affirmation of a falsehood, in common consecration of a myth.

Sociology is not now and never has been any kind of objective seeking out of social truth or reality. Historically, the profession is an outgrowth of nineteenth-century European traditionalism and conservatism, wedded to twentieth-century American corporation liberalism.

That is to say that the eyes of sociologists, with few but honorable (or honorable but few) exceptions, have been turned downward, and their palms upward.

Eyes down, to study the activities of the lower classes of the subject population—those activities which created problems for the smooth exercise of governmental hegemony. Since the class of rulers in this society identifies itself as the society itself—in the same way that Davis and Moore in their infamous 1945 propaganda article identified the society with those who run it—therefore the problems of the ruling class get defined as social problems. The profession has moved beyond the tearjerking stage today: "social problems" is no longer the preferred term; but the underlying perspective is the same. The things that are sociologically "interesting" are the things that are interesting to those who stand at the top of the mountain and feel the tremors of an earthquake.

Sociologists stand guard in the garrison and report to its masters on the movements of the occupied populace. The more adventurous sociologists don the disguise of the people and go out to mix with the peasants in the "field," returning with books and articles that break the protective secrecy in which a subjugated population wraps itself, and make it more accessible to manipulation and control.

The sociologist as a researcher in the employ of his employers is precisely a kind of spy. The proper exercise of the profession is all-too-often different from the proper exercise of espionage only in the relatively greater electronic sophistication of the latter's techniques.

Is it an accident, to name only a few examples here, that industrial sociology arose in a context of rising "labor troubles," that political economy grew when elections became less predictable, or that the sociology of race relations is flourishing now?

As sociologists you owe your jobs to the union orgainzers who got beat up, to the voters who got fed up, to the black people who got shot up. Sociology has risen to its present prosperity and eminence on the blood and bones of the poor and oppressed; it owes its prestige in this society to its putative ability to give information and advice to the ruling class of this society about ways and means to keep the people down.

The professional eyes of the sociologist are on the down people, and the professional palm of the sociologist is stretched toward the up people. It is no secret and no original discovery that the major and dominant sectors of sociology today are sold—computers, codes, and questionnaires—to the people who have enough money to afford this ornament, and who see a useful purpose being served by keeping hundreds of intelligent men and women occupied in the pursuit of harmless trivia—and off the streets. I am not asserting that every individual researcher sells his brain for a bribe—although many of us know of research projects where that has happened literally—but merely that the dominant structure of the profession, in which all of its members are to some extent socialized, is a structure in which service to the ruling class of this society is the highest form of honor and achievement. (The speaker's table today is an illustration.) The honored sociologist, the big-status sociologist, the jet-set sociologist, the fat-contract sociologist, the book-a-year sociologist, the sociologist who always wears the livery, the suit and tie, of his masters—this is the type of sociologist who sets the tone and the ethic of the profession, and it is this type of sociologist who is nothing more or less than a house servant in the corporate establishment, a white intellectual Uncle Tom not only for this government and ruling class, but for any government and ruling class—which explains to my mind why Soviet sociologists and American sociologists are finding, after all, they have something in common.

To raise and educate and train generation after generation of the brightest minds this country's so-called educational system has let survive to this sociological ethic of servility, to socialize them into this sociocracy, is a criminal undertaking: one of the many felonies against youth committed by those who set themselves up in a loco parentis situation that is usually far more oppressive than any real parental relation. The crime which graduate schools perpetrate against the minds and morals of young people is all the more inexcusable because of the enormous liberating potential of knowledge about social life. Unlike knowledge about trees and stones, knowledge about people directly affects what we are, what we do, what we may hope for. The corporate rulers of this society would not be spending as much money as they do for knowledge, if knowledge did not confer power. So far, sociologists have been schlepping this knowledge that confers power along a one-way chain, taking knowledge from the people, giving knowledge to the rulers.

What if that machinery were reversed? What if the habits, problems, secrets, and unconscious motivations of the wealthy and powerful were daily scrutinized by a thousand systematic researchers; were hourly pried into, analyzed, and cross referenced; were tabulated and published in a hundred inexpensive mass-circulation journals and written so that even the fifteen-year-old high school dropout could understand them and predict the actions of his landlord, manipulate and control him?

Would the war in Vietnam have been possible if the structure, function, and motion of the U.S. imperial establishment had been a matter of detailed public knowledge ten years ago?

Sociology has worked to create and increase the inequitable distribution of knowledge; it has worked to make the power structure relatively more powerful and knowledgeable, and thereby to make the subject population relatively more impotent and ignorant.

In the late summer of 1968, while the political party currently in power is convening amidst barbed wire and armored cars, the sociological profession ought to consider itself especially graced and blessed that its own deliberations can still be carried on with a police-to-participant ratio smaller than one to one. This may be because the people of the USA do not know how much of their current troubles stem, to borrow Lord Keynes's phase, from the almost-forgotten scribblings of an obscure professor of sociology. Or it may be that sociology is still so crude that it represents no clear and present danger.

In 1968 it is late, very late; too late to say once again what Robert S. Lynd and C. Wright Mills and hundreds of others have long said: that the profession must reform itself. In view of the forces and the money that stand behind sociology as an excerise in intellectual servility, it is unrealistic to expect the body of the profession to make an about face.

If the barbed wire goes up around the ASA convention in a future year, most of its members will still not know why.

Chapter 16

Women's Caucus Statement and Resolutions to the General Business Meeting of the American Sociological Association
September 3, 1969

FOR ALL OUR commitment to studies on social change, the record of the sociological profession has been poor indeed when it comes to predicting and explaining the emergence and the course of major social and political change. We anticipated neither the sharp rise nor the fall of fertility rates in the past twenty-five years and have only a partial retrospective understanding of why these changes have occurred. We neither predicted nor explained the critical turing points in the civil rights or the New Left movements during the past ten years. And unless sociology has a sharp and dramatic awakening rather soon, this predominantly male field will show the same blindness in the late 1960s to the emergence, scale, and significance of the women's liberation movement in this country.

Where women are concerned, the majority of men sociologists still engage in the put-down, via ridicule, exclusion masked as sexual flattery, and overt as well as covert denial of the civil rights of women in hiring and promotion. The same white men who experienced embarrassment and outrage in old screen stereotypes of the superstitious, foot-shuffling servility of a Steppin Fetchet still accept and act upon a stereotyped set of expectations of male intellectual and social dominance and female intellectual and social dependency that is as outrageous to women as the Negro stereotype is to blacks. Sociological research and scholarship are rife with a complacent, conventional acceptance of the "what is ought to be" variety, nowhere more apparent than in theory and research on women, marriage, and the family. There is a great and pressing need for critical reassessment of many psychological and sociological assumptions in the area of sex role and family structure. To cite but one example: in a world bursting with the potential economic and political chaos of population excess, the demographic applied branches of sociology tinker with technological contraceptive gadgetry, despite the fact that research has suggested that the population problem is far more one of how to reduce

wanted pregnancies than of avoiding unwanted ones. To effect a reduction in wanted pregnancies hinges on the critical issue of what women
do with their lives. Any attempts to thwart the aspirations of women for
achievement in nonfamily roles is not only a violation of their basic human rights but a blind encouragement of a bountiful maternity the world
no longer needs.

As sociologists we should be capable of distancing ourselves from the
dailiness of public and private life, and to work with rather than against
any movement dedicated to an expansion of individual opportunity and
human rights. It is a failure of the society and of the sociology profession
in particular to find, as the women's caucus survey of graduate departments did this spring, that women were 30 percent of the doctoral students in graduate school this past year, but only 4 percent of the full-time
full professors in graduate departments, or to find that women were 39
percent of the research associates in the elite graduate departments but
only 5 percent of the associate and 1 percent of the full professors in
these same top departments. It is outrageous that a custom persists
whereby a woman research associate or lecturer with a Ph.D. and ten years
or more of research experience cannot apply for research funds as a sole
principal investigator, while a young man with a brand-new assistant professorship but no prior responsibility for conducting research can readily
do so.

Women are tired of the rationalized litany of their male colleagues:
"but women drop out of graduate work to marry and rear a family." In
1969, the question is: What are *you*, the men in graduate sociology departments, doing to retain these highly selected women graduate students? Since these women are carefully selected, else they would not be
in your departments, it is more a failure of a department than of the
student if they leave without a degree. Do you permit easy transfer of graduate credits to another university? Do you suggest part-time study with
stipend support to ease study-home combinations of responsibilities? Has
any department studied its Ph.D. dropouts, much less established policies
aimed at reducing this loss of talented young people? Has any sociologist
surveyed his own university student, employee, and faculty body to gauge
the need that might be met by the establishment of university day care
centers for preschool youngsters?

The Women's Caucus does not seek any new committees, new sym-
posia, new conferences on the status of women or the presumed role
conflict or identity problems of women. Many of us have attended or
contributed to dozens of such ventures already. We have already gathered the empirical facts concerning the distribution of women among

students and faculty of graduate sociology departments. What we seek is effective and dramatic action; an unbiased policy in the selection of stipend support of students; a concerted commitment to the hiring and promotion of women sociologists to right the imbalance that is represented by the current situation in which 67 percent of the women graduate students in this country do not have a single woman sociology professor of senior rank during the course of their graduate training, and when we participate in an association of sociologists in which NO woman will sit on the 1970 council, NO woman is included among the associate editors of the *American Sociological Review* or the advisory board of the *American Journal of Sociology*, and NO woman sits on the thirteen member committees on publications and nominations.

RESOLUTIONS

WE urge the individual sociologists attending this convention, the departments to which you will shortly return, and the officers, council and committees of the professional association, to consider and to take effective action on the following resolutions from the Women's Caucus.

1. That every sociology department give priority to the hiring and promotion of women faculty until the proportion and rank distribution of women faculty at least equals the sex ratio among graduate students with a long-range goal of increasing the proportion of women among graduate students. In working toward such a goal, this must supplement rather than detract from departmental effort to train, hire, and promote black and Third World personnel and students.

2. That equitable stipend support be given to graduate students regardless of sex, for both full- and part-time programs of study, with additional allowances for student support and household expenses incurred because of absence from home.

3. That sociologists collaborate with others from the relevant disciplines in proposing and assisting in the establishment of day care centers for preschool children of employees, faculty, and students at all colleges and universities.

4. That women sociologists be given the encouragement and the support to establish new courses on the history of women and the analysis of women's movements for social and political change in all colleges and university sociology departments. In departments in which their male colleagues are sufficiently accessible to personal education, they should be welcomed as auditors in such courses.

5. That sex inequality be added as a topic to all courses and texts

which cover social inequality but are now confined to race, religion, and ethnicity.

6. That flexibility guide the appointment of both men and women to department faculties, facilitating easy transitions between full- and part-time appointments, to increase the career continuity of women with family responsibilities or to permit men to play significant roles in their families and communities. Twenty six percent of the full-time male faculty in graduate departments today are joint appointments at a senior rank. If a department can thus share a man with another department, it can as readily share a man or a woman faculty member with a family. It should be noted that an increasing number of young men and women sociologists wish to contribute significantly to a variety of life areas, and to avoid a twenty-four-hour-day career commitment to sociology.

7. That women sociologists be added as rapidly as possible to all committees, advisory, or editorial boards within or related to the American Sociological Association, as the case may be.

8. That sociology endorse the principle of parental leave and family sick leave for all employees, faculty, and students at colleges and universities.

9. That sociology consider the findings of their own research—the effect that social performance predicts school performance, but not adult success in work—and examine the contribution that the present patronage and sponsorship techniques make to these research results. Professors may feel pride in all-round good student performers and obligation to helpful research assistants, but this is no necessary harbinger of future success as sociologists. We urge the field to dispense with the patronage system of employment and substitute a strict adherence to an open employment system based on performance and creative potential in both scholarship and teaching. Further, we urge that employers stop violating the privacy of women and men applicants by inquiries into actual or potential marital status, fertility plans, or political values, and confine interviews to an exchange of professional qualifications and job characteristics.

10. Lastly, to facilitate communications and assure continuity between annual conventions, we urge the council, the editor and the editorial board of *The American Sociologist*, to establish a new section in this journal, to be entitled the Women's Caucus Newsletter, to be handled by an editorial representative of the Women's Caucus.

The Contributors

CAROL A. BROWN is associate professor of sociology at Lowell University in Lowell, Massachusetts.

NORMA STOLTZ CHINCHILLA is professor of sociology and women's studies at California State University at Long Beach.

HOWARD J. EHRLICH is a member of the Great Atlantic Radio Conspiracy collective and is the editor of *Social Anarchism*.

HENRY ETZKOWITZ is associate professor of sociology at the State University of New York at Purchase.

LYNDA ANN EWEN is professor of sociology at West Virginia Institute of Technology in Charleston, West Virginia.

DICK FLACKS is professor of sociology at the University of California at Santa Barbara.

HARDY T. FRYE is associate professor of sociology and former associate dean of social sciences at the University of California at Santa Cruz.

ALFRED McCLUNG LEE is professor emeritus of Brooklyn College and the Graduate Center, CUNY, and Visiting Scholar at Drew University, Madison, New Jersey.

RHONDA F. LEVINE is associate professor of sociology at Colgate University, Hamilton, New York.

MARTIN J. MURRAY is professor of sociology at the State University of New York at Binghamton.

ROBERT G. NEWBY is associate professor of sociology at Central Michigan University in Mt. Pleasant, Michigan.

MARTIN NICOLAUS is practicing law in the San Francisco Bay area of California.

MARTIN OPPENHEIMER is associate professor of sociology at Rutgers University, New Brunswick, New Jersey.

ANTHONY M. PLATT is professor of social work at California State University at Sacramento.

ROBERT J. S. ROSS is associate professor of sociology at Clark University in Worcester, Massachusetts.

EVAN STARK teaches public administration at Rutgers University in New Brunswick, New Jersey, and directs the Domestic Violence Training Project in New Haven, Connecticut.

Index